I find that many books about ⟨...⟩ books about books. Yet, while in the guise of being a book about books, *Wild Things and Castles in the Sky* is actually a book about imagination. This is an inspiring and immensely practical gift from forty wise and well-read people to those who want to bring up children marked by meaning.

—BRIAN LAWRENCE BROWN, executive director of the Anselm Society

Wild Things and Castles in the Sky brings together a remarkable assembly of voices sharing wisdom and guidance in one beautiful volume. It captures the best of what we might receive at a fabulous educator's conference mixed magically with having coffee one-to-one with a friend discussing what they love best in children's books. A joy to read, it is a pure, wondrous gift for those of us who love the young and the literature we introduce to them!

—LANCIA E. SMITH, founder of The Cultivating Project.

A welcoming and thorough guide to having a deeper and richer experience with great kids' literature. I wish I'd had access to this wonderful book while raising my own children.

—JOE SUTPHIN, illustrator of *The Wingfeather Saga* and *Little Pilgrim's Progress*

As a person who has spent my life selecting children's books to sell, I can't think of a better person to have put together a book to inspire you to read children's literature. I can't remember a time that Leslie Bustard wasn't reading and excited about children's books. If you want to be inspired to read to your children, grandchildren, or students you need to read this book.

—LAURIE DETWEILER, executive vice president of Veritas Press, Inc.

There are enough good books mentioned by these thoughtful writers to fill a childhood, and a grand childhood it would be, if it were filled with books such as these. Alas, childhood is too short, and I find myself making a new list of books, inspired by these authors.

—SHAWN SMUCKER, author of *The Day the Angels Fell*

This is a book for those who suspect that shaping a child's mind and heart is something more than just explaining the rules. With gracious clarity and a collective twinkling eye, these authors make the case that children, as full image-bearers, are made for and in need of story. By offering their favorite stories of goodness, truth, and beauty, they lay a feast for the imagination and ask everyone to pull up a chair and be changed. Be it a wardrobe, a shire, or a wizarding school, the stories we read to our children will become the foundation for what they chase, defend, and love. Let's offer them worlds in which virtue sparkles and the light stretches over the darkness, so they can better see and join in this same work in our own world.

—AUTUMN KERN, host of *The Commonplace* podcast

Children's books are never just for children. They are also for anyone who remembers what it means to be childlike. Children's stories return us to the heart of things as little else does, and give us language to talk about the bigger things. *Wild Things and Castles in the Sky* is a sweet reminder of why literature for children is essential for us all. You will find friends here in these pages.

—SARA GROVES, singer-songwriter

Reading through *Wild Things and Castles in the Sky* was like rummaging through an eclectic warehouse full of rich wisdom and perspective. It both motivated and moved me. As a parent of young children who wants the stories they ingest to enrich their lives, I was incredibly thankful for the suggestions and the inspired reasoning behind them. As a lover of stories myself, it rekindled my desire to explore new books and revisit forgotten favorites. This book is a gift for anyone looking to expand and enrich their library!

—KRISTEN BREWER, writer and director at Sight & Sound Theaters

Over the years when I have spoken to parents and teachers, frequently they have asked me to help them identify editions of fairy tales and children's stories that are whole and have not been bowdlerized or altered to suit one harmful ideology or another. This lovely book, composed of graceful and informative essays, written by persons who teach or are parents themselves, is a much needed guide through the bewildering plethora of children's books, old and new, that are out there. It belongs in the hands of everyone who, in these troubling times, cares for the souls of our children.

—VIGEN GUROIAN author of *Tending the Heart of Virtue: How Classic Stories Awaken a Child's Oral Imagination*

We are lead by the hand by this thoughtful guide into the deeper layers of community life by way of story, a help for how to choose books for children. What we read at a young age shapes us, and it matters. Beautifully done, this collection is sure to be a well-worn reference.

—SANDRA MCCRACKEN, singer-songwriter

Some of my most cherished childhood memories are of sitting on the floor with my brother and sister as my mom and dad read aloud to us. Not only did these story hours bond us with our parents, they also created a life-long bond between us and good books. It's my prayer that *Wild Things and Castles in the Sky* will spur on many parents to pick up this time-honored tradition. The volume you're holding in your hands isn't just about great books, it is itself a great book.

—DUSTIN MESSER, pastor for Faith Formation at All Saints Dallas

Together, the essays of *Wild Things and Castles in the Sky* make a work of great breadth and nuance. Whether your love for good books is lifelong, new-found, or still aspirational, here you'll find a hundred doors thrown wide in welcome—and a banquet hall full of ideas, encouragement, and friends to help you find your place at the table.

—JAMES D. WITMER, managing editor of Story Warren

When Leslie Bustard recommends a book, I read it. Period. I have always been impressed by her inimitable instinct for identifying great literature. *Wild Things and Castles in the Sky* is a treasure that will help you wade through the vast opus of children's literature and spend your time reading the truly worthy ones with your children.

—BRUCE ETTER, founder of The Alyosha Society

What a treasure of ideas and information. The book's many articles from differing points of view are a feast for the mind. And, if you are looking for recommendations in children's books (or even if you weren't before you started), you and your reading list will be excited with all the suggested titles. I found among the titles lots of old friends and many new ones. I think I'll soon be reading a few children's books, with or without my grandkids.

—SUSAN K. BEATTY, author of the *Faces of Courage* series

This book is a treasure! More than simply a resource guide, *Wild Things and Castles in the Sky* feels like the most sumptuous, sacred gathering you could imagine, a treasure trove of encouragement from story-loving kindred spirits coming together to celebrate the power of stories to nurture the good, true, and beautiful. These are wise words, written to guide seekers toward books which will carry the banner of goodness in the lives of young people they know. It's a collection you'll return to again and again, throughout the seasons of your life. It's a book I'll want to share with everyone I know, and I think you will too!

—GLENN MCCARTY, author of *The Misadventured Summer of Tumbleweed Thompson*

A charming, informed, literate, and uplifting collection of essays. William Wordsworth said, "What we love, others would love." The contributors to *Wild Things and Castles in the Sky* love exceptional literature. As you read their contributions I believe you will partake of their ardor for reading edifying books to and with your family.

—STEVE DEMME, creator of MathUSee/founder of Building Faith Families

Wild Things and Castles in the Sky is a treasure trove of children's books! Where was this when my son was young? Finally, a rich collection of essays recommending great writing to share with the children in your life (and grownups too). How did I not know there was an adaptation of Father Brown mysteries for nine- to twelve-year-olds? Now I know. You will find something for every child in your life to stretch their imagination and help them find inspiration and hope. As the host of a radio show for kids, I can't wait to share these recommendations with my listeners.

—LISA LANDIS-BLOWERS, host of the Kids Cookie Break (WJTL 90.3 FM)

Have you seen the look in children's eyes when you read to them? Their minds are building worlds with your words. Their hearts are learning to navigate emotional complexities with every turn of the page. They are sorting out if and how righteousness triumphs over evil. They are taking what you give. This book is an excellent guide for choosing not only what to read to children, but how. You won't find another book like it.

—RUSS RAMSEY, pastor and author of *Rembrandt is in the Wind*

WILD
THINGS
AND
CASTLES
IN THE
SKY

A GUIDE TO
CHOOSING THE
BEST BOOKS
FOR CHILDREN

WILD THINGS AND CASTLES IN THE SKY

A GUIDE TO CHOOSING THE BEST BOOKS FOR CHILDREN

EDITED BY

LESLIE BUSTARD
CAREY BUSTARD
THÉA ROSENBURG

SQUARE HALO BOOKS

In Christian art, the square halo identified a living person presumed to be a saint. Square Halo Books is devoted to publishing works that present contextually sensitive biblical studies, and practical instruction consistent with the Doctrines of the Reformation. The goal of Square Halo Books is to provide materials useful for encouraging and equipping the saints.

©2021 Square Halo Books, Inc.
P.O. Box 18954
Baltimore, MD 21206
www.SquareHaloBooks.com

ISBN 978-1-941106-24-2
Library of Congress Control Number: 2021952112

Printed in the United States of America

TO CAREY, MAGGIE, AND ELLIE—
MY FAVORITE "WILD THINGS," AND TO
CHARLOTTE BYRD AND LUCI SHAW
FOR THEIR STORIES AND POEMS

LESLIE BUSTARD

TO THE PEOPLE WHO
SHAPED MY LOVE OF BOOKS:
MOM, DAD, JOY LOUISE STRAWBRIDGE,
AND MISS REGINA THE LIBRARIAN

CAREY BUSTARD

TO LYDIA, SARAH, PHOEBE, AND JOSIE
—OUR EXPERT CASTLE ARCHITECTS.

THÉA ROSENBURG

CONTENTS

THE BEST STORIES

LUCI SHAW

As any of those parents, grandparents, aunts or uncles knows, a child's appetite for stories is a ravenous, gargantuan, never-satisfied craving. I experienced the thrill of this, myself, many years ago, when my own Aunt Lucy would create, out of her own fertile imagination, an almost-endless accumulation of toothsome tales. She knew how, at bed-time, to leave my brother and me with a story's cliff-hanger crisis that could magically be resolved the following evening, at which point the next chapter would issue from the bubbling cauldron of her inventive imagination.

In my childhood I also loved Christopher Robin, Piglet, and Eeyore. I introduced my own kids and grandkids (and now, great-grandkids) to Narnia, and to other fantastical books like George MacDonald's *The Light Princess* and *The Golden Key,* as well as to Katherine Paterson's *Bridge to Terebithia,* and to *Peter Rabbit* along with Flopsy, Mopsy, and Cottontail. And, of course, to Madeleine L'Engle's *A Wrinkle in Time*—all vivid characters and imaginary events that gleam in a child's creative thinking and feeds her mind with the fruits of an author's imagination. And poems! How could we ever forget Robert Frost's magical "Stopping by Woods on a Snowy Evening"? The rhythms and images are models from which a child's own imaginative understanding of beauty and meaning is formed;

they stimulate a passion of possibilities.

Story is to a growing mind what a grilled cheese sandwich and a crisp apple is to a young and hungry mouth. Story is how language is learned, how dynamic relationships are encountered and enlivened, how problems are resolved and give way to solutions. My guess is that even the adults in the room will find immense gratification in the way these stories yield their magic.

And so, for any parent or grandparent, any aunt or uncle, this generous guide for What to Read Next to your beloveds is a heartwarming, mind-enlarging, appetizing pathfinder to the wide range of available kid-lit. To fill this gap and cater to a child's essential hunger for story, the legendary publisher Square Halo Books is coming to your rescue.

Luci Shaw is a poet, an editor, a retreat leader, a lecturer, and the author of forty books, including her first kids' book, The O in Hope: A Poem of Wonder. *Luci and her husband live in Bellingham, Washington, where she enjoys sailing, tent camping, knitting, gardening, and wilderness photography.*

BEHIND THE CURTAIN

PREFACE

CAREY BUSTARD

I dragged my friend, Annalise, to a library book sale one summer Saturday. I teach junior kindergarten at a classical Christian school in New York City, and I jump at any chance to grow my little classroom library. After we made our way down to the basement of the public library, I made a beeline to the picture books. I don't know if you have ever been to a library book sale, but it is an experience like no other: rows and rows of used books, either stuffed in bins or on shelves, themes and topics spilling into one another. To some, this scene is overwhelming. To others, it's pure magic. Annalise held my coffee as I quickly thumbed through the bins. Every few books, I would stop, flip through a few pages, hand it to my friend, and keep going. Finally, Annalise stopped me. "How are you doing that?"

I looked over, confused. "What do you mean?"

She stared at me. "How do you know which books are good and which are not? You are barely looking at them!"

I didn't really know what to say. I just *knew*.

I have to credit my mom for this ability to "just know." She was very intentional about not just giving my sisters and me a love for the written word, but about helping us find the good stuff. The stuff that makes your heart soar when you read that final sentence. The kind of words that make you weep because somehow the author could see into your soul. Words that make you feel uncomfortable in the best way, so that you will yearn for something greater, something more—for justice, peace, and restoration. For love, kindness, and hope. For the type of world we are graciously welcomed into with the very first chapters of Genesis. This love and knowledge is not exclusive to my family—it is a skill and passion that can be learned and passed around to all. The desire for everyone to have the ability to share good, true, and beautiful words was what birthed this book.

So welcome to an adventure of discovering great writing. This journey—through poetry, fantasy, history, the classics, modern literature, and more—is guided by forty different voices. There is an essay encouraging grandparents to pass a love of great books on to their grandchildren, as well as essays about telling stories, reading fairy tales, and seeking out diverse characters in literature. You will find essays for those guiding children through adversity, or for those hoping to introduce children to poetry, Shakespeare, or art. There are essays on reading with toddlers, elementary school children, middle schoolers, and high schoolers. Each essay features a list of five book recommendations that fit with the essay's genre or theme, not to mention dozens of other books mentioned throughout the essays. You can find a sequence/reading level guide in the back of the book featuring the books recommended at the end of each chapter.

The lists you find here form a collection that we have carefully curated, alongside our diverse group of writers, with the desire to give you a more well-rounded selection of inspiration than you would find by just googling key words. Of course, every writer featured here would have gladly recommended more books, so we encourage you to look up the essayists whose words resonate most deeply with you—they all have much more to say on this subject than we could feature here. We also plan to add more recommendations in the future on the Square Halo Books blog.

But how do these essays work together? And if you are not in a certain season of life, can each essay be relevant to you? There is a central thread that binds us all together: a shared faith in Christ, and a deep desire to be formed by Scripture and to share our love of Christ and His word with the generations after us. This is the lens through which each writer has determined which authors and illustrators to highlight, and it has served as the ultimate guide to help them choose books that are good, true, and beautiful. Not all the books featured in this anthology were written by Christians. However, they are held together by our belief that we are all made in the image of God and have shared human experience. We believe that stories and imagination are key to a child's growth. The good, the true and the beautiful, by God's grace, can be found in any of His image-bearers.

This provides value to the written word, since He is the Word made flesh and breathes life into words, regardless of who pens them.

We want to thank all our writers for crafting such beautiful essays and for curating book lists that are thoughtful and specific. Thank you for sharing your joys and insights on the written word with us and with our readers. Thank you for being courageous and sharing your stories about how the Lord has used words in your lives. My mother Leslie and I wanted to give the biggest thank you of all to Théa Rosenburg for her amazing edits and for working alongside us to make this book a treasure. We could not have done this without her! She is a master of editing and writing, and we are so grateful for her time and wisdom. I also wanted to give a personal thank you to my mother for inviting me to join her on this journey and for instilling a deep love for the good, the true, and the beautiful in my life. She has stamped a passion for literature, poetry, and art in my heart and in the hearts of many others who have had the honor of crossing her path.

And thank you, dear reader, for being curious and for diving deeper into the world of words. We hope this treasure trove will inspire you to create traditions and habits that will last in the hearts of your children, whether you're a parent, teacher, aunt or uncle, grandparent, unofficial family member, or a student yourself. We hope that this will be a tool in your tool belt to help you just *know* when you find the next great book. Our deepest desire, though, is that you will see God's creativity and fingerprints throughout these essays and that they will give you a peek behind the curtain.

So, welcome. We are so glad you're here.

LOVE. THINK. SPEAK.

LESLIE BUSTARD

> Far overhead from beyond the veil of blue sky ... either from the sky or
> from the Lion itself, ... the deepest, wildest voice they had ever heard
> was saying: "Narnia, Narnia, Narnia, awake. Love. Think. Speak.
> Be walking trees. Be talking beasts. Be divine waters."
> —C.S. Lewis, *The Magician's Nephew*

These three words—*love, think, speak*—grabbed my attention the first year
I guided my seventh-grade literature class through C.S. Lewis's *The Magician's
Nephew*. Aslan's call to his newly-ordained talking animals to awaken and to
love, think, and speak was a call to image him to the rest of Narnia. This reminded me of the awe-inspiring truth that humanity being is made in God's image;
we love, think, and speak because the Creator did so first.

Not only do these three commands of Aslan remind us we are image-
bearers of God to the world, but they also show us that the words we use and
the various ways we use them are part of our image-bearing work. The use
and importance of words is woven throughout Scripture as we see God acting
for and speaking to His people, as well as commanding and teaching them
(and us) how to speak with love and wisdom.

As a parent, church member, teacher, aunt, and friend, I am called to the
imaginative and intentional work of shepherding, in large and small ways, the
hearts and minds of the children around me. And so are those who find themselves in communities with little ones, tweens, and teenagers. As we love, think,

and speak in our communities, we also need to bring into our children's lives life-giving words, good stories, and meaningful conversations so that they, too, can grow as image-bearers of God. Bible reading, worship, service, outdoor time, movies and plays, stories, books, poetry, humor, artwork—these are seeds we plant in our children's lives that can add to the treasure in their hearts. As Jesus taught, "Out of the abundance of the heart his mouth speaks" (Luke 6:45).

In her book *Caring for Words in a Culture of Lies*, Marilyn McEntyre says,

> Words are entrusted to us as equipment for our life together, to help us survive, guide, and nourish one another. We need to take the metaphor of nourishment seriously in choosing what we "feed on" in our hearts, and in seeking to make our conversation with each other life-giving."[1]

The way our taste buds grow accustomed to the foods we eat and how those foods affect the health of our body is an apt metaphor for how we decide which words and ideas to offer our children. A child accustomed to sweet foods and cheese-covered vegetables (I am very sympathetic to this) might struggle to appreciate the variety of flavors and textures found in nutritional foods. A steady diet of dumbed-down stories, illustrations, and conversations will not prepare them for all the glorious ways words can be used in times of joy and delight and in times of sorrow and suffering.

The stories we offer our children are important to their growth as people. As James K.A. Smith says, "My feel for the world is oriented by a story I carry in my bones."[2] These stories are experienced through a variety of written and visual forms, including history, poetry, fiction, memoir, and songs. Children also learn an orientation to the world through advertisements, social media platforms, video games, TV shows, celebrity culture, and music videos. Smith elaborates,

> The imagination is acquired. It is learned. It is neither instinctual nor universal ... Rather, the imagination is a form of habit, a learned, bodily disposition to the world. Embodiment is integral to imagination ... This is why the arts are crucial to our collective imagination. Grabbing hold of us by the senses, artworks have a unique capacity to shape our attunement, our feel for the world.[3]

C.S. Lewis's words about stories solidified what I intuitively knew about children and books when I became a mother. In his essay "On Stories" Lewis states,

"No book is really worth reading at the age of ten which is not equally (and often far more) worth reading at the age of fifty."[4] This became my guide for how to choose good books. I found, over time, that if I was reading a book out loud and its illustrations or words were insipid or banal, I would get a knot in my stomach. These books did not stay long in our home.

Lewis's belief that stories have formative power is intertwined throughout *The Chronicles of Narnia. Prince Caspian,* the second book in the series as Lewis wrote them, highlights the power of stories. The young Prince Caspian, whose nurse and then his tutor told him stories of Old Narnia—full of talking animals, high kings and queens, and Aslan—felt a strong connection with and loyalty to Narnia, so that later he longed to be crowned its rightful king. On the other hand, King Miraz—as well as previous Telmarine kings—perpetuated fear in his subjects by insisting that the stories of Old Narnia and Aslan were myths and that only evil came from across the waters and forests. His subjects lived in this fear and kept away from the seas and woods as much as they could.

"There was a boy named Eustace Clarence Scrubb, and he almost deserved it," begins *The Voyage of the Dawn Treader,* the book following *Prince Caspian.* It is a story that fleshes out Lewis's belief concerning the negative, formative power that the lack of good stories can have on a child's heart and mind.

From the very beginning of the book, we know that Eustace is truly an insufferable boy. His teachers and parents—whom he called by their first names—gave him facts and opinions, not stories or edifying conversations. "He liked books if they were books of information and had pictures of grain elevators or of fat foreign children doing exercises in model schools."[5] When Eustace entered into an adventure on the high seas, he had no imagination for its possibilities and lacked the largeness of heart necessary to welcome new people (or talking mice) into his life. He was full of disdain and self-righteousness—he needed a heart change.

Stories can train our imaginations and help us grow in empathy and sympathy, but stories can also help us understand how we fit into the kingdom of God, as well as prepare us for a life of being molded by the word of God. As Marilyn McEntyre writes,

> We derive our basic expectations from the narrative patterns we internalize . . . Stories provide the basic plotlines and in the infinite variations on those plots help us to negotiate the open middle ground between predictability and surprise.[6]

By reading an abundance of diverse stories—from *Beowulf* to *The Tempest* to *The Lord of the Rings* to *A Wrinkle in Time* to *Harry Potter*—children learn that although they may be a central character in a story, the story is not only about them; there is a bigger story and outside themselves of which their story is part. Although Sam, in J.R.R. Tolkien's *The Lord of the Rings*, wishes for future storytellers to sing tales of his and Frodo's quest with the Ring, we know that he is one part of the epic fight for the life of Middle-earth. His part is vital, but he is not the only one to make brave sacrifices and face his enemies. When we get to the end of the story, we celebrate Sam, but we also celebrate the other heroic characters as we marvel at the story's victorious conclusion.

In the overarching story of God's kingdom and its chapters of creation, fall, redemption, and consummation, every individual is important. Every believer has a salvation and sanctification story that is part of eternity's new creation story. No one human, however, is the center or the hero of this ongoing plot. The Kingdom Story is about God drawing near to and dwelling with His people through the life, death, and resurrection of Jesus Christ. The Kingdom Story is about the Triune God. Reading stories that show protagonists as part of something bigger than themselves helps us see, even at a slant, that though we are important, the story is not only about us.

Reading widely and deeply can also bear fruit in how children enter into Scripture. Through stories, children encounter not just facts and ideas, but also poetic language, motif, foreshadowing, metaphor, and symbolism. God's word is divinely inspired truth that comes to us not only in historical accounts and commands, but also in poetry, prophecy, and parables. Understanding how a story works will help our children intuit how Scripture works as a large true story, full of connections, conflicts, and resolutions.

We are people who have words and stories deep down in our DNA. Our God created the world through His words, and He brought us into life and fellowship with Him through the Word-of-God-Made-Flesh. Jesus embodied to those around Him the life and light of God the Father. Through His words and stories, and then through His death and resurrection, our hearts, minds, and imaginations can be enlarged for the glory of God. As Paul writes, "For God, who said, 'Light shall shine out of darkness,' has shone in our hearts to give the light of the knowledge of the glory of God in the face of Jesus Christ" (2 Cor. 4:6). We can help our children be formed by Scripture as we help them enlarge their imaginations and minds through both reading Scripture and experiencing a multitude of well-told stories.[7]

Scripture is what can truly change hearts, minds, and souls, so knowing it should be a priority for us. Throughout Psalm 119, the psalmist declares the need for and the goodness of God's laws. All 176 verses focus on God's testimonies and instructions as the writer's life-blood. Verses 36 and 37 sum up this prayer:

Incline my heart to your testimonies,
     and not to selfish gain!
Turn my eyes from looking at worthless things;
     and give me life in your ways.

These young image-bearers of God will be formed by many, many things. Therefore, we must provide the children in our lives with words, conversations, and stories that will plant the seeds of abundance in their hearts and minds. As Marilyn McEntyre affirms, "To accept the invitation of good stories is to enter into deep and pleasurable reflection on very old philosophical questions: what can we know and what must we do."[8] And with these seeds growing in their lives, our children will have deeper roots to draw from in how they love, think, and speak.

What a good work for all of us to participate in.

My Very First Mother Goose
Edited by Iona Opie | *Illustrated by Rosemary Wells*

All my memories of reading this book to my daughters are happy ones— someone sitting on my lap as we recited the words together and enjoyed the bright, colorful, whimsical illustrations. Rosemary Wells has taken Mother Goose rhymes and made them better with her lovable characters and pictures. No longer do these famous verses seem dry and distant—instead they are fun and enjoyable to memorize. Even though my daughters are grown, we often randomly recite "To Market to Market to buy a fat pig / home again home again ...jiggity jig" to each other.

A Child's Calendar
John Updike | *Illustrated by Trina Schart Hyman*

The stunning paintings in this book follow the members of a multi-genera-tional, multiracial family through the months and seasons with their friends.

I cannot imagine a better introduction to poetry for young ones. This Caldecott Honor book has been in our family for twenty years. Even after many, many rereads, the verses, rhymes, and meter still feel fresh and magical.

Mr. Putter and Tabby Pour the Tea
Cynthia Rylant | *Illustrated by Arthur Howard*

This is the first book in a charming series that my family enjoyed as much as I did, despite the fact that one of the main characters is a cat and we are a dog family. Arthur Howard's rumpled illustrations capture Mr. Putter to a tee. In later books, his neighbor and her dog join in their everyday adventures. This story affirms friendship, old people, and good food.

The Father Brown Reader: Stories from Chesterton
Adapted by Nancy Carpentier Brown | *Illustrated by Ted Schluenderfritz*

Brown adapts four of the Father Brown mysteries for nine- to twelve-year-olds. These include "The Blue Cross," "The Strange Feet," "The Flying Stars," and "The Absence of Mister Glass." But the real mystery is: Who borrowed our copy and when will we get it back? What a fun way to introduce these classic detective stories to the next generations. And kudos to the author for making Chesterton's writing accessible without dumbing it down.

Twig
Elizabeth Orton Jones | *Illustrated by Elizabeth Orton Jones*

This is the kind of book that you discover one day in a used-book store and wonder where has this been your whole life. Twig has a number of adventures in her backyard, with birds, an elf, and other wee folk. Elizabeth Orton Jones pairs this magical story with charming illustrations that will remind you of the work of Garth Williams or Joe Sutphin. This story has continuously satisfied everyone I have read it out loud to.

I'm taking editor's privileges and also sharing my favorite books for teenagers.

The Mysterious Affair at Styles
Agatha Christie

This was Agatha Christie's first book—her debut novel, as well as the book that introduced the character of Hercule Poirot. She started working on it while serving as a nurse during WWI; it was published it after the war. Like all her future mysteries, this story has clever twists and turns and a surprise ending, making it a truly good place to start reading this famous murder-mystery writer.

Parables and Paradox
Malcolm Guite

Guite writes, "All poetry avails itself of the wider symbolic reach of everyday experience which is the basis of any parable, and poetry is especially fitted to point towards and deepen that experience of paradox which pierces us so often when we try to grasp a spiritual truth."[9] In this collection of fifty sonnets, Guite allows poetry to help us experience afresh the sayings of Jesus in the Gospels.

Peace Like a River
Leif Enger

This highly praised, award-winning novel is a quest, a tragedy, and a love story. Leif Enger is a master storyteller. Many folks disagree over which of his books is the best, but this is my favorite. I am always happy to return to it, and several scenes still make their way into my thoughts often. I love how Enger puts words together, and how he builds both the ordinary and extraordinary into his tale. This book is rooted in the heartland of America and will make you believe in the possibilities of both murder and mystery in one family's story. But the foundation of this story is one dad's love for God and for his family—and the sacrifices he makes for both.

The Day the Angels Fell
Shawn Smucker

I discovered this book several years ago, after reading that Shawn Smucker's writing was like a mixture of Madeleine L'Engle, Chaim Potok, and Leif Enger. Since these are three favorite writers of mine, I quickly ordered his book. A little while later, I learned that Shawn and his family lived close by and that we even had several mutual friends. The happy ending to that story is now we are friends ... and I am still a big fan of his. Shawn writes the types of sentences that make me say "Listen to this!" to whoever is close by. Like Leif Enger, Shawn creates hyper-realistic American landscapes in which out-of-the-ordinary events grow up and you don't question them. This story will make you laugh and cry and tremble. The sequel, The Edge of Over There, takes you to a place you didn't expect to go—it's a cannot-put-it-down type of story, too.

My Name is Asher Lev
Chaim Potok

My Name is Asher Lev is about a practicing Hasidic Jew who, from a very early age demonstrated a gift in drawing as well as the deep soul of an artist. For the rest of his life, as he pursues growth as an artist while also practicing his faith, he comes in direct conflict with the ones he loves as well as with his faith community. Although this story rests on a particular faith (Judaism) and calling (artist), the story's many universal struggles become real for the reader. I first read *My Name is Ashur Lev* in high school. Images from several scenes stayed with me for years, and when I later reread the book, I was delighted to find them again. Recently my love for Potok's stories and his writings have been passed on to a couple of my daughters, which makes me very happy.

ENDNOTES

1   Marilyn Chandler McEntyre, *Caring for Words in a Culture of Lies* (Grand Rapids, MI: William B. Eerdmans, 2009), p. 2.

2   James K.A. Smith, "Healing the Imagination: Art Lessons from James Baldwin," *Image Journal*, accessed October 25, 2021, https://imagejournal.org/article/healing-the-imagination-art-lessons-from-james-baldwin/..

3   Ibid.

4   C.S. Lewis, "On Stories," in *On Stories: And Other Essays on Literature* (New York: HarperOne, 1982, orig. publ. 1966), p. 20.

5   C.S. Lewis, *The Voyage of the Dawn Treader* (New York: HarperTrophy, 1952), p. 1.

6   McEntyre, *Caring for Words*, p. 124.

7   Eugene Peterson in *Eat this Book: A Conversation in the Art of Spiritual Reading* says, "The Holy Scriptures are story-shaped. Reality is story-shaped. The world is story-shaped. Our lives are story-shaped ... We enter this story, following the story-making, storytelling Jesus, and spend the rest of our lives exploring the amazing and exquisite details, the words and sentences that go into the making of the story of our creation, salvation, and life of blessing" (Grand Rapids, MI: William B. Eerdmans, 2006), p. 62.

8   McEntyre, *Caring for Words*, p. 115.

9   Malcolm Guite, *Parable and Paradox: Sonnets on the Sayings of Jesus and Other Poems* (London, UK: Canterbury Press Norwich, 2016), p. xi.

THROUGH HIM AND FOR HIM

GOSPEL STORIES

THÉA ROSENBURG

When the crackling emotion of the Easter service burned out; when I was alone at last in my bedroom, bewildered, I rummaged through my desk, looking for the Teen Devotional Bible that my mom had given me years before, and that I—ashamed to own such a thing because I didn't need it, thank you, I was *fine*—had buried in the back of a bottom drawer.

I was seventeen. I hated church, hated having to attend with my parents, so in protest I wore knee-high Doc Martens, a dozen studded cuffs, and eyeshadow in a shade named "Acid Rain." But that Easter morning, a fissure had formed in me, and that opening was apparently all the invitation God needed: I'd peeked into the wardrobe, just to see—and He'd whisked me through it into Narnia. I knew nothing of Bible studies or reading plans, only that there was magic in the world after all and that the Bible was somehow a part of it. So once I liberated mine from the bottom drawer, I treated it the way I treated every other book: I opened to the first page and began to read.

I can't say that I recommend this approach to reading Scripture for the first time to everyone—I don't know. I don't think I'd discourage someone who wanted to from trying it. But I do think it was one of God's mercies to me that I started His story at the very beginning and read it all the way through, though I wouldn't understand why until much later, when I began reading Bible stories to my daughter.

During the years between my rebirth and my daughter's birth, I read and re-read the Bible.

I got married, and my husband and I attended Bible studies, some of which called upon us to memorize whole passages and some of which called for craft beer. At one church we heard Scripture used as a supporting argument; at another, as a main text the pastor preached through book by book. Still, I struggled to see how the whole thing held together: What did Ruth have to do with Isaiah? Leviticus with Luke? Or Job—why was Job even in there?

But once our daughter was big enough to sit and listen, we started reading to her every night from *The Jesus Storybook Bible*. I don't know if she enjoyed it as much as we did—she wiggled quite a bit, so we had to read quickly—but we read to her anyway, because we enjoyed it and because it seemed like a good thing to do. And as I sat there in the rocking chair, reading around her hands as she patted the pages, I began to see it—the thread that ran through the whole book, stitching the stories together.

Sally Lloyd-Jones wrote *The Jesus Storybook Bible* for toddlers and preschoolers, but as I read to our daughter the book worked on me, too. It drew the threads of Ruth and Isaiah, Luke and Leviticus together, and taught me to watch the big story as it wove in and out of the shorter, more notorious stories of Scripture. It gave me an eye for foreshadowing throughout the Bible and an ear for Jesus' approaching footsteps. Gradually, I began to grasp the truth behind the *The Jesus Storybook Bible*'s subtitle, "Every Story Whispers His Name."

In the book's introduction, Lloyd-Jones explains:

> There are lots of stories in the Bible, but all the stories are telling one Big Story. The Story of how God loves his children and comes to rescue them.
>
> It takes the whole Bible to tell this Story. And at the center of the Story, there is a baby. Every Story in the Bible whispers his name. He is like the missing piece in a puzzle—the piece that makes all the other pieces fit together, and suddenly you can see a beautiful picture.[1]

Sometimes, like when my daughter put a dead housefly under a microscope and its abdomen lit up like a mermaid's tail, zooming in reveals the beauty hidden within something mundane. But sometimes we only see the wildness and wonder of a thing when we zoom out—when we consider that a burnt-red chestnut holds within it the makings of a tree as massive as the one it fell from. And that there were dozens of chestnuts where we found that one, each with the potential to be giants.

Which is to say: word studies, meditation on particular verses, memorization—these are all excellent (and necessary) ways to study Scripture. They reveal one sort of beauty. But there is another vantage point not to be missed, and that is the one that gives us the height and distance we need to see the whole arc of Scripture, from rising tension to resolution. But to spot it, we have to know what we're looking for.

The Bible is a collection of sixty-six books, written over the course of about 1,500 years[2] by more than thirty-five different authors.[3] Among those sixty-six books are historical narratives, letters, prophecies, poems, and songs. Some works are ancient Hebrew literature; others were written during the Roman Empire. The variety within them all is staggering—so much so that as a seventeen-year-old more familiar with MTV than with any kind of ancient text I found the Bible bewildering.

And yet. I say "thirty-five different authors," but in truth, just one Author inspired the biblical writers to tell different portions of a single story (2 Tim. 3:16–17). Vern Poythress writes, "One unifying thread in the Bible is its divine authorship. Every book of the Bible is God's word."[4] Despite the variety in genre and historical context, no part of Scripture stands alone; no part is purposeless or isolated from that overarching story of God's plan for our redemption. Greg Gilbert describes it this way:

> The story of the Bible is beautifully complex; dozens of themes and hundreds of symbols weave together like a symphony until they all come to rest on the shoulders of one man, a carpenter named Jesus from a little town called Nazareth. And then, just like those who saw him with their own eyes, we begin to realize that this man has been the goal of everything, right from the very beginning. The promises are about him; the crown has been forged for his head; the prophets have spoken about him. As the last prophet himself cried out, "Behold! . . . This is he" (John 1:29–30).[5]

Which is, I think, a more grownup way of saying "Every story whispers His name."

Jesus is the protagonist of this story[6]; He is the one the story follows, from that first hint of His coming in Genesis 3:15 to His return at the end of

Revelation—"all things were created through him and for him" (Col. 1:15–20). When you read the genealogy at the beginning of the book of Matthew in isolation, as though it is only the first chapter of the book of Matthew, it looks like a list of names. But when you consider where it sits within the whole Bible—about three-quarters of the way through, right where the tension of a story usually begins to rise rapidly toward a climax—it becomes clear that it's not just a list of names, but a tightening of the Old Testament stories into a single, unified thread.

That genealogy says what Sally Lloyd-Jones said, too: "He is here!" The One who fulfills God's promise to Abraham, His promise to Jacob, to David (Rom. 1:1–6); the One who redeems the stories of Rahab and Uriah, and of the Israelites sent into exile; who will restore the kingdom God's people had broken. The One who keeps all covenants, who will rescue His people from the slavery of sin—He is here! (Eph. 1:7–10) A new exodus has begun.

But how do we keep that big story in mind as we read smaller portions of Scripture? Consider *The Lord of the Rings*. The first time I read that series through, I was caught up in the story itself—what would happen next? I wanted to know. But when I reread it, I noticed that J.R.R. Tolkien had built little signposts throughout the story, starting all the way back in *The Hobbit*. Those signs couldn't tell me what would happen next, but once I'd read all four books, I recognized what they pointed toward. The ring Bilbo won from Gollum, for example. In *The Hobbit*, that's a full story—entertaining and complete. Bilbo takes the ring home and keeps it as a trophy. But in the greater story of *The Lord of the Rings*, that gold band was never just a ring, and it was not his wit that brought the ring to Bilbo. The ring was a signpost pointing forward to a bigger, grander story.

So it is with Scripture: if you read Genesis without knowing the rest of Scripture, it's full of stories that are fascinating, stirring, and disturbing. Many of them could stand alone, and they often do when authors trim away the context and convert them into picture books. Like Joseph—what a great guy! His story, told without the earlier chapters of Genesis or anything at all about Jesus, becomes a riveting, adventure-filled tale of . . . what? Forgiveness? Brotherly love?

But if we consider that story a chapter within a greater story—not a book in its own right—we see that it is not the climatic event itself but a signpost, like the ring, appearing early on so that when the true climax arrives, we are ready for it. When Jesus comes and shows mercy to those who betrayed Him, when He gathers around Himself twelve disciples, when He makes a way for His people to pass safely through death's famine, we see the beauty and cohesion of Scripture.[7]

The best picture books—and the best Bible studies—tell their stories with the beginning and end of Scripture in mind. They may focus on the life of Joseph, but the author points ahead to Jesus, either overtly or quietly, through the images she chooses and the themes she leans upon. These authors recognize that Joseph's story isn't a single framed painting of a tree but a sliver of a mural depicting a borderless forest.

Here is the truth: our stories aren't neatly framed, individual paintings either. We live somewhere between the final verses of Jude and the book of Revelation. The story's climax came with the death and resurrection of Christ[8]—that was the moment that changed everything and determined in which direction the rest of the story would flow.[9] We live now in the shades of the denouement: we look back at all He accomplished, and as we look forward, we wait to see how all things will resolve, how God will bring about that final battle and clear away the last tatters of sin and death.

We don't have to wonder how things will end—His victory is certain (Rev. 21–22). But we're here looking at those signposts, thinking, "Ah! How interesting." We don't know yet exactly how God will use them. But we do know that He will redeem all things, that through Christ He will bring us into His kingdom, and that this is the best story we could tell our children, because it is the one they are living through. This is the story that makes sense of all the others.

The Garden, the Curtain, and the Cross
Carl Laferton | *Illustrated by Catalina Echeverri*

Through the images of the Eden, the temple curtain, and the cross of Christ, *The Garden, the Curtain and the Cross* tells the big story of Scripture in eighteen pages. Carl Lafterton explains a fairly abstract idea—sin, and the way it keeps us from God—through a visible symbol: the temple curtain. God hung the curtain when He lived among the Israelites; Jesus tore it for good when He died. Catalina Echeverri's illustrations illuminate the story for young readers in a way both winsome and inviting.

But best of all, this book belongs to a series of picture books (*Tales That Tell the Truth*) that strive to share the big story with small readers: each volume in the series looks at a specific Bible story or theological concept through the lens of the big story and points readers to God's plan for the salvation of His people.

The Biggest Story
Kevin DeYoung | *Illustrated by Don Clark*

In ten chapters, this book takes a swift trip through the whole Bible, focusing on how Jesus ("the Snake Crusher") fulfills the promise of Genesis 3:15 and several others along the way.

In his author's note, DeYoung explains that *The Biggest Story* began as a sermon series, delivered to his congregation of all ages, but when writing the book, he focused on the youngest readers. DeYoung writes, "The Bible's biggest story—the story of our snake-crushing King and our destined-to-die Deliverer—is the best story that's ever been told."[10] And so it's worth telling to our children: DeYoung articulates that story in a way that is warm, engaging, and easy to follow, while Don Clark's vibrant, richly-symbolic illustrations speak directly to the child studying the art as a parent reads aloud. This is a beautiful introduction to the big story for readers old and young.

The Gospel Story Bible
Marty Machowski | *Illustrated by A.E. Macha*

Like *The Jesus Storybook Bible,* this book tells the stories of Scripture in a way that connects them to one another and to the big story of Scripture. But *The Gospel Story Bible* is written for older children and includes longer, more detailed versions of Bible stories, well-known as well as obscure.

In choosing how to frame the different stories contained within this story Bible, Machowski writes, "Old Testament stories point forward to Jesus. New Testament stories point to the cross. The goal is to thread each of the 156 Bible stories like beads on the silk thread of the gospel, creating one picture with them all."[11] Rather than focus on that big picture alone, *The Gospel Story Bible* dives into the individual stories of Scripture and shows where each bead fits on the thread.

Bible Infographics for Kids
Harvest House Publishers | *Illustrated by Brian Hurst*

True, this book doesn't actually tell any stories, big or small. But through infographics, illustrations, and maps, the authors translate information about the Bible into graphics that are both illuminating and fun to read.

From "Noah's Ark—How Big Was It?" to "Jesus' Family Tree," *Bible Infographics for Kids* zooms out so readers can see how different pieces of Scripture fit together. Perhaps the best way the authors accomplish this is through a board game, tucked between the Old and New Testament portions, that follows the Bible's main narrative from Genesis to Revelation. Many of the books I'm recommending here are books to read with your children, but this is a great one for kids to pore over on their own.

The Whole Story of the Bible in 16 Verses
Chris Bruno

The title of this book makes a bold claim, but then it makes good on that claim: Chris Bruno uses sixteen key verses from Scripture as pinpoints along the roadmap of the big story. "This book," Bruno writes, "is an attempt to see the forest by looking at the trees"[12]—that is, by studying these sixteen verses we can learn plenty about the story they belong to.

This book is aimed toward teens and adults, and each short chapter ends with a summary of "The Story So Far," so readers can become fluent in their understanding of and ability to articulate the big story of Scripture. By exploring both the forest and the trees, Bruno teaches readers to approach Scripture with the big story in mind. (I can only imagine what a help a book like this would have been when I got mired in Leviticus at seventeen.)

ENDNOTES
1   Sally Lloyd-Jones, *The Jesus Storybook Bible* (Grand Rapids, MI; Zonderkidz, 2007), p. 17.
2   Gordon D. Fee and Douglas Stuart, *How to Read the Bible for All Its Worth,* 4th ed. (Grand Rapids, MI: Zondervan, 2014), p. 27.
3   Jeffrey Kranz, "The 35 Authors Who Wrote the Bible." *OverviewBible,* August 9, 2018, https://overviewbible.com/authors-who-wrote-bible/.
4   Vern S. Poythress, "Overview of the Bible: A Survey of the History of Salvation," in *ESV Study Bible* (Wheaton, IL; Crossway, 2008), p. 23.
5   Greg Gilbert, *ESV Story of Redemption Bible: A Journey Through the Unfolding Promises of God* (Wheaton, IL: Crossway, 2018), p. vi.

6   Michael D. Williams, *Far As the Curse is Found: The Covenant Story of Redemption* (Phillipsburg, NJ: P&R Publishing Company, 2005), p. 14: "Christ is the center of the biblical story."

7   For a beautiful example of how the "signpost" of the Old Testament priesthood points to Jesus, see Hebrews 7:11–8:7.

8   Poythress, *ESV Study Bible*, p. 23: "The work of Christ on earth, and especially his crucifixion and resurrection is the climax of history; it is the great turning point at which God actually accomplished the salvation toward which history had been moving throughout the [Old Testament]. The present era looks back on Christ's completed work but also looks forward to the consummation of his work when Christ will come again."

9   Timothy Keller, *King's Cross: The Story of the World in the Life of Christ* (New York: Penguin Group, 2011), p. 221: "The truth of the resurrection is of supreme and eternal importance. It is the hinge upon which the story of the world pivots."

10   Kevin DeYoung, *The Biggest Story* (Wheaton, IL: Crossway, 2015), p. 129.

11   Marty Machowski, "Introduction," *The Gospel Story Bible* (Greensboro, NC: New Growth Press, 2011).

12   Chris Bruno, *The Whole Story of the Bible in 16 Verses* (Wheaton, IL: Crossway, 2015), p. 11.

SHARING WORLDS

READING ALOUD

LYNETTE STONE

Twenty-two fourth graders have bustled back into my classroom from outdoor recess that had the nip of fall in the air. Their cheeks are flushed, their chatter a little loud...

"Grab your read-aloud notebooks," I announce.

"Shiloh!" the excited cry comes back as they move toward the reading corner of the room.

"Alright, circle up. We left off with how Marty was doing just about anything to keep Shiloh a secret from his whole family so he wouldn't have to take the poor abused dog back to his owner, and we'll pick up here..."

I move my arms off my face after a while and let him rest his paws on my chest, and I'm lying there petting his head and he's got this happy dog-smile on his face. The breeze is blowing cool air in from the west, and I figure I'm about as happy right then as you can get in your whole life.

And then I hear someone say, "Marty." I look up, and there's Ma.[1]

An audible gasp.

"Right?" I agree with their shocked reaction. "So, let's write about that." And the heads bow down over composition books, pencils scribbling, the concentration palpable until one hand shoots in the air. The boy with the tousled brown hair, sparkling chocolate eyes, and grin as wide as the Shiloh Bridge itself has a new realization, and he's ready to share.

Sharing: that's the entire magic of the read-aloud experience. Whether it happens in a classroom of elementary school children, or while tucked under blankets for my own toddler's bedtime ritual, or sitting knee-to-knee on the floor of the church youth room, the experience is unique to that moment. Together the listeners laugh or heave a sigh, cringe or gasp, recoil or feel their hearts warmed. Then there's a moment when the author has revealed just enough clues about his characters, and the listener looks around to see if . . . *Yes! We're on the same page.* And a bond is formed in that moment amid the whole group experiencing that revelation at the same time.

A more intimate bonding that occurred in my own household involved a single word from *Winnie-the-Pooh.* My husband and I adopted our daughter from Ethiopia when she was nearly six years old, and she barely knew even ten words of English. The 24–7 onslaught of language immersion brought her to a point of absolute mental exhaustion. So, the nightly ritual of snuggling in bed and reading piles of books was not, to her, the treasured end of the evening it had been with my older boys but rather a bit of a chore. However, she did like to cuddle up under blankets with me as she looked through pictures, and she would let me read maybe a few pages of a book. Although she didn't understand what I was saying in those early months, she liked that she could count on certain cadences that I repeated with particular books. One of her favorites was when Pooh said "Indeed!" and I'd drag out each half of the word. She started mimicking my up-and-down inflection, and we giggled and threw the sheet up over our heads, letting it billow down on us as we repeated the word. She loved the silly action so much that *Winnie-the-Pooh* became nearly a nightly request. She'd let me read a little longer, and we'd end up devolving into fits of giggles as we dove into the sheets with exclamations of Pooh's "Indeed!" To this day, if we hear that word used when we are together, or if we use it ourselves, we glance at each other and repeat it with the exaggerated enunciation and grin.

In the act of hearing an author's creation come alive through someone's spoken interpretation, we come together in a special way that's different from participating in other activities with a body of people. There's a stillness in the air, with ears perked to catch the nuances of the dialogue or description. There's a watchfulness as well—watching the reader's facial expressions or maybe hand gestures—and watching each other, imperceptibly nodding as the reader captures the tone of a character just right.

Sometimes the act of reading aloud nearly graduates to a form of reader's theater. My memories of reading through the *Harry Potter* series with one of my sons falls into this category. While my older son devoured each novel as it came out, my younger son couldn't quite read them himself, much to his frustration. So, I offered to read *The Sorcerer's Stone* aloud to him. This was long before any of the films were made, but the characters and descriptions were so vivid, there was a running movie in my head. I wanted to make this come alive for my son, so naturally I gave each of the characters a "voice" and found I needed plenty of room for all the hand gestures along the way. How could I possibly cry out, "Expelliarmus!" without jabbing the air confidently? Once my son had honed his reading skills enough to read *Harry Potter* on his own, we were fairly entrenched in our version of the series, with all the drama we'd worked, so we took turns reading, but at times he'd ask me to read longer so I would continue the voices.

The movies had started to come out by then, but we decided we would only see one in the theater if we had finished that book in the series, and we had to go together. Then one summer, when he was traveling with his youth group on a mission, they had chosen to use their day off to see the sixth movie in the theater. He called me before purchasing a ticket and asked if he should just stay in the lobby since we'd planned to see it together when the trip was over. Of course I told him to go with the group, but I loved that he felt that committed to our shared experience of *Harry Potter,* a commitment that had been forged through years of reading aloud and imagining together. Years later, when he met his now wife, I knew they were meant to be when I heard they were reading the whole *Harry Potter* series aloud to each other.

Listening to a text read aloud is different than reading to oneself because every ounce of energy can be devoted to creating the vision in our minds that is being created by the author's words and the reader's delivery. Additionally, because reading aloud takes longer, we find ourselves even more invested in the story because we've given so much of our time to these characters in this setting with this problem. We've had more time to mull over the decisions the character has made and to consider the resolution. There's no "cheating" and flipping to the end of the book because we just can't wait to know how it ends. And finally, as the reader rounds into the last page with just the right inflection, we have time to absorb the ending in what is both the most satisfying way and yet disappointing as well, because we know we are saying good-bye to these characters that have, in their way, become a part of our lives.

One such moment has occurred collectively each time I have read *Wonder* by R.J. Palacio to my classes. After sharing Auggie's fifth-grade year with him and his peers, watching as he navigated a world that was not ready to accept his unusual appearance, and seeing him change from victim to hero, we finally move to the final dialogue with his mother at the end of his graduation ceremony.

> "Thank *you,* Auggie" she whispered softy.
> "For what?"
> "For everything you've given us," she said. "For coming into our lives. For being you."
> She bent down and whispered in my ear, "You really are a wonder, Auggie."[2]

Even my most hardened anti-readers have sighed after that last word and begged to read the companion book *Auggie and Me,* in which Palacio shares three short stories from the points of view of three of the other characters in *Wonder.* Without fail, it would then become the most sought after book in the classroom library.

While I'm sure my educator mother read aloud to me, my memory of falling in love with a good read-aloud started in the elementary grades with an amazing school librarian who could bring every text to life, causing me to escape to whatever world the author had created in that moment. The joy was something I wanted to share, so I practiced on my many stuffed animals through my childhood, eventually with my own children, and then with my students throughout my years of teaching in both elementary and middle school grades. Through our read-alouds, we have shared warmth and laughter and tears and lots of good discussion. I am very grateful for those moments that have helped us grow together in a world that seems to want to divide us. Even more, I'm grateful to the many authors that have brought these magical experiences into my shared world.

A Fly Went By
Mike McClintock | *Illustrated by Fritz Siebel*

A wild and crazy chase begins when a fly whizzes by a young boy. The repetitive nature of the story and the rhythmic writing (as editing by Dr. Seuss will ensure!) made this a favorite in our household when my children were young. Laughter and genuine excitement were always a part of cruising through this picture book together.

Love That Dog
Sharon Creech

This novel, written in free-verse poetry, brings the reader on a journey of learning to love poetry as well as sharing the main character's memories of his first dog. Because poetry can be so tightly packed with meaning, reading this aloud gave students time to think more deeply about what was really happening throughout the story. And it helped them understand that part of the joy of poetry is simply the sound of how the words work together. My students loved unraveling the mystery of the boy's memories and were often inspired to write poetry themselves as we moved through this book together, modeling their work on what the main character, Jack, had been learning.

Wringer
Jerry Spinelli

This realistic fiction book shows a young boy learning to stand up for his own values amidst tremendous peer and community pressure, as he faces the expectation to become a wringer of pigeons—as all the local boys do—during the town's annual pigeon shoot. Spinelli's vivid writing has caused many audible reactions from my listeners, and the more complex characters have yielded amazing conversations among the students with whom I have read this book.

The Watsons Go to Birmingham: 1963
Christopher Paul Curtis

This historical fiction novel leads the readers from Flint, Michigan into the Deep South during a time of significant civil unrest, which is shown through the eyes of Kenny, the middle child of a Black family, the Watsons. The book is full of memorable characters and outstanding dialogue, which makes reading it aloud a great experience. Especially when read with an eye toward understanding the history of race relations in our country, this book gives an up-close view of both the everyday and historic disruptions and terror that Black families have suffered. Curtis makes the characters accessible, and as the story delves into the more difficult pieces of the journey, my students have felt connected to the story and want to learn more. Again, this book has made for important talk in both my home and my classroom.

The Giver
Lois Lowry

The Giver is a dystopian story about a world in which everyone conforms at all times to keep their community functioning in what they believe is utopia. The main character Jonas, however, discovers he has some ability to think and see differently, and that brings him into a darker world of understanding. Lowry's ability to detail a world that has never existed allows readers to envision every corner, which makes it an especially great read-aloud. The content has provoked a great deal of discussion about independent thought and action—as well as about how we are governed—amidst the middle schoolers with whom I have read this.

ENDNOTES
1   Phyllis Reynolds Naylor, *Shiloh* (New York: Aladdin Paperbacks, 2000).
2   R.J. Palacio, *Wonder* (London: Random House, 2012), p. 310.

SORROW AND GRACE
IN TOLKIEN'S WORKS

VULNERABILTY

MATTHEW DICKERSON

I cry when I read books. Also when I watch movies. Even sometimes when I listen to music. Not every book or movie or song makes me cry, but certain ones do—some even bring open weeping.

I used to be embarrassed by my tears. Adult males crying at books and movies doesn't fit the cultural stereotypes of strength or masculinity. My wife and I have three sons, plus a fourth young male who isn't legally our child but who has spent considerable time in our home over the past decade-and-a-half. They have all watched me cry at books and movies. I think they think it's funny, or at least they used to. There were times we'd be watching a movie and would come to a scene I found particularly moving, and I'd realize they were watching me to see whether I was crying.

My sons have had plenty of opportunity to hear me choke up over passages in books. When my oldest son, Thomas, turned ten, I read *The Hobbit* aloud to him over the course of a couple months. I'm not sure I had a plan when I started it, but by the time I finished I had one. After I read it aloud to him, he had to read it by himself. After he finished, I read *The Lord of the Rings* aloud to him. Then he read *The Lord of the Rings* by himself. Finally, as the culmination of the experience, I read *The Silmarillion* aloud to him.

As you might guess, this took not just days or weeks, but almost three years. By the time we had completed the experience, Thomas was approaching his thirteenth birthday, and his younger brother Mark was approaching his tenth. The night Mark turned ten, I started the process over again: reading *The Hobbit* aloud to Mark, followed by Mark reading it to himself, followed by *The Lord of the Rings*, and ending with a reading of *The Silmarillion* aloud.

The gap between our second son, Mark, and our third son, Peter, is four years, so I had several months off before starting the three-year adventure over again with Peter on his tenth birthday. Our foster son Israel, by contrast, was twenty-two years old when he moved in with us permanently after a decade of shorter summer and holiday visits. I only had time to read *The Hobbit* aloud to him before he headed off to college. During my readings aloud to Peter and Israel, the other brothers would sometimes listen in. They knew when the tears were coming. (I usually did too.) With one or another of my sons watching me choke with emotion, four times I read aloud Thorin's harsh words to Bilbo recanting their friendship, and four times read his dying words of reconciliation; three times I read aloud Aragorn's parting words to Boromir; three times I wept as Húrin stood before the throne of Thingol and Melian and was freed from the lies of Morgoth.

I repeatedly relived the scene of Pippin gazing at Gandalf during one of the darkest moments in the entire Third Age of Middle-earth, seeing at first "lines of care and sorrow" in the wizard, but then looking more closely and perceiving "great joy: a fountain of mirth enough to set a kingdom laughing, were it to gush forth."[1] Those are simply the scenes I know will consistently move me to tears, whether of joy, loss, sorrow, hope, or some other inarticulate emotion. But I could go on—there are many others. By the end of it, my sons were used to hearing me cry at readings.

The funny thing, though, is that as they have grown to adulthood—my three sons are now married and have flown from the nest—I've begun to catch *them* crying at certain scenes in movies or television shows. I don't tease them when they do. I'm delighted—even proud. All my sons and daughters-in-law watched all seven seasons of Marvel's *Agents of S.H.I.E.L.D.*, often viewing episodes together. After the final episode had aired, we discussed who had cried and at which point in the episode. The expectation was that we all would have cried at some point. And none of us were embarrassed about it.

I have said often over the past many years: *If you don't ever read books that make you cry, then there is a problem with either the books you are reading or with you as a reader.*

I'm not talking about the cheaply bought tears of sentimentality in a Disnified book or film; I'm referring to the more profound tears of joy and sorrow that well up when an author or director or songwriter taps into the deepest wells of meaning and emotion. Not every book you read should make you cry, of course. But some should. If none do, you need to expand the range of books you read. Or you need to soften your heart.

There are two things required of a book for it to move us to tears at a profound level. One is that it must deal with things that really matter in life. And the second—the central point of this essay—is that it must build our empathy.

Good fiction teaches empathy. Indeed, it does far more than *teach* empathy, as though empathy was a mere abstract principle we could learn intellectually. Good storytelling, with compelling characters, engages and nourishes our imaginations so that we enter into the lives of others and see the world through their eyes. In doing so, we come to care about people who are different from us and who see the world very differently than we do. We come to care about them because we come, imaginatively, to understand them. We shed tears precisely to the extent that we care about them. We don't so much cry *about* them—we cry *with* them.

A great work of literature does that for us: shapes our hearts with empathy. Of course Tolkien's works have many other values that, even apart from building empathy, make them worth reading. I could write another essay about how Tolkien's works engage our imagination to see moral virtue as heroic. They prompt us to ask, *What would Faramir do?* Giving my children heroic models of virtue to imitate was certainly a big reason for my reading Tolkien to them. Twenty years ago, it might have been the primary reason.

Tolkien also gives a clear moral picture of what Good looks like, and what Evil looks like. Contrary to popular shallow readings, Tolkien's portrayal includes not just the obvious colossal world-dominating evil of Sauron, but also the countless little temptations to seek worldly power (perhaps for good ends) and to justify the small compromises required. Along with the demonic Sauron, he gives us the more modern figure of Saruman with all his rational political rhetoric, as well as the pettiness of Ted Sandyman. He even gives us the complex Boromir whose fall into destructive pride is mingled so closely with a real love of his people and a self-sacrificial bravery.

And despite the lack of traditional signs of religion in his work, Tolkien's works also shape our imaginations to see a world in which there is a spiritual reality as well as a physical one—a world in which a great, loving creator God is active in the world (even when most people don't see or recognize him). Tolkien's books give reason for hope and help readers see that hope is a choice.

These are all good reasons to read Tolkien's works and to read them to our kids. Since my first read-aloud to Thomas, however, I have also come to appreciate the value of reading to children books that build empathy or that imaginatively shape them to be empathetic people. Our world needs empathy. We need to see through the eyes of others. We need to shed tears and to know that it's good to shed tears—not just for our skinned knees, but for the pain and sufferings of others, even when their suffering is caused by their own choices. We need to shed tears over injustice. The empathy that fiction can imaginatively form in a young mind is an empathy that carries into the nonfiction world in which we live.

I said at the start that our culture doesn't value tears. They are not portrayed as signs of strength. Sadly, that's sometimes true within the church. I know many Christians who don't like to read books that make them cry. The gospel message is one of hope and joy, they say. So oughtn't we be full of joy? They want to read something "uplifting."

Yes. The gospel is a message of hope and joy. Deeper than the care and sorrow that Pippin saw in Gandalf was that great joy, that fountain of mirth. But care and sorrow were there also. And, indeed, the care and sorrow were the more evident in his face, at least at first glance. Gandalf was full of empathy—empathy even for Smeagol and Saruman. In Tolkien's creation myth (the Ainulindalë), shortly after the scene in which rebellion against the Creator first infects the world with loss and sorrow, Tolkien's narrator states, "It seemed at last that there were two musics progressing at one time before the seat of Ilúvatar, and they were utterly at variance. The one was deep and wide and beautiful, but slow and blended with an immeasurable sorrow, from which its beauty chiefly came."[2] I wondered at that when I first read it, but I've come to see it as true.

Some of the most beautiful and tearful moments in Tolkien's stories are moments of great loss. Yet like the gospel story itself, in which the Creator takes incarnate form within His own creation and takes the suffering of the world upon Himself, those moments of sorrow in Tolkien's works are also often the moments when grace is most clearly seen. It is when Boromir, in all his pride, has had his greatest failure that he can then taste the grace in the forgiving words of Aragorn. It is when Húrin has lost everything and stands before the throne of Thingol and Melian a completely broken man that he experiences grace through Melian and is freed from the lies of the great deceiver. It is at the darkest moment of Gimli's life—after he has discovered the downfall of the great Dwarf kingdom and the loss of his kin; after Gandalf has fallen; and after he receives scorn and mistrust, rather than welcome, from the Elven king Celeborn—that he tastes grace so deeply through the words of Galadriel.

Tolkien shows us that along with the tears of loss that come to us when we learn empathy are mingled tears of joy. In reading to my children stories that bring tears of sorrow, I am also exposing them to beauty—in particular the beauty of grace.

Brendan: A Novel
Frederick Buechner

Saint Brendan was an Irish abbot who was called "The Navigator" due to his famous sailing expeditions to the West. Some believe he discovered the New World in the early 500s. In this award-winning book, history and legends swirl about the early saint of Ireland. Buechner utilizes a first-person narrator—Brendan's childhood friend, Finn—which allows the miracle and mystery to happen for us, even when Brendan is uncertain.

The King Raven Trilogy
Stephen Lawhead

Although I think his Arthurian stories—especially *Taliesin* and *Merlin*—are the best Arthurian legends I've read, I recommend Stephen R. Lawhead's *King Raven* series as a good starting point for this author. These retellings of Robin Hood stories are creatively and uniquely set in Wales, after the Battle of Hastings and coinciding with the Norman invasion of Wales. Through the books *Hood, Scarlet,* and *Tuck,* Lawhead reimagines these familiar stories in a fresh way, rich with historical detail and vivid descriptions.

Auralia's Colors
Jeffrey Overstreet

Although not as well-known, Overstreet's works belong in a category with the fantasy writings of Lawhead and Madeleine L'Engle. He offers us well-crafted prose with characters who are both real and compelling. From the moment when a pair of thieves find an abandoned child lying in a monster's footprint, the settings, situations, and choices of the characters matter in these tales. What follows is a suspenseful tale of wizards, dungeons, and more.

The Book of the Dun Cow
Walter Wangerin, Jr.

The Book of the Dun Cow and its sequel The Book of Sorrows had a profound impact on me when I was in high school and college. They are works at the intersection of fairy tale, heroic romance, and grand myth—that is, works that blur the distinctions between those genres. When you are reading this story you truly won't know what kind of book it is, but you will be glad you read it. It has talking barnyard animals and the most evil monster ever described in a fairy tale. It's a high-water mark for contemporary Christian literature.

The Necessary Grace to Fall[3]
Gina Ochsner

Gina Ochsner is a writer whose works are most often labeled "magical realism." Like the works of Madeleine L'Engle, Oschner's stories are definitely set in this world but with an otherworldly influence. I didn't read Ochsner until I was well into my adult years, but I found her writing not only beautiful and compelling but also something that could appeal to young adults. This book won the Flannery O'Conner Award for Short Stories in 2001.

ENDNOTES
1   J.R.R. Tolkien, The Return of the King (New York: Houghton Mifflin Harcourt, 1955), p. 742.
2   J.R.R. Tolkien, The Silmarillion (London: HarperCollins, 2013, orig. publ. 1977), p. 5.
3   Editors' note: These stories are lovely and mysterious, but they do contain adult content and themes that some readers may find troubling. We encourage you to preview this book to determine if it is a good fit for your teen.

THE GRANDCHILDREN'S LIBRARY

FAMILY READS

ANDI ASHWORTH

A few years ago, in the after-Christmas days of pajamas, reading, and late afternoon matinees, I discovered jigsaw puzzles. I knew about them, of course —I'm a mother and a grandmother. But I hadn't worked on one by myself since I was a child. Suddenly, I felt the urge.

I went poking around a closet dedicated to games, puppets, Legos, dress up clothes, and kids' puzzles before finding a 500-piece puzzle my daughter left behind over twenty years ago. I settled in, enjoying every satisfying moment of locking one shape into another. I was hooked! I wanted more!

In my search, I discovered book puzzles: scenes of book-filled rooms, covers of classic novels, and my favorite, a 1,000-piece collage of children's book covers—the Bedtime Stories puzzle.

The wonderfully illustrated original covers took me back to stories I've read as a child, a mother, and a grandmother—*Charlotte's Web*, *Corduroy*, *The Wind in the Willows*, and *Goodnight Moon*. I've been in love with books for as long as I can remember, and sharing that love with those I hold most dear has been one of my greatest pleasures.

When our first granddaughter was born in 2003, I began collecting books for a new season with children. I bought board books, picture books, and books with textures that she could feel. I sat with Bridget on my lap, reading simple stories and identifying objects, just as I had with her father, Sam, and her Aunt Molly. Her baby fingers recalled theirs as she pointed to the pictures and I gave them names: tree, flower, butterfly, moon.

As Bridget grew from baby to toddler, we brought the little red rocking chair down from our storage closet. It first belonged to my husband, Chuck, when he was a small California boy in the late 50s and early 60s. His parents gave it to Molly on her first birthday in 1978, lovingly restored and adorned with a bow. When our kids outgrew it, we put it away, moving it from house to house and eventually across the country to Nashville, where we made a home, recording studio, and gathering place from a century-old church. Chuck named it the Art House. And there the chair rested in the closet until it was time to bring it out for a new generation of children.

After the necessary repairs and a fresh coat of paint, I put the chair and a large basket of picture books in our chapel-turned-living-room near the bookshelves. I wanted to create a space for Bridget, and the three grandchildren yet to come, that spoke a simple message. *Books are treasured here. These are for you. Sit in this sweet red rocking chair with the vintage circus decal. It's just your size. Choose a book, or three, from the basket. Experience the pleasure of holding a book on your lap, looking at the pictures, turning the pages to see what's next. I'll read to you whenever you want and we'll enjoy the stories together.*

Reading to a child is one of the best things I know. The feel of their warm little bodies next to mine, their rapt attention given to a good story with great illustrations, the sharing of time with no other distractions—it's a wonderful gift, not to be missed.

In the summer of 2011, Chuck and I were on vacation in Rosemary Beach, Florida. We spent mornings writing at the local coffee shop and afternoons under a beach umbrella. When I tired of my laptop screen and latte, I walked next door and browsed the bookshop, losing myself in the exploration and lingering in the children's section.

One afternoon, fresh from an ocean swim, I settled into my beach chair with a novel. As I lay there, digging my toes in the sand, I thought of the happy hours I'd spent in the library as a kid—the anticipation, the search, the haul of books to read when I got home.

Then the idea came to me. A grandchildren's library!

It was simple. I'd clear a space in our floor-to-ceiling shelves and dedicate one long shelf to children's literature, with an emphasis on books for advancing readers. The basket of picture books would stay put, but the books on the shelf could be checked out, taken home, and returned for someone else to read.

Back home from the beach, I went to McKay's, Nashville's wonderful used-book store and purchased inexpensive copies of titles I knew: *A Wrinkle in Time, Anne of Green Gables, Mary Poppins, The Borrowers.* I bought two Beverly Cleary books and one Judy Blume. From my own stash I added Katherine Paterson's *Bridge to Terabithia* and *The Great Gilly Hopkins.* I'd been saving them since we attended her inspiring lecture at the Calvin Festival of Faith and Writing in 1998. To those books and more, I threw in my childhood copy of *Heidi* and one of Chuck's *Hardy Boys* mysteries. I continued to glean from books my children had left behind and made a few selections from the basket to add to the library for the youngest kids—*How Rocket Learns to Read* and *Planet Earth* among them.

When I'd compiled enough books to start, I did the most important thing. I drove to Staples and bought a red hardback journal with lined pages, an inkpad, and a date stamp. Checking books in and out the old-fashioned way was the biggest draw of all! The kids wrote their names, the title of the book, and stamped the date of check out and return.

On a day their dad was in the studio, Bridget and her little brother, Alfie, came to help me launch the library. They were eight and six, with a new baby sister named Brinsley. We made a festive day of it, which is easy with kids—get out the face paint, crayons, and drawing paper! We piled the books in the middle of a long table in the sunroom, I decorated their faces, and we made signs to tape on the wall with their words "Party for library reading kids!" When Alfie got bored and drifted off to the Lego box, Bridget and I wrote "Grandchildren's Library" on the inside cover of each book. She used the label maker from the studio, which made it a little more fun for her to stay with the project, and I wrote by hand. At lunchtime, we made BLTs and invited the studio crew to eat and celebrate with us, raising our glasses for a toast to "library reading kids!"

Four years later, our grandsons, Robert and Alfie, came for a sleepover. It was just the two cousins—Robert's first time to be away from his parents for a whole night.

I picked them up from opposite areas of town in the afternoon and took them to Phillip's Toy Mart, a wonderfully old-fashioned store with an elaborate electric train to watch and bunnies to pet during Easter season. At our house, they worked on a scavenger hunt their grandfather had created. When the last mystery was solved, we went out for tacos and ice cream. Back home, they played until they were exhausted.

Before the kids fell asleep, sandwiched between layers of blankets on the floor of our room, they climbed up on the bed with me. With one tired little boy tucked under each arm, I read two stories, *The Little Black Truck* and *Steam Train, Dream Train.*

Books provided the opportunity to be physically close to both boys at the same time and that filled my grandmother heart. Robert and I usually played kickball or hide-and-seek. He loved to be on the move and I loved to join him. And though I'd had many opportunities to read to Alfie, he was growing up fast. There wasn't a lot of time left to tuck him in with a story.

Reading to the boys that night created a memory of time and place that was never repeated in quite the same way.

We moved out of the Art House a few months later, packing up twenty-five years of life and work, to take up residence in a more urban neighborhood. Our whole family felt the pain of saying good-bye to a place that held so many years of memories: dancing under the disco ball in the living room, large gatherings at Thanksgiving and Easter, the cottage garden in bloom. Of the four grandkids, Bridget and Alfie had the most intense reaction, sobbing when we told them we were selling. They had the longest memory of their grandparents' magical home.

Bridget went with us when we took a second look at the house we live in now and found an alcove upstairs, with a skylight in the slanted ceiling. As soon as she saw it she exclaimed, "This would be a great reading room!"

We wanted our new house to be comfortable and fun, a place to make new family memories. So we added some fresh traditions to the old ones, and I created Bridget's reading room.

We brought the original church pew from our old house and used it as a bookshelf. I made a sitting room with a love seat, chair, side table, small rug, and two vintage lamps—all items we brought with us. Two framed pages from a wonderfully illustrated vintage copy of *The Three Little Pigs* hang on the wall. The little red rocking chair with its basket of picture books completes the room.

In the years we've lived here, Brinsley, our youngest grandchild, has used it the most. She and I settled in to read together only a week before COVID-19 began spreading across the US, requiring us to sacrifice being up-close for the sake of love. That was twelve months ago. As hugs, gatherings, and sitting next to each other on the couch temporarily disappeared, we've looked for ways to stay connected in our family. Books have played a role.

In the late summer of 2020, Bridget and I read *Little Women* together. At sixteen, she was hungry to read "everything" and moved rapidly between classics and modern literature. Since *Little Women* was on both our "to read" lists after viewing Greta Gerwig's film adaptation earlier in the year, we formed a book group of two. Bridget had a beautiful copy given to her as a Christmas gift, and I found a copy in the reading room upstairs that I had bought on my first trip to McKay's years ago.

On a hot, sweaty day in September, we sat across from each other under a tree in Bridget's back yard, and talked about Louisa May Alcott and her complex but gently told story of the March family. And, as happens when people read the same book, we were inspired to share from our own lives. It was special and connecting, just what we needed that hard summer. We decided to do it again in the fall.

Our son Sam joined us for the next round. We chose *The Great Gatsby* and had a meaningful screened-in porch discussion about the care-filled life versus the careless life, spurred on by the story of Tom and Daisy Buchanan, two of the main characters. It was the perfect topic for the fall of 2020. I loved the conversation so much I offered an idea to my whole family. Would anyone be up for reading *A Christmas Carol*?

For my sixty-fifth birthday on December 21st, the night the Christmas Star shone bright in the sky, the Bonfire Birthday Bookclub was born. Normally we practiced a beloved tradition of gathering with our large extended family to decorate Christmas cookies. Instead, we circled the fire in Molly, Mark, and Robert's back yard, eating burgers and fries from Hugh Baby's, toasting marshmallows for s'mores, and talking about *A Christmas Carol*—what we liked or didn't like, the ways it had moved us to think and feel and want to be in the world. As I looked around the firelit faces of those I love the most—Chuck, Molly, Mark, Robert, Sam, Ruby, Bridget, Alfie, and Brinsley—I knew I would never forget this birthday. It was a gift to have three generations willing to read the same book and make a party of it.

As to the future, whatever literary fellowship and book-inspired conversations lie ahead, I'll be there with a grateful heart, championing words on a page and the stories that bring us together."

The Little Black Truck

Libba Moore Gray | *Illustrated by Elizabeth Sayles*

Chuck once bought a 1949 Chevy truck because the interior smelled like our grandfathers' trucks. After seeing it parked in our driveway, a friend gave us *The Little Black Truck* to read to our grandkids. Along with *The Little Engine that Could*, it was our grandsons' most requested book.

The little black truck went happily about its business, carrying flowers, vegetables, fat orange pumpkins, and bushy green Christmas trees to the sturdy, steepled church, the small brown store, and the yellow farmhouse. Years after the truck was worn out and abandoned, a young man found it in the woods. Reminded of his grandfather's old black truck, he restored it to life. The illustrations of country life are lovely, and the story is fun to read again and again. The boys liked to chime in on the sing-songy verses—*Beepedy beep, Chug chug, and Hummedy hum, Toot toot.*

The Alfie Books

Shirley Hughes | *Illustrated by Shirley Hughes*

Children's books are excellent gifts for grandparents! After our grandson Alfie, was born, two families gave us three books we'd never heard of: *The Big Alfie and Annie Rose Storybook, All About Alfie,* and *The Big Alfie Out of Doors Storybook.* Each book contains several mini-stories about Alfie, his little sister, Annie Rose, and their parents, neighborhood friends, grandmas and grandpas, and the adventures of daily life in a family with small children. Each one is a treasure and all were favorites at bedtime. The stories are beautifully relatable, and the wonderful illustrations, with messy kitchens and toys on the floor, bring each one to life.

Blueberries For Sal

Robert McCloskey | *Illustrated by Robert McCloskey*

Robert McCloskey's books are perennial favorites, loved by generations of children and those who read to them. McCloskey, a two-time Caldecott Medal winner, was awarded a Caldecott Honor for *Blueberries for Sal* in 1949. As the story begins, Little Sal and her mother go to Blueberry Hill to pick berries to can in preparation for winter. Little Bear and his mother are on the other side of the hill, eating berries to grow fat and store up food for the long, cold winter they will face in the outdoors. What happens when the little ones are so busy eating berries they begin to follow the wrong mother? This is a charming and gentle story, with beautifully detailed, black-and-white artwork. The illustration of Little Sal and her mother in their old-fashioned kitchen, deep in the messy process of canning blueberries, is worth the price of admission.

How to Get a Job . . . by Me, The Boss
Sally Lloyd-Jones | *Illustrated by Sue Heap*

Sally Lloyd-Jones, author of the beloved and best-selling *Jesus Storybook Bible,* has also written many other wonderful picture books for children. Brinsley loves choosing Sally Lloyd-Jones's books for bedtime, and this one is a favorite. "Some jobs are very BIG. Like President of the WORLD. Some jobs are very small. Like Balloon Holder. (Except sometimes your balloon can pop and then you are Un-employed, which means now you don't have a job.)" This book is fun, witty, and utterly enjoyable whether you are the reader or the one being read to.

Pretzel
Margaret Rey | *Illustrated by H.A. Rey*

This is the story of Pretzel, the longest dachshund in the world, and his love for Greta, the little dachshund who lives across the street. "Pretzel was very pleased with himself because it is very distinguished for a dachshund to be so long." But Greta doesn't care for long dogs. Pretzel will have to prove his love and win her heart. This sweet story, published in 1944, is one of the first books I bought for my grandchildren's collection after Bridget was born.

CONNECTING WITH STORIES

NARRATION

REBECCA BECKER

As people who love children and know how formative stories are to their minds and imaginations, how can we build the bridge from the written page to their hearts? We want to see our boys and girls build relationships with various authors and their words; we want to see them own books, not just as space holders on shelves but as extensions of their spirits. The respected Victorian educator Charlotte Mason had the same concern, which led her to develop the practice of narration as that bridge. Narration makes it possible for children to move beyond answering basic comprehension questions and helps them train their minds to be attentive to the plot and details of a story so that they, as the readers, may find what interests them in the story, thus building their own relationships with books and authors.

Mason made it her life's goal and effort to improve the quality of education in Britain from the 1860s through the 1920s. At that time she observed that from the homes of the privileged to the poorer, underprivileged sections of the country, children were not being educated as "persons,"—meaning they were not being given, as humans made in God's image, the tools necessary for gaining and enjoying a real education. She found that parents and teachers lacked the training to intertwine students' image-bearing humanity with the work of growing in knowledge—knowledge of God's world and their relationship to it.

Charlotte Mason understood that it is hard to be a loving, effective, and diligent parent or teacher. Our own brokenness mixed with that of our children gets in the way. We often have the best of intentions and good ideas, but any honest parent or teacher knows it is not uncommon for good intentions and ideas to go awry.

But Miss Mason had her pulse on the whole picture—the beauty, wonder, sublimity, stubbornness, and weakness—of being human. She worked her whole life at developing a curriculum as well as a way of helping teachers with their own weaknesses and strengths, so that they could help *their* students establish a relationship with everything in God's creation; in fact she called education "the science of relations."[1]

Seeking to guide teachers and parents, Charlotte Mason's vision was to help children "get to" the rich nuggets of a book. Her main tool was narration. She wrote the following about this practice:

> Narrating is an art, like poetry-making or painting, because it is there, in every child's mind, waiting to be discovered, and is not the result of any process of disciplinary education.... "Let him narrate": and the child narrates, fluently, copiously, in ordered sequence, with fit and graphic details, with a just choice of words, without verbosity or tautology ... This amazing gift with which children are born is allowed to lie fallow in their education. Bobbie will come home with a heroic narrative of a fight he has seen between "Duke" and a dog in the street. It is wonderful! ... but so ingrained is our contempt for children that we see nothing in this but Bobbie's foolish childish way ... Whereas here, if we have eyes to see and grace to build, is the ground-plan of his education.[2]

In my teaching experience I have found this habit and practice of narrating to be an invaluable tool to help the student really engage with the ideas of the author—much more effective and long-lasting than a comprehension worksheet. In his retelling of the text, the student is compelled to remember and recall in sequential order the details and vocabulary of a text, and by doing so, he does not easily forget it.

In her development of this skill, Charlotte Mason outlined helpful and doable steps.

First, the reading should come from a well-chosen book from Scripture, literature, history, poetry, science, music appreciation, art appreciation, or even math. A well-chosen book does not talk down to a child or dilute the information. It does not undervalue the intelligence of a child by making the reading too easy. The chosen story is not a goody-goody book or a highly-spiced, titillating adventure.

Before the reading, the teacher can properly prepare her students by reviewing any vocabulary that the children may need in order to understand what they will be reading. If they are reading something connected to previous reading, reviewing is done together.

A few paragraphs to two to three pages will be read (whatever is needed to include an episode or the main idea of the text). Then the teacher can call on the students to narrate, in turns if there are several students. Children generally help each other remember, and their own memory is strengthened as they hear from each other.

Ideally the children would be encouraged to narrate in the proper sequence of the narrative, using as many of the author's words as possible. By doing so, they will be narrating in the style of the author. Some lively debates on the accuracy of another's narration may even take place.

The teacher ends the lesson with a little discussion of some of the moral points or possible connections to past ideas; also, the teacher can use pictures or diagrams to illustrate the lesson.

Although Miss Mason encourages teachers and parents to start narration after six years of age, I have seen five-year-old kindergarteners narrate with accuracy, in sequential order, and using the author's vocabulary.

Depending on the discipline being studied and the book used, children in kindergarten through second grade can do a combination of oral narration and picture narration. Third through sixth graders can use oral and written narrations, as can junior and senior high students.

Picture narration is an engagement with ideas where the student illustrates a narrative or idea from the text. In my experience, literary books such as *Charlotte's Web* or *Black Beauty* work well for picture narration with younger students. In this activity, the teacher chooses the part of the text to be drawn.

Written narration, where the teacher leads the students through writing down a narrative of the text, is meant for third graders and above. This is the foundation for composition writing.

In my experience, the more individuals listening and responding to a text, the better the activity goes. Because we all are created differently, we all perceive the same text in different ways and can help each other glean from the text.

Homeschool settings often involve fewer students than classroom settings. Narration can be successful in this setting with some of these options:

If there is one student, it is not wise to expect that child to do all the narrating alone. The adult should share some of the responsibility (and by doing so, may remain empathetic to the student's task of narrating).

Children who are close in age can take turns narrating, depending on the text. Keep in mind age appropriate narrating.

A few homeschool families could come together to make a small group of children who could read and narrate a well-chosen book together.

Being a consistently loving, effective, and diligent parent or teacher is difficult work. Our own brokenness coupled with that of our students can make for some rough days amidst the moments of joy and illumination.

Miss Mason, as a follower of Jesus and one who was devoted to the Scriptures, observed and believed that we are all weak and prone to waywardness, foolishness, and sloth, and that we are bound in insecurities. Her philosophy of education accounted for the weaknesses of humans. And so she developed the idea of habit formation.

Another essay could be devoted to this idea of habit formation—that is, the development of the habits of the mind: the habits of attention, application, thinking, imagining, remembering, and strong execution. Of the moral dimension, she focused on habits of truthfulness, reverence, and even-temperedness.

When it comes to narration, continually-improved habits of the mind are at the crux of its success. Is the child paying attention to the text, whether it's being read aloud or read silently? Is she thinking about these ideas, or just hearing or reading words on a page? Can he imagine the text in his mind? Can the child use her powers of memory to recall the text? Is the child able to apply the text and make connections to ideas learned heretofore?

Developing habits of the mind in students (and in oneself as an adult) comes from daily, diligent work. Our nature is to find the easiest route and to do the least amount of work possible. In our present culture, it is almost the norm for a student to just tick off the boxes to get the task finished and hopefully receive the highest grade possible.

As Charlotte Mason proposed, when children practice narration and develop these habits, they strengthen their minds, critical thinking skills, and imaginations, as well as their ability to catch and integrate beautiful, true, and good ideas. They learn to live fully, as persons created in the image of God, and to grow in their knowledge of God, His world, and their place in it.

I, Juan de Pareja
Elizabeth Borton De Trevino

When the great Diego Velázquez was painting his masterpieces at the Spanish court in the seventeenth century, his colors were expertly mixed and his canvases carefully prepared by his slave, Juan de Pareja. This vibrant novel depicts both the beauty and the cruelty of this time and place, as well as the story of Juan, who was born a slave and died an accomplished and respected artist.

This is an excellent book to use for oral and written narration. It gives the student an opportunity to tell back the story in sequential order, recall details, and use vocabulary from the text. This is a very moving narrative of the life of Juan de Pareja, and a student will glean much more of the affect of his story by reading and narrating it. *I, Juan de Pareja* won the 1966 Newbery Medal.

Black Beauty
Anna Sewell

From his carefree days as a foal on an English farm, to his difficult life pulling cabs in London, to his happy retirement in the country, this beloved fictional story is narrated by the horse Black Beauty. Along the way, he meets with many hardships and recounts tales of cruelty and kindness. Each short chapter tells an incident in Black Beauty's life containing a lesson related to kindness, sympathy, or an understanding treatment of horses.

There are segments in this book that can stir up deep emotions in children; by allowing them time to narrate the story, they can experience it together, processing the hard bits corporately and coming to a greater understanding of Black Beauty's life.

Misty of Chincoteague
Marguerite Henry

Misty of Chincoteague begins with an account of the wreck of a galleon off the coast of Virginia. The ponies in the hold swim to Assateague Island and become feral as generations pass. Centuries later, Paul and Maureen earn money to buy a Chincoteague pony mare named Phantom. Paul is able to capture her and also acquire Misty, Phantom's foal. From here, more action with the children and the horses take place.

Narration in this book can help children keep track of the fast-changing plot and the characters. The practice of recalling vocabulary will also be very useful when dealing with "horse" terms.

A Wrinkle in Time
Madeleine L'Engle

For five years, ever since Mr. Murray disappeared, Meg Murray and her little brother, Charles Wallace, have been without their scientist father. Joined by Meg's classmate Calvin O'Keefe and guided by the three mysterious astral travelers known as Mrs. Whatsit, Mrs. Who, and Mrs. Which, the children brave a dangerous journey to rescue Mr. Murray.

This book is geared toward upper elementary and junior high students and is not recommended for children under nine years of age. Oral narration is an effective way to get at some deeper ideas about good versus evil. The ideas in this book, especially those on love and self-sacrifice, should not be rushed through.

The Saturdays
Elizabeth Enright

The Saturdays is the first in a series about the Melendy family.

This book centers around four siblings living in New York City during the early 1940s. Each sibling, from the five-year-old up to the thirteen-year-old, has a separate Saturday adventure. If you are beginning the practice of narration in your home or classroom, this book is a solid place to begin. The story has a definite time arc and is descriptive in details from clothes to people to places. Plus, the action is lively and warm.

ENDNOTES

1   Charlotte Mason, *Home Education*, 5th ed. (Australia: Living Book Press, 2017, orig. publ. 1886), p. x.
2   Mason, *Home Education*, p. 231.

OLDEST OF OLD FRIENDS

TELLING STORIES

THÉA ROSENBURG

> What I wanted in a story was the same thing I longed for in a friend—I wanted
> understanding ... I wanted to make sense of a world that was frightening and
> chaotic. I didn't want a lecture, I wanted a story—a story that could make me laugh
> and cry and, when I had finished, would give me hope for myself and the world.
> —Katherine Paterson, *A Sense of Wonder*

When I was a child, we wrote a book—my dad, my brother, and I. Our book skipped along to the cadence of *Brown Bear, Brown Bear, What Do You See?*, but our story started like this:

Red Fred, Red Fred, what do you see?
I see an orange horse looking at me.

Instead of yellow ducks and white dogs, we filled our book with purple gerbils, green queens, and silver tigers. I drew some of the pictures (which explains why the black bat is wearing high heels and a hairbow); with my little brother's help, Dad drew the others and lettered the text. When it was finished, he had the book spiral bound at Kinko's.

I was five when we wrote *Red Fred*—I know because I wrote 1988 on the cover of the book, but it came out 8891. I hadn't figured out yet which e's in my name have accents (one each in my first and middle name), so on the title page, I wrote my full name and accented all four e's. But I also wrote my brother's name, and my dad's, and my mom's. Had I started kindergarten by then? My dad can't remember and neither can I, but Dad does remember where we were when we wrote *Red Fred*: at his house, the one he moved into right after my parents' divorce.

"No kind of writing lodges itself so deeply in our memory, reverberating there for the rest of our lives, as the books that we met in our childhood," William Zinsser writes, "and when we grow up and read them to our own children they are the oldest of old friends."[1]

This is true. The first time I read Virginia Lee Burton's *The Little House* to my own daughters, I was struck by how deeply this story—which I hadn't recognized when I grabbed it off a library display—had embedded itself in my childhood imagination. Ah! I thought. *This* is why I love old houses and why I think every one of them must have a personality. That little house had been one of my oldest of old friends.

But *The Little House* arrived in my hands fully formed: a book written, illustrated, and published long before I was born. When I read it, I was smitten with the world it contained, where houses had dreams and desires, endured hardship, and (revelation!) could be moved from one place to another. But the making of it was a mystery, Virginia Lee Burton's name no more specific to me than something I might have seen printed in a newspaper.

Red Fred, on the other hand, is a book as deeply embedded in my imagination as *The Little House*, but I don't feel some deep connection with *Red Fred*. What I feel is a connection with my dad; what I remember more than the book itself is the fact that he wrote it with me. As our home divided into two houses that my brother and I visited every few days, my dad set up two small desks next to his and showed us how to tell a story. He reminded us that laughing together was still something we could do. He assured us that whatever else changed, our dad was still our dad.

He was not, however, the first grownup to tell a story to a child. Remember Pa Ingalls and his stories, their wildness a delicious contrast to the warm, bright cabin in the Big Woods? Or Nokomis, in *The Birchbark House*, telling stories to sustain her grandchildren through the hungry months before spring? Freshly invented stories; Bible stories or fairy tales retold; family stories—I like to think of the world humming, right now, with the voices of adults telling stories to restless children, reminding those children who they are, where they came from, and how much they are loved.

These days, though, we have professionally narrated audio books. We have picture books so handsomely illustrated that I like to sit and look through them after my daughters are in bed. We have social media, perpetually reminding us that whatever we do, some other parent is out there doing it better and more photogenically. I find it awfully tempting, most nights, to leave storytelling to the professionals.

But *Red Fred* is the pebble in my shoe that won't let me relinquish the role of storyteller entirely to published authors, much as I admire them. My parents, teachers, and babysitters must have read dozens of picture books to me around the time we made *Red Fred,* and many of those books were probably just as enchanting as *The Little House.* Probably, unbeknownst to me, they too tint my imagination to this day.

But I barely remember them.

Red Fred, simple as it was, looms large in my memory—a tangible reminder that my dad loves me. The tidy, edited, published books had their moment, but *Red Fred,* in its humble spiral binding, outlasted them all.

All four of my daughters love stories about my childhood, however mundane. They love stories about their grandparents, back when they were just *my* parents, as enigmatic to me as I must sometimes seem to my daughters now. They love stories about themselves doing ordinary things—so long as those stories end with a dragon coming to tea or with a sudden trip to the top of the clouds. I'm sure they would love stories about their great-grandparents, if only I knew more of them.

But I am a better story-writer than spur-of-the-moment storyteller, so every now and then I write a story for my daughters—like *The Story of Maggie and Blankie,* written for one daughter after her favorite baby doll went missing. Or *So Long, Binkie!,* written for another in an attempt to persuade her that it was, in fact, time to retire her binkie. (She loved the book but kept the binkie for another six months.)

Madeleine L'Engle writes, "The author and reader 'know' each other; they meet on the bridge of words."[2] These stories for my daughters—I want them to be bridges. Raising children and growing up are both demanding tasks, and often those tasks seem to be at odds with each other. But these stories are places of safety spanning the space between us, where we can meet and be, for a while, fellow artists, crafting a world we can explore together.

And so I have written an anthology of poems about our family (one for every month of the year), and stories to celebrate birthdays or the arrival of a new sister. The girls have illustrated some; I've illustrated others. Some I've had bound as photobooks, while many remain staple-bound pamphlets of printer paper, illustrated with Sharpie markers. But they all live on our bookshelves, every bit as real to us as the glossy, hardcover picture books.

At the start of this year, I realized that though I had told them a smattering of bedtime stories, my youngest two daughters hadn't yet had starring roles in any of the written ones. So we collected costumes and props, pinned a white fleece blanket to the wall in our bonus room, dusted off my camera, and began.

Our subject was *Beauty and the Beast*. The littlest wore a bunny costume and dragon cape to play the beast; we cast the cat as the villain. The older girls employed make-up, costumes, and a lot of enthusiasm to transform themselves into an enchanted candelabra and a teapot. My third daughter for once played the lead—she made a delightful, giggling, six-year-old Beauty. We photographed a dozen or so different scenes, cleaned up our mess, and then I began writing the story: "In the distant land of Bonusroom, there lived a selfish prince..."

A few weeks later, someone in our county tested positive for the coronavirus, and our city retreated into quarantine. Our school and church emptied; our routines blurred around the edges. My husband wedged my grandma's sewing table into a corner of the living room and called it a desk. Through it all, I wrote. I left drafts of the story lying around for the older girls to read; I edited photos and we laughed at the cat, and at the girls' collective inability to keep a straight face.

This was, by far, the most elaborate book we've made. It took a few months for me to finish the story and design the book layout, but I couldn't have timed which months to spend on it better: my daughters had encountered uncertainty for the first time, that sensation of putting their full weight down on the last stair and hitting the floor hard instead. I had little to give them during that time but myself and constant, gentle encouragement to look upward to the One writing our story.

And one of the best ways I could think of to give them myself was to write for them this story about a girl who suffers willingly so her father can go free, who spends months locked in a castle, and whose imprisonment eventually leads not only to her release but to freedom for everyone around her.

When our copy of the finished book arrived in the mail, the girls squeezed into our window seat, and my second daughter read it aloud. They laughed in all the places I'd hoped they would and loved seeing themselves in the pages of the book. On a whim, I had invented a publisher's name and logo and included it on the spine, and later my eldest daughter told me, "I know which book they'll publish next!"

By which she meant her book—the fantasy saga she has been writing. The one I hear her reading aloud to her sisters upstairs and on video chats with her grandparents. And she is not alone: my middle two daughters are writing stories as well. My third daughter can't write much yet so she dictates her story to an older sister, and the result meanders and sparkles, hilarious as only a first-grader's invented plot could be.

I cannot fix the world for my daughters. I cannot promise them that this is the last time they'll encounter uncertainty, or that I will always be here with them to share their stories. But as my dad did for me, I can show them that stories can be made as well as purchased. I can remind them that the imagination behind the story we're living through is infinite, holy, and eternal—that whatever comes, He is always certain, and His endings always satisfy.

The Tale of Peter Rabbit
Beatrix Potter | *Illustrated by Beatrix Potter*

When the son of one of Beatrix Potter's good friends fell ill and was confined to bed, Potter wrote him a letter, illustrated and filled with the story of a disobedient rabbit that looked suspiciously like her own pet rabbit, Peter. She began, "I don't know what to write to you, so I shall tell you a story about four little rabbits whose names were—Flopsy, Mopsy, Cottontail, and Peter."[3]

Later Potter revised the story and prepared it for publication—after the boy's mother suggested she give it a try[4]—and that letter written for a bedridden boy became Potter's first published children's book, *The Tale of Peter Rabbit.*

(It wasn't her only book to begin that way: the day after she wrote the Peter Rabbit letter, Potter wrote a story to the boy's brother, as well. His letter was about a frog named Jeremy Fisher; his story, too, would eventually be published as *The Tale of Mr. Jeremy Fisher.*[5])

The Swiss Family Robinson
Johann Wyss

Johann David Wyss was a pastor, not a published children's author, when he began telling his four young sons a series of stories about a family shipwrecked on a desert island. While many of the books available to his sons at that time tended to be educational, Wyss's story was a genuine adventure—one of the first written for children. He wove lessons about virtue, faith, and the natural world throughout the family's adventure and told it in bedtime installments. Wyss eventually wrote the story out for his sons, and one of them illustrated the manuscript.[6]

It was only toward the end of Wyss's life that this story found its way to public bookshelves: with the help of another son, Wyss published his first and only book, *The Swiss Family Robinson.*[7]

The Green Ember Series
S.D. Smith

S.D. Smith's series about rabbits who beat back their world's darkness with hope and with swords began as a story he told for his daughter. At first, he told "simple and innocent" stories about a little girl rabbit. But as Smith's family grew, so did the stories: they "developed more peril and danger, and higher stakes," Smith says. "We told the stories at bedtime, or on walks. Originally, the rabbits' names were Hannah and Joe, based off of Anne and Josiah's names—since the stories were for them."[8]

Eventually, those stories became *The Green Ember* and its companion books, a series that also seems to grow in depth and beauty as its readers grow. Smith says, "I feel like the story belongs to our kids—it belongs to our family," Smith continues. "But as I wrote it out, we decided that we wanted to share it. We want to share what we love with others."

Letters From Father Christmas
J.R.R. Tolkien | *Illustrated by J.R.R. Tolkien*

When J.R.R. Tolkien's eldest son was three, he received a beautiful letter from Father Christmas. So began an annual tradition that continued over the next twenty-three years—through the childhoods of all four of Tolkien's children—and that grew more elaborate and delightful as Father Christmas's letters lengthened from simple greetings into descriptions of his adventures with the North Polar Bear, the Red Elves, and others. The handwritten, illustrated letters often arrived with postage stamps from the North Pole, tucked into the postman's usual deliveries; sometimes they simply appeared in the house Christmas morning.[9]

After Tolkien's death, his children published these letters as *Letters From Father Christmas*. Though Tolkien wrote them for his children's enjoyment and not with publication in mind, that intimacy is part of what makes *Letters From Father Christmas* so enjoyable: Tolkien clearly did not reserve his craft for the public but shared it generously with his children.

Roll of Thunder, Hear My Cry
Mildred D. Taylor

Mildred D. Taylor's powerful story about a family living in the South during the Great Depression was shaped by the stories her father told—so much so that she acknowledges in her dedication that many of the events in it are drawn from his stories of his own childhood.

"My father was a master storyteller," Taylor writes in the book's introduction. "By the fireside in our northern home or in the South where I was born, I learned a history not then written in books but one passed from generation to generation on the steps of moonlit porches and beside dying fires in one-room houses, a history of great-grandparents and of slavery and of the days following slavery; of those who lived still not free, yet who would not let their spirits be enslaved. From my father the storyteller I learned to respect the past, to respect my own heritage and myself."

Taylor writes that his stories informed both who she became and the books she wrote: "Without his teaching, without his words, my words would not have been."[10]

ENDNOTES

1   William Zinsser, *Worlds of Childhood: The Art and Craft of Writing for Children* (New York: Houghton Mifflin Company, 1990), p. 3.

2   Madeleine L'Engle, *Walking on Water: Reflections on Faith and Art* (New York: Farrar, Straus and Giroux, 1980), p. 34.

3   Linda Lear, *Beatrix Potter: A Life in Nature* (New York: St. Martin's Press, 2007), pp. 85–86.

4   Lear, *Beatrix Potter*, p. 142.

5   Lear, pp. 86–87.

6   "Johann Wyss." *Penguin Random House,* https://www.penguinrandomhouse.com/authors/33872/johann-wyss.

7   Johann David Wyss, *The Swiss Family Robinson* (United Kingdom: Penguin Random House Children's UK, 2009), pp. 476–477.

8   Ellie Cummins, "S.D. Smith: An Interview Revisited." *Wonderment,* April 26, 2018, https://elliecummins.com/interview-with-s-d-smith/.

9   J.R.R. Tolkien, *Letters From Father Christmas* (Boston, MA: Houghton Mifflin Company, 1999), p. 5.

10   Mildred D. Taylor, "Author's Note," in *Roll of Thunder, Hear My Cry* (New York: Penguin Books, 1976).

WINDOWS AND MIRRORS

REPRESENTATION

KIMBERLY GILLESPIE

> If someone had taken
> that book out of my hand
> said, *You're too old for this*
> maybe
> I'd never have believed
> that someone who looked like me
> could be in the pages of the book
> that someone who looked like me
> had a story.
> —Jacqueline Woodson, *Brown Girl Dreaming*

With eyes wide in astonishment, the little girl gripped three of her mother's fingers with a diminutive hand as they entered the auditorium. This was nothing like her classroom. Her wildly beating heart betrayed her feeble attempts to appear calm. She felt small, so she stood taller as she willed herself to "look like a grown-up." She *was* on a college campus, after all.

Finally. There she stood. The reason the little girl's mother brought her to the college campus: Gwendolyn Brooks. The poet. The Chicago legend who published her first poem at thirteen and was the first African American to win the Pulitzer Prize.

With admiration, the little girl smiled as her pecan-hued pointer finger reached up and pushed her new glasses up the bridge of her nose. It was as if she was staring into a mirror that foretold the future.

In that moment, she finally believed her mother: "You can be a writer."

There has been a trend in recent years of more people of color emphatically proclaiming "Representation matters!" This cry is, disappointingly, sometimes met with hesitation and rebuttal. However, closer examination of various images throughout history reveal that for centuries cultures have utilized whatever medium is available at their disposal to promote particular imagery and concepts—both positive and negative. A perusal of different forms of media reveals a myriad of ways people have made alterations to popular images or promoted their own communities—both to make such images more relatable (mirrors) and to provide exposure in ways that perhaps would not occur otherwise (windows).[1]

A universal example of this is found in the various cultural depictions of Jesus Christ. Jesus would have likely had an olive skin tone, dark curly hair and beard, and brown eyes, consistent with historical findings regarding typical Jewish men residing in Palestine two thousand years ago.[2] However, different cultures have made adaptations to His image.[3] Some have done this in an effort to make Him appear more relatable, but others have done so for the more nefarious purpose of domination and oppression.

In an Algonquin nativity scene, a sun-kissed baby Jesus is wrapped in a papoose, while Mary is draped in deer skin. Reverend Tamura Naoumi, a late nineteenth- and early twentieth-century Japanese pastor, employed local artists, determined to ensure that his Sunday-school books would be filled with Japanese depictions of Jesus and His disciples.[4] The 16th Street Baptist Church in Birmingham, Alabama holds two images of Jesus.[5] A restored stained-glass window depicting a traditional Western Jesus—with a peaceful demeanor, long straight brown hair, and European features—serves as a memorial to four little brown-skinned girls killed in a bombing in 1963. The face of Jesus was blown out in the original window during the bombing.[6] In 1965, after hearing of the tragic bombing, the people of Wales donated a different stained glass window to the church, one with a crucified Jesus in mourning—arms outstretched, eyes closed, head hanging low in sadness, clothed in a white robe . . . and with skin the color of milk chocolate.[7] If adults are this intentional in providing mirrors and windows for themselves, how much more vital is it that we do the same for our children?[8]

America has been described as a "melting pot" because of the various ethnicities and cultures found within her borders. As a whole, however, the country is
relatively segregated. First Nations people are found primarily in specific states,
the result of the "Indian Removal Act" of 1930. When taking a drive around many
major cities one may encounter neighborhoods such as "Little Ethiopia," "China-
town," "Little Italy," or "Greektown," the result of immigrants settling in communities that were familiar—sometimes out of necessity and preference, but sometimes
because they were forced to by governmental involvement. The Great Migration
of 1916–1970 saw millions of African Americans move from the rural South to
industrial cities in the North, West, and Midwest and settle in Black communities
for similar reasons. A drive on "one side of the track" or a "Division Street" could
reveal a completely different experience than driving on the other side.

With all of this separation and isolation, how can children gain exposure
to and appreciation for cultures that are different than their own? How could
a child in a major city get a peek into life for a child on a farm? For children
with limited resources who cannot travel to other cities or states, let alone other
countries, what could provide a "window" into a world beyond their own? Books.
Specifically, books written about people who are different than they are, written
by people who represent those communities.

One challenge with this is availability. While there has been some improve-
ment in the number of children's books published by people of color, in general,
the percentages pale in comparison to their representation in America, and to
those books written by and about the majority culture.

According to a study conducted by the Cooperative Children's Book Center in
2019, they received 4,035 published children's books. Of those books, 232 books
(5.7%) were written and/or illustrated by Black or African people, but about 471
were written about them. Forty-six (1.1%) were written by Indigenous/First Nations/
American Indian authors, and 65 were written about them. Asian/Asian American
authors wrote 429 books (10.6%), with 357 books written about them. Latinx
authors wrote 243 books (6%), and about 236 were about them. Only 5 (0.1%) were
written by Pacific Islanders, and only 5 books were written about them. Twenty
(0.5%) books were written by Arab/Arab American authors, and 35 books were
written about them. By comparison, 3,060 (75.8%) children's books in 2019 were
written by white authors, and 71% of children's books had main characters that
were white children, or animals, monsters, vehicles, etc. This list gives a glimpse
into the challenges of providing windows into other cultures and ethnicities.[9] It
also provides a window through which to view the challenges that children who

are a part of these cultures have in readily accessing images of themselves in books, and in seeing people who look like them writing these books—their mirrors.

The ability to read books that reflect one's own culture creates connection and relatability. That was illustrated in the previous examples of the various depictions of Christ. A child who is able to read books with main characters that look like her will be encouraged as she sees her community represented, celebrated, and valued. For a little boy who can read stories about communities similar to his, written by authors from his community, books can provide a sense of belonging as well as context and historical background. Such stories can also serve as windows for cultures with similarities, reinforcing the truth that regardless of appearances, not all people are the same. This provides the opportunity for readers to celebrate and rejoice in our similarities, even as we appreciate and learn from our differences. And, let's face it. Children just enjoy seeing images that look like them. It's fun!

There is one final benefit to having books that not only reflect the reader but that were written and/or illustrated by someone who looks like the reader. Those books provide hope. Hope that the little brown boy can grow up to be an inventor like Garrett A. Morgan or that the little brown girl can be like Dr. Patricia Bath. Hope that the little girl can be appreciated for her kindness, like the princess Nyasha in the African tale *Mufaro's Beautiful Daughters,* or that the little boy can take his responsibilities seriously like Jackson in *The Ring Bearer.* Or hope that the little pecan-hued girl whose mother took her to see Gwendolyn Brooks share her work could one day grow up to be the writer of this essay.

Brown Girl Dreaming

Jacqueline Woodson

Brown Girl Dreaming is a brilliant autobiography written in verse. In this high school novel Jacqueline recalls stories of being a brown girl growing up in Greenville, South Carolina and New York City in the 1960s and 1970s. Her descriptions transport you back in time, either to a time of reminiscing or to a time and space previously unknown, yet now knowable. Each memory is a poem, with each poem weaving together to create a tapestry of Woodson's childhood experiences, inner thoughts, and journey to becoming the writer she is today.

ColorFull
Dorena Williamson | *Illustrated by Cornelius Van Wright and Ying-Hwa Hu*

ColorFull is the first in a series of three books written by Dorena Williamson. In this vividly illustrated book, Dorena leads children on a journey of celebrating God's creativity demonstrated through color. In this sweet story, Granny Mac shares wisdom with her grandchildren and one of their friends, opening their eyes to the colors found everywhere in God's creation—from nature, to the color of our skin and hair. God's gift of color shows that His aim was not that we would be colorblind but that we be color*full.*

Grandpa's Face
Eloise Greenfield | *Illustrated by Floyd Cooper*

As one who has fond memories of conversing with my grandfather while sitting on his lap in his favorite chair, this book is nostalgic and heartwarming. *Grandpa's Face* is an endearing story about a little girl's relationship with her grandfather. Tamika loves her grandfather and is reassured of his love by watching his facial expressions. One day, while rehearsing for a play, he makes an expression that frightens her. Eloise Greenfield captures this loving relationship perfectly, while providing parents with a glimpse into child's mind. This is an excellent book to read with younger children to talk about facial expressions and emotions.

Little Leaders
Vashti Harrison | *Illustrated by Vashti Harrison*

Harrison states in the introduction that this book was birthed from a drawing challenge to herself. During Black History Month she purposed to draw one historical woman a day and post the drawing with a summary of the woman's life. The result is this amazing educational and enlightening gift to little girls and women alike. There are forty women included; among them are scientists, educators, doctors, artists, etc. Some are familiar names, like Rosa Parks and Harriett Tubman, but others are not as well known, like Alice Ball and Charlotte Ray. My childhood inspiration, Gwendolyn Brooks, is included as well. Every time I see one of my own little ones reading a story about a woman who has left—and is still leaving—an indelible mark on this world, I am encouraged, knowing they are being inspired to dream.

Garvey's Choice
Nikki Grimes

Nikki Grimes chose to write *Garvey's Choice* entirely of tanka poems because she wondered if it was possible. The result is a beautifully written story about a young boy's journey to find his identity despite the taunts and discouragement of enemies and loved ones alike. Garvey struggles with his weight and confidence, and Nikki ingeniously uses limited words to tell his story. She evokes sadness and disappointment in one moment and guides readers to hope, joy, and pride by the end. *Garvey's Choice* is a redemptive story showcasing the beauty of friendship and complexities of family.

ENDNOTES

1   Kimberley Moran, "What Are Mirrors and Windows?," *We Are Teachers*, July 12, 2018, https://www.weareteachers.com/mirrors-and-windows/.

2   Sarah Pruitt, "The Ongoing Mystery of Jesus's Face," *History*, April 2, 2020, https://www.history.com/news/what-did-jesus-look-like.

3   Nikki Tundel, "Societies Create Jesus in Their Own Image," *MPRNews*, December 23, 2008, https://www.mprnews.org/story/2008/12/23/societies-create-jesus-in-their-own-image.

4   Eric V. Copage, "Searching for a Jesus That Looks More Like Me," *New York Times*, April 4, 2020, https://www.nytimes.com/2020/04/10/arts/design/jesus-christ-image-easter.html.

5   Erica Wright, "The Preservation of Historic Sixteenth Street Baptist Church," *Birmingham Times*, October 18, 2018, https://www.birminghamtimes.com/2018/10/the-preservation-of-historic-sixteenth-street-baptist-church/.

6   Jeremy Gray, "16th Street Baptist Church Bombing: Photos of the Tragedy," AL.com, February 19, 2020, https://www.al.com/news/erry-2018/09/2712124b2d2518/16th-street-baptist-church-bom.html.

7   Jon Eastwood, "Iconic Wales Window Inside 16th Street Baptist Church," *Birmingham Times*, October 18, 2018, https://www.birminghamtimes.com/2018/10/the-iconic-wales-window-inside-16th-street-baptist-church/.

8   Christena Cleveland, "Why Jesus' Skin Color Matters," *Christianity Today*, March 13, 2016, https://www.christianitytoday.com/ct/2016/april/why-jesus-skin-color-matters.html.

9   Data on books by and about Black, Indigenous, and People of Color published for children and teens compiled by the Cooperative Children's Book Center, School of Education, University of Wisconsin-Madison, https://ccbc.education.wisc.edu/literature-resources/ccbc-diversity-statistics/books-by-about-poc-fnn/.

ENCHANTED PLACES

IMAGINATION

ELIZABETH HARWELL

When I was around eight or nine years old, I fell in love with a certain children's sing-along series on VHS. The opening scene of each movie had the same set-up: children participating in their normal activities, playing hide-and-seek with friends, or coloring with siblings. And then, after the intro music had faded into the background, these children would somehow find themselves stumbling into a parallel world full of color, whimsical creatures, and silly songs.

I was fascinated by the thought of another more vibrant world existing independent of mine; I was also obsessed with figuring out how to get there. I looked for signs of passage everywhere: maybe behind that tree I spied in the backwoods on a walk with my mom, or perhaps there was an entry under my grandmother's bed. Once, in a desperate attempt to get myself to this other world, I dragged a plastic toddler slide into my bedroom. To create a tunnel, I draped a blanket over an easel and set it up at the bottom of the slide. I pulled my three-year-old sister into my lap and together we made dramatic slides down, and down, and down, forever landing onto the gray carpet of my plain old bedroom. My disappointment grew, alongside my temper with my sister, as I kept rediscovering the same sunflower wallpaper and wrought-iron bed after each attempt. "Close your eyes tighter!" I would plead with her, "You aren't believing hard enough." I was convinced that the problem couldn't be that the other world didn't exist, but that our belief was not steady enough to get us there.

All of this happened for me before I knew Christ—before I understood that He had an invisible kingdom at work in the world and to which I belonged.

This acute awareness of a world both far and near was written on my heart, and it was affirmed by children's books like Maurice Sendak's *Where the Wild Things Are* and A.A. Milne's *The House at Pooh Corner*. These stories didn't give me a certain formula to apply to my imagination. They served to reinforce things I already knew to be true about the world: that it didn't exist on its own; that there were truer things about it than I could see. And so, without my being conscious of it, these books were training and strengthening my imagination so I could participate in imagining the kingdom of heaven. This is why I believe that our children need to read books—or maybe even more importantly, to be read books—in which children make easy passages into parallel worlds. These stories strengthen muscles in their imaginations and prepare them to believe that the veil between this world and the kingdom of God is thin, and that there are truer things about this world than we can see.

In his book, *Imagining the Kingdom*, James K.A. Smith suggests that,

> Christian worship needs to be an incubator for the imagination, inviting us into "the real world" by bringing us aesthetic olive leaves from the kingdom that is coming, helping us to then envision what it would look like for God's will to be done on earth as it is in heaven.[1]

His point here is that our worship services should feel less like the world in which we move about in every day, and more like the real and everlasting world that Christ will bring in His fullness. These "olive leaves" from the coming kingdom help us to reorient our lives to what is true, and they send us out to participate in the world with strengthened imaginations. Of course, he is talking about worship here, and I'm not suggesting we substitute story-time for our children's participation in worship, but the emphasis stands that imagination is our invitation into understanding what is true about the world. We love Lewis's Narnia because it serves as an olive leaf to us and to our children from Christ's kingdom. It tells us: there is a world both far and near, and it is not impossible for you to one day be there.

Our world does not give our children the tools they need to comprehend such an improbable thing, and sometimes even the church does a poor job at this task. We ask our children to know their catechisms. "Where is God?" we ask. "God is everywhere," they reply. "Can you see God?" we inquire. "No, I cannot see God, but He can always see me." I love catechisms and will continue to teach them to my children, but this is an incredible statement we are asking them to repeat.

Does memorization alone do the work of bridging the gap in our children's minds between the seen and the unseen? It cannot. Story is a vehicle that can help get them there.

G.K. Chesterton, in his great work *Orthodoxy*, says, "Poetry is sane because it floats easily in an infinite sea; Reason seeks to cross the infinite sea and so make it finite. The result is mental exhaustion."[2] I think something similar could be said of storytelling. It's impossible to comprehend an already-but-not-yet kingdom by reason alone. When we give our children stories of passages into fantastical worlds, we give them the tools they need to cross this infinite sea. We don't try to make good sense of it, but we help them make boats in which to float across. We acknowledge that the world is full of mystery instead of trying to solve it. What is true is different than what is measurable.

When we read books to our children that speak of passages to other worlds, we prepare their imaginations to believe that beauty could be unfolding beyond what they can see. The world in Narnia was unfolding whether or not Lucy opened that wardrobe. The Wild Things were roaring their terrible roars before Max's ears were there to hear them. Helping our children to imagine these other worlds is a way to stretch their muscles of faith and to build bridges over the unexplainable.

What I also love about these sorts of stories, in which characters make passages into other worlds, is that they leave this new world with a sort of kinship to it. They return, in a sense, with two homes, and with a longing to go back again someday. Christopher Robin feels a citizenship to the Hundred Acre Wood; Wendy still waits for Peter Pan and word from Neverland; Harry can hardly wait for holidays to be over so that he may return to Hogwarts. Young children will have no trouble identifying with this sort of longing, even if they are quite happy and well-cared-for in their current home. C.S. Lewis says, "If I find in myself desires which nothing in this world can satisfy, the most probable explanation is that I was made for another world."[3] These sorts of books can help to awaken these desires in a child and assure him that even the most comfortable of us are exiles here—that it's okay, good even, to not feel completely at home in this world.

I'm writing this during a season of complete upheaval, when the world seems to be deteriorating underneath our feet. We are in the middle of a global pandemic and the political climate of the United States is more tense than ever before. What has benefited me the most during this time, besides my hope in Christ, is the ability to imagine a truer world. This imagination lends a hand to my hope, telling me that there is something greater at work here than what I can see. And because of this hope, I am able to engage with the broken world around me, since I am not clinging to it for safety. It's like having a ledge on which to sit, so that I am able to engage with God in His work of redemption. I don't know of a better gift we could give to our children right now than to sharpen their awareness of a truer and better kingdom growing beneath their feet.

In the great Hall of Faith chapter of Hebrews, the author reminds us of our forefathers and mothers who operated out of this conviction of things not seen:

> These all died in faith, not having received the things promised, but having seen them and greeted them from afar, and having acknowledged that they were strangers and exiles on the earth. For people who speak thus make it clear that they are seeking a homeland. If they had been thinking of that land from which they had gone out, they would have had opportunity to return. But as it is, they desire a better country, that is, a heavenly one. Therefore God is not ashamed to be called their God, for he has prepared for them a city. (Hebrews. 11:13–16)

If these great heroes of faith really wanted their homeland, the author says, they had the opportunity to go back. But they were imagining a better country, and their hope kept them moving toward it. When we give our children stories of ventures into other worlds, we give them the imagination they need to greet this Better Country from afar. Children familiar with these stories will find the kingdom of God more accessible and more probable. Through these stories, we can ignite their imagination for our coming Home, and as we do that, we ignite their hope.

––––––––––––––––––––––––––––––––––––

Chirri & Chirra, Under the Sea
Kaya Doi | *Illustrated by Kaya Doi*

This charming picture book, originally published in Japan in 2004, is part of a larger series of stories about two adventurous young girls, presumably twins, who go on fantastical adventures in the natural world. These books, which are intended for children ages 4–8, are vibrant in color and charming in content. In *Under the Sea*, Chirri and Chirra ride their bicycles into a cave, which leads them to the ocean floor. Here, an octopus serves them sea-spray parfait and schools of fish put on a musical in a large underwater theater. The girls enter into and out of this magical world as naturally as they would enter into and out of a regular school day, and the confident and curious way in which they engage with an enchanted world is what makes this book so endearing.

Christopher's Garden
Elsa Beskow | *Illustrated by Elsa Beskow*

Elsa Beskow is the most popular children's illustrator in Sweden, where her picture books have been known and loved for over a century. In *Christopher's Garden*, Christopher is led into a secret world within his own garden by a magical little boy named September. Through warm illustrations, delightful songs, and witty dialogue, Beskow introduces us to the characters in Christopher's garden that he has known but never truly *met* before—characters like Mrs. Cabbage, Mr. Scarecrow, and the Strawberry Family. This is a wonderful book that engages the imagination and leaves children wondering if entire secret worlds exist in their own backyard, right underneath their noses.

Flotsam
David Wiesner | *Illustrated by David Weisner*

This book is one of three Caldecott winners by David Wiesner. Wiesner is best known for these wordless picture books, which enthrall children and adults alike. *Flotsam* tells the story of a young boy who finds an old camera washed up on the beach shore. When he develops the film, he discovers documentation of a fantastical world of creatures, engaging in unbelievable activities, on the bottom of the ocean floor. The developed film also gives evidence of children from all over the world who have discovered these same hidden truths. What makes this book so enjoyable is that it lets the reader discover and delight in the incredibly detailed photographs alongside the main character. It leaves children with the questions "What if?" and "How could we rule it out?" That sense of mystery is a wonderful gift for our children.

Roxaboxen
Alice McLerran | *Illustrated by Barbara Cooney*

This classic picture book is illustrated by two-time Caldecott-winner Barbara Cooney and written by Alice McLerran (who was retelling a story from her mother's childhood). *Roxaboxen* celebrates the imagination of children and gives them permission to take their imaginations seriously—so seriously, in fact, that entire cities must be created to house their imaginary worlds. In *Roxaboxen*, neighborhood children set up a town on a rocky hill complete with a bakery, a mayor, and even its own currency. In this beautiful story the narrator affirms the significance of the children's imagination and even elevates its importance. One can expect children, after reading this story, to run off into the backyard with sticks and boxes and a readiness to build the world already alive in their minds. My children certainly did.

Here, There Be Dragons
James A. Owen

Three strangers are thrust together during World War I and entrusted with *The Imaginarium Geographica*—a rare atlas of all the lands of myths and legends—which enables them to cross over into the Archipelago of Dreams. Discovering the identities of these characters is quite a delight; through their travels they encounter a wide range of characters, including Mordred, Captain Nemo, and even H. G. Wells. James A. Owen has written an enjoyable and enchanting adventure, which begins an entire series.

ENDNOTES

1   James K.A. Smith, *Imagining the Kingdom: How Worship Works* (Grand Rapids, MI: Baker Academic, 2013), pp. 177–178.

2   G.K. Chesterton, *Orthodoxy,* in *Heretics and Orthodoxy: Two Volumes in One* (Bellingham, WA: Lexham Press, orig. publ. 1909), p. 180.

3   C.S. Lewis, *Mere Christianity* (New York: HarperCollins, 1952), pp. 136–137.

TASTE AND SEE

TODDLER BOOKS

THÉA ROSENBURG

Toddlers take an interest in everything: a stray Lego, the ceiling fan, the twitching end of a sister's braid. They may not have a full vocabulary yet, but with their hands and inquisitive faces, toddlers continually ask questions. If I poke the cat, what will he do? If I make this face, will Mama laugh? Where is my sister going, and can I go there too? Parents of toddlers know that much of the work required in those early years involves redirecting the child's curiosity toward things that aren't likely to electrocute or bite her—things that will do her good, not harm. And so, for the toddlers who want to touch, taste, and tear into everything, I present: the board book—a feast for all five senses!

What to us looks like another run through *Fifteen Animals* before naptime—blessed naptime—arrives is, for a toddler in the right sort of mood, a deeply satisfying experience. The illustrations give him something visual to explore; the pages themselves are a toy—something to turn, gnaw on, or slam shut on a parent's hand. The language in the best board books is musical, whether it reads like a Sousa march or a lullaby. And the child can't help but notice that a board book is often the last thing an adult grabs just before inviting the child to the couch for a good snuggle.

In this way, listening to a board book may be a child's first experience of the deep pleasure of reading. Alan Jacobs writes,

> Forget for a moment *how* books should be read: *Why* should they be read? The first reason . . . is that reading books can be intensely pleasurable. Reading is one of the great human delights.[1]

Yes—forget *how*. When our children are small, it is easy to fixate on *how*. We are busy with *how* every day: How should we feed our children? How should we discipline them? (How do our friends feed and/or discipline their children?) Perhaps you are a more enlightened parent than I am, but I am still—though my daughters are well out of the toddler stage—consumed by the question *how*. But when we read to our children simply for the pleasure of reading to them, we set aside the question of *how* reading ought to be done and show our children that words are enjoyable. Better still, they are meant to be shared.

Our world was made by words, and we are meant to enjoy them—God's word, first of all, but also the words He's given us to share with one another. Through words, we're able to communicate not only with those around us but also with those who have lived before us; through the written word, we are capable of time travel. God gave words power, but He also made them delightful, with different sounds and flavors. So when we read with toddlers, let us give them their first taste of that enjoyment. In her prayer "For Delight in Books and Learning," Kathleen Nielson expresses this beautifully:

> Help me teach my child delight in words—your words, all first and foremost, but as well the words we humans speak and read and write because we're made by you.
> So, as I read aloud, and lead my child to read, please let us savor words, with all their rhythms, sounds, and meanings; may we taste and learn and grow.[2]

So, why read together? Because it is very good.

Another question worth asking is *what*. What should we read to our toddlers? To start with, books that you enjoy reading aloud. Few toddlers consider a book properly read if they've only heard it once, so if you find yourself shaking your fist at a board book and mouthing, "If I have to read you *one more time*," smuggle it into the donation pile. Some picture books are worth revisiting over the years, on the chance that they've grown on you or you've grown into them. But if a board book doesn't win you over by the first five readings, it had its chance. Even if it's a book all your friends adore—don't keep it. If reading to your toddler is meant to be an introduction to reading for pleasure, then it's only right that you should enjoy reading aloud too.

That said, Sandra Boyton's books are a great place to start—we have an entire
shelf of them, their edges gnawed and their text forever emblazoned on our
collective family memory. (Call out "Blue hat, green hat, red hat—" in our kitchen,
and somebody's bound to answer, "Oops!") Nina Laden's *Peek-a-Who* uses cut-
outs and creative wordplay to give toddlers something to grasp as well as a mystery to solve. Margaret Wise Brown's *Big Red Barn* is lyrical, lovely, and littered
with animals—and what toddler doesn't love animals? These are all delightful
introductions to reading board books for pleasure.

But in these early years, children are learning so much about the world
around them and their place in it. When we choose books to share with them,
let's also look for books that help toddlers get their legs under them theologically
and prepare them to love the word of God when they one day meet it in full. In
her classic *Honey for a Child's Heart*, Gladys Hunt puts it plainly:

> Your children need to know how to relate to God, how he relates to them,
> what he has done for us, and the whole story of the birth of Jesus Christ, the
> purpose of his coming—the Cross and his Resurrection. [Books] will give
> you opportunities to talk about these important truths.[3]

Does your child need to know all these things by his third birthday? No, of
course not. These are truths that grow upon us as we age—truths that seem to
deepen as our understanding of them deepens. My children aren't old enough
yet for me to speak authoritatively on this, but I assume we'll go on teaching our
children about them as best we can for the rest of our lives. Just as we need to
hear the good news of the gospel every day, so will they.

So much of the calling of Christian parents involves returning to this work
of discipleship again and again—dusting off our hands, and getting back to it.
Good books are an essential tool in this work. But unfortunately, it often feels as
though we're expected to choose between reading books that introduce these
important truths and reading books that we actually enjoy. I'll just say it: when
it comes to Christian books for readers under three, the selection is lamentably
sparse and regrettably prone to syrupy rhyme schemes.

Perhaps I am too critical. But when looking for books about God for a toddler
with an attention span three heartbeats long, I want meat. I want the author
to invite us into a feast that is worth savoring for, say, six heartbeats. I want
illustrations so rich that they make the toddler hesitant to turn the page; I want
language that even I can luxuriate in.

Is that too much to ask? For a while, I thought maybe it was. But lately, there seem to be more beautiful books cropping up for young readers, and over the course of the decade when one or the other of my daughters was under three, I did find some Christian books that bore reading and rereading gracefully. These are retellings of Bible stories in which the author, to quote Katherine Paterson, aims "not to make us good but to tell us who we [are]"[4]; they are books that reveal the character of God, as though the message has sprouted organically from the story's soil. These books make reading together a pleasant experience: one to which we can—when our child slaps a book in our lap and asks "Please?"—gladly say yes over and over again.

Found
Sally Lloyd-Jones | *Illustrated by Jago*

In paraphrasing Psalm 23 into a moving poem for readers big and small, Sally Lloyd-Jones draws out the tenderness and warmth of our Good Shepherd. The text for this large-format board book comes from Lloyd-Jones's classic *The Jesus Storybook Bible*, but *Found* features new illustrations by Jago that are filled with color, movement, light, and sheep—all things sure to catch a toddler's eye.

Little Seed: A Life
Callie Grant | *Illustrated by Suzanne Etienne*

This book follows a single seed as it is plucked up and carried and dropped and buried and left to lie dormant for a time. But, Callie Grant reminds us, God gave the seed everything it needed to endure the winter and prepare for spring. *Little Seed* is a perfect example of a simple, engaging story that communicates deep truth: the seed goes through death to bring life to others, and its faithful growth sends forth a flurry of new seeds. Suzanne Etienne's brushstrokes seem almost tactile, they're so vivid and richly textured.

Prayer for a Child
Rachel Field | *Illustrated by Elizabeth Orton Jones*

This Caldecott winner walks through a simple prayer line by line, touching on the different parts of a child's life that are worth thanking God for: parents, shoes, a favorite chair. The author's emphasis on gratitude and the lilting cadence of the prayer make this a lovely read-aloud. The illustrations are a little on the nostalgic side, but consider this: *Prayer for a Child* was published in 1944. The classic look of the illustrations underscores the fact that this prayer is timeless, as applicable for children of our era as it was for the children of World War II.

Let the Whole Earth Sing Praise
Tomie dePaola | *Illustrated by Tomie dePaola*

This is a beautiful book, short and eloquent, based around verses drawn from the book of Daniel and Psalm 148. Tomie dePaola is the author and illustrator of many, many beloved children's books (such as *Adelita and Look and Be Grateful*), but this is one of my favorites. From the joyful rhythm of the text to the vibrant illustrations, this book carries a perfect message for busy toddlers: "Hey, everybody! Praise God!"

God's Very Colorful Creation
Tim Thornborough | *Illustrated by Jennifer Davison*

As he retells the story of creation, Tim Thornborough revels in the sound and feel of words. God does not simply make land, He makes a land that is "brown and beige, chestnut and chocolate, tan and taupe." Through descriptive colors and plenty of interesting adjectives, Thornborough invites toddlers and parents alike into a vision of creation that teems with color and creativity—then he sends them out with an invitation to explore that creation. Jennifer Davison's illustrations harmonize with the text, making this book as delightful to look at as it is to read aloud.

ENDNOTES

1   Alan Jacobs, *The Pleasures of Reading in an Age of Distraction* (New York: Oxford University Press, 2011), p. 10.

2   Kathleen Nielson, "For Delight in Books and Learning," in *Prayers of a Parent for Young Children* (Phillipsburg, NJ: P&R, 2021), p. 39.

3   Gladys Hunt, *Honey for a Child's Heart: The Imaginative Use of Books in Family Life*, 4th ed. (Grand Rapids, MI: Zondervan, 2002, orig. publ. 1969), p. 215.

4   Katherine Paterson, *A Sense of Wonder: On Reading and Writing Books for Children* (New York: Plume, 1981), pp. 183–184.

THE NEED FOR GRACE

K.C. IRETON

Even now that my two oldest children are in high school, our family still reads together almost every evening. Tonight, we finish a chapter of our current read-aloud, and I ask the kids what classic picture books they recall. My oldest son, who is seventeen and wants to move to the Alaskan bush, says promptly, "*Owl Moon*." When I ask why, he says, "I like the way it sounds. It feels like winter."

My daughter walks to the bookshelf and hands me *Thundercake* by Patricia Polacco. "Remember when we made thundercake?" she says. I do. Then she hands over James Herriot's *Treasury for Children*, a collection of beautifully illustrated stories about a country vet in mid-century England that we have read countless times. One of my ten-year-old boys says, "*Drummer Hoff.* I loved doing the KAH-BAH-BLOOM at the end." His twin says, "*The Napping House.* I always tried to find the flea on every page."

I am surprised by how quickly they come up with their responses, and by how clearly I can see the ways in which the books they name reflect their personalities and interests. I realize yet again how deeply picture books ingrain themselves into children's hearts and minds. Read again and again, picture books become a part of the foundation of children's lives. For that reason, it is important to read books that feed their minds and their imaginations, that fill their heads and hearts with good stories and beautiful images—books that are strong enough to stand on for a lifetime.

In this essay I will be focusing on classic children's picture books. Defining a classic is always a bit tricky, but for our purposes, I'm going to say that a classic picture book is one that was published before 1990. Thirty years is a long time in children's publishing—at least three generations of children. It's also arbitrary. Taken as a hard rule it would mean that *Roxaboxen*, illustrated by Barbara Cooney and published in 1991, is not a classic, but *The Year of the Perfect Christmas Tree*, also illustrated by Cooney, *is* a classic, simply because it was published three years earlier. Also, it would mean my daughter's choice, *Thundercake*, doesn't count as a classic, simply because it was published in 1990. I don't intend to be quite that granular. Mostly my goal here is to talk about older picture books—the ones that were around when I was a child—and why we should read them to our children.

Before I begin, I want to address one large and legitimate complaint about classic picture books, which is that they lack cultural diversity. This is sadly true. In the decades when the books I am calling "classic" were created, almost all picture book writers were white. When classic picture books depict human characters, those characters are mostly white. There are a few shining exceptions—the books of Molly Bang, Don Freeman, Gyo Fujikawa, and Ezra Jack Keats show children from non-European backgrounds—but they are, as I say, few and exceptional. In the past thirty years, picture books have come to represent a wider diversity of voices and cultural experiences, and that is an excellent thing. So just to be clear, I am not advocating that we *only* read classic children's picture books. I am advocating that we *also* read them.

But why? Why does it matter that we read these classics to our children?

Well, in the first place, classic picture books have stood the test of time. As a proportion of the number of books published, I suspect there was just as much of what British educator Charlotte Mason called "twaddle" in 1920 as there is today. The difference, of course, is that today we have to wade through all the contemporary twaddle, looking for the gems. The twaddle published in 1920 has fallen by the wayside. Thus, classic picture books have already been vetted by generations of readers who continue to find them worthwhile. That's a large part of what makes them "classic."

Additionally, opening a classic picture book and reading it with a child allows what C.S. Lewis calls "the clean sea breeze of the centuries"—or at least the decades—to blow through. The past is a different country. Take, for example, *Play With Me* by Marie Hall Ets, a story about a girl who wants to play with the wild creatures of the meadow near her home. This book would not (and possibly could not) have been written today: most modern children don't have the outdoor solitude that Ets assumes. Her book comes from a different time, with different norms and assumptions, and those differences are as much a part of its value as is its message about stillness and patience. Those differences call into question *our* norms and obliquely show that they are not really normative—or necessary. They might in fact be getting in the way of our ability to be still, to be alone, to enjoy the company of wild things, and to see that wild things exist for their own sake and not for our convenience.

And that brings me to my third reason to read classic picture books. Like many classics, Ets's *Play With Me* is visually quite different from the lush illustrations of today's books. Its simple spare illustrations are comprised of only three colors: yellow, brown, and green. The illustrations for Robert McCloskey's *Blueberries for Sal* are entirely in dark blue block print. Its sequel, *One Morning in Maine,* along with McCloskey's Caldecott-winning *Make Way for Ducklings,* are both illustrated in charcoal. Clement Hurd's illustrations for Margaret Wise Brown's *Goodnight Moon* and *The Runaway Bunny* alternate pages of full-color with pages of black-and-white, as does Irene Haas's *The Maggie B.* Virginia Lee Burton's *The Little House* and *Mike Mulligan and His Steam Shovel,* despite featuring full-color illustrations on every page, are still more subdued than the picture books that we're used to in the digital age. Generally speaking, the illustrations in classic picture books are quieter and less color-saturated than in their contemporary counterparts. They can thus stretch and form our children's ability to appreciate subtleties of color and simplicity of form.

Another reason I recommend classic picture books is that they almost always keep their message, whatever it is, implicit. Their authors trust that readers will pick up on the moral of the story without being told what it is. You could, for instance, read Wanda Gág's *Millions of Cats* a hundred times and never say to yourself, "Oh, I see. This book is about the dangers of pride." Partly that's because it's *not* about the dangers of pride. It's about an old man and an old woman who want a cat, and the adventure that ensues when the old man goes off in search of one. Embedded in the story is a quiet reminder that the meek shall inherit the earth—or at least the cream bowl—and that those who exalt themselves will be humbled and those who humble themselves will be exalted. But that reminder is *quiet.* It's not shoved down your throat or hammered into your head. In fact, you could go your whole life and never consciously realize it's there. But it *is* there, and it's working on you, subtly, shimmering at the edges of your consciousness, shaping your view of the world. I find that is true of most classic children's picture books. Whatever lesson they hold, they hold it behind their backs and focus on telling a good story—and on letting the story speak for itself.

In a similar vein, classic picture books are generally uninterested in cleverness for its own sake—a stark contrast to our contemporary milieu which tends to emphasize, even idolize, cleverness. By cleverness, I mean wit with no substance. Books that are solely clever often revolve around an interesting or original idea, but they lack depth. The whole appeal of the story is its novelty. As a result, these books tend to operate on a single level, the level of a glib and shallow cleverness.

In contrast, classic picture books are never glib, though many of them are quite clever. Virginia Lee Burton's *Calico: The Wonder Horse, or The Saga of Stewy Stinker,* for instance, is a rollicking comic-book-style western, chock-full of melodrama and derring-do, featuring a horse who "wasn't very pretty … but she was very smart" and a villain who's "so mean he would hold up Santa Claus on Christmas Eve."

Maurice Sendak's *Where the Wild Things Are* is an imaginatively original exploration of a child's warring longings to seek adventure and to be in charge on the one hand and to seek security and to be cared for on the other. These are both extremely clever books. But they are not *only* clever books, and they don't draw attention to their own cleverness. They don't need to. They are first and foremost satisfying stories with so much else going on that you might not even notice how very clever they are.

Finally, classic picture books tend to emphasize our need for others. The main character nearly always requires assistance, even rescue and deliverance. Contemporary children's books, on the other hand, tend to emphasize self-reliance and self-help. It is almost a canon of contemporary publishing that the main character of a children's book must solve his or her own problem. Contrast this to a classic picture book like *Corduroy* by Don Freeman, in which the bear Corduroy, despite his best efforts, cannot find his missing button. It is Lisa who redeems him from the department store, just as he is, and gives him the button he lacks. Similarly, in Marjorie Flack's *The Story of Ping,* about a duck on the Yangtze River, Ping attempts to avoid a spanking and ends up being captured for a family's dinner. Unable to save himself, he only escapes death by the intervention of a boat-boy.

Classic stories like these show us that we cannot rescue ourselves—and that our striving to do so will ultimately get us into worse trouble than we were in to begin with. They teach us that left to ourselves, we are lost. But they don't stop there. They show us that we are *not* left to ourselves, that others will come alongside us in our need. Lisa redeems Corduroy. The boat-boy rescues Ping. These characters reflect the reality of a higher and better Redeemer and Rescuer. They show us, in the words of Gerard Manley Hopkins, that "Christ plays in ten thousand places, / lovely in limbs, and lovely in eyes not his."[1] A steady diet of such stories, in which the main character is saved not by works but by the kindness of another (which is ultimately the kindness of Another), teaches our children a great deal about their need for grace.

The Tale of A Fierce Bad Rabbit
Beatrix Potter | *Illustrated by Beatrix Potter*

Potter is the grandmother of classic picture books. Her most famous book is the delightful *The Tale of Peter Rabbit,* but my personal favorite is the lesser known *The Story of A Fierce Bad Rabbit.* Like his cousin Peter, the fierce bad rabbit is quite naughty, but in true classic form, Potter never stoops to moralizing—she lets the rabbit's misadventures speak for themselves. Potter wrote and illustrated over two dozen books. Her complete works are available in an omnibus edition, but some of the impact of the stories is lost in the larger format (this is especially true of *A Fierce Bad Rabbit*). So check your library for the individual books, as Potter designed the text and illustrations for these child-sized originals.

The Runaway Bunny
Margaret Wise Brown | *Illustrated by Clement Hurd*

This is the story of a mother bunny's relentless love for her little bunny—and the lengths to which she would go to bring her runaway bunny home. The boundless mother-love portrayed in this book is reason enough to read it—again and again—to a child. But the story is also an allegory of the soul, showing the lengths to which God will go to find His wayward children and bring us Home. Few children will pick up on this level of the story—and that's fine! The message of a love that never fails and never gives up will still get through and sink deep into their pysches.

The Clown of God
Tomie dePaola | *Illustrated by Tomie dePaola*

In this retelling of an old legend, the street urchin Giovanni grows up to be a famous juggler, then grows old and is forgotten. But his final performance is his most spectacular—for he juggles for the Christ Child on Christmas Eve. The story both explicitly and implicitly teaches that everything sings of the glory of God—even juggling! The illustrations are reminiscent of stained glass, evoking the early Renaissance time period in which the book is set.

Autumn Story
Jill Barklem | *Illustrated by Jill Barklem*

This is one of eight books about the mice of Brambly Hedge. The whole series features delightfully detailed illustrations of mid-nineteenth-century English country life, all at a diminutive scale. In *Autumn Story* we meet the busy mice as they prepare for the coming winter. Young Primrose wanders off, and as night falls, she is alone and afraid. But a search party has gone out looking for her, and she is brought safely home. This tale of getting lost and being found has strong undertones of the parable of the Good Shepherd. The other seven books in the series follow this cozy community of mice through the course of a year as they have a good many other adventures, whether they stay close to home or travel all the way to the sea.

Miss Rumphius
Barbara Cooney | *Illustrated by Barbara Cooney*

Little Alice lives with her grandmother and grandfather beside the sea. She tells her grandfather that, when she grows up, she will travel to faraway lands and then come back to live by the sea. Her grandfather tells her that is all well and good, but she must do one thing more: she must make the world a more beautiful place. This is the story of how Alice does just that. A truly beautiful book.

ENDNOTES
1   Gerard Manley Hopkins, "As Kingfishers Catch Fire," in *Poems and Prose of Gerard Manley Hopkins* (New York: Penguin Books, orig. publ. 1953), p. 51.

TRUTH, GOODNESS, BEAUTY ...AND PICTURE BOOKS

TRANSCENDENTALS

CAREY BUSTARD

When I was five years old, my mom and I would go to the open-air food market for hot dogs and lemonade. Every two weeks, we moseyed over to a park surrounded by brick office buildings, where we would sit near a beautiful water fountain and eat our hot dogs, drink our lemonade, and dive into the large canvas bag full of library books. The local library was always our first stop on this adventure. My mom and I would spend the morning going through shelf after shelf of children's picture books, finding the best of the best and putting them into the canvas bag. Five-year-old me was sure we left with one hundred books every time. Some would be repeat check-outs; others would be new discoveries. All were equally loved and cherished while they visited our home.

There were some criteria to our choices. They must be good. They must be true. They must be beautiful. They couldn't make Mom's stomach hurt, as any Barbie or Clifford book would. The odds that I was allowed to return home with a paperback retelling of a Disney movie were very low. Just because a book was old didn't mean the book made my mom's stomach feel any better. Regardless of publication date, the books from the library shelves that made it into our canvas bags had one magical qualification that I couldn't always put my finger on. Beautiful but not trite; written decades before, but bursting with delight; worn and paperback, sure, but rich with detail, story, and character. Now I realize that the books my parents were nudging my little sisters and me toward, on those library days, were good not because they were old but because they were classical books.

What is classical, though? Ty Fischer, headmaster at Veritas Academy and editor of the book *Teaching Beauty,* has said,

> Classical education has always been committed to forming the hearts, minds, and tastes of the young. Those tastes or desires are formed by living in a community that conveys a common understanding of what it means to be human and how to value and love those things that are true, good, and beautiful.[1]

This classical education movement took flight over twenty years ago because of the influence of authors such as Dorothy Sayers. Sayers encouraged educators (and, therefore, parents) to embrace the "Lost Tools of Learning" by spreading out a map and pointing out where culturally we had made a wrong turn. She suggested that, in order to reroute, we must look back in the direction whence we came. She was not, however, suggesting that we throw out the modern baby with the cultural bathwater. Her suggestion was not to revert back to only going about town in a horse and buggy when modernity has gifted us with perfectly fine cars. Her suggestion was to look at the good in the past that created a whole person and marry it with the gifts of contemporary life.

Some of those who embraced this education model—with its study of Latin and the Great Books—often conflated *old* with *good,* and therefore considered old books the only books worth their time because old books are just better. This view merely falls into the age-old error of assuming that everything in the "good ole days" must, by definition, be "good." In many areas, this is true. A book that stands the test of time survives because of its goodness. But that does not mean every old book passes this test. Classic and timeless do not necessarily equal good, let alone also true and beautiful.

Obviously I'm not saying to get rid of old books. The classical movement believes that there are great works of literature that we need to look back on and learn from. Every library should have copies of *Winnie-the-Pooh, Charlotte's Web, The Story of Ferdinand, The Snowy Day, Oxcart Man, Blueberries for Sal,* and *Bread and Jam for Frances.* These books are important for our children's imagination and for their understanding of where we come from. Yet if these great works are the only meals you feed your child's imagination, I argue that you are doing a disservice to that important muscle. If you restrict the definition of the good, true, and beautiful to only old books, you will miss out on the current works that will eventually stand the test of time. These books provide current pictures of goodness that your child can use to work through how her world works. On the flipside, if your view is too wide you will fall down a Berenstain Bear hole that you won't be able to escape. This calls for a rubric for choosing books that help train your child's gravitational pull towards classical books.

In his book *Art for God's Sake*, Philip Graham Ryken gives us a good outline for how to be discerning in creation and consumption. He is talking about the visual arts here, but I believe his words ring true for the written word as well. Ryken states, "Using Exodus 31 as a guide ... God's aesthetic standards include goodness, truth, and beauty. And these standards aren't relative; they are absolute."[2] This doesn't mean that you always get all three every time. That is a dynamic balance that will only be perfected in Jesus. You may only find a book that has two out of three. That's okay. This is just the lens we have been gifted to look through to find the best we have on this side of heaven.

According to Ryken, "Goodness is both an ethical and an aesthetic standard."[3] Looking for goodness captures both content and quality. "The difference," Ryken continues, "between good art and bad art is not something we learn from the Bible, primarily, but from the world that God has made. But what the Bible *does* tell us is that God knows the difference, and that he has a taste for excellence."[4] Much goodness can be found in the work of Shirley Hughes. An award-winning author and illustrator from England, Hughes has published over fifty books about various children in an English village. Her beautifully illustrated work depicts the simple joys and adventures of Alfie, Tom, Lucy, and their families. What happens when the pipes break? What about when the sheep get loose? How does one navigate getting a new sibling? Hughes explores the goodness of everyday life in a quality way. This simple excellence, in story, poetry, and illustration, informs a child's imagination of the deep richness in the ordinary world that God has created.

In a beautiful combination of this goodness standard of ethics and aesthetic, Stephanie Parsley Ledyard and Jason Chin take the reader on a journey through the different emotions and actions of sharing in their book *A Pie is for Sharing*. This book gently encourages kindness and hospitality through experience and examples—dessert, a book, a tree, or time—that are easy for children to recognize and grasp. Ledyard and Chin's pictures, both written and illustrated, quietly celebrate the goodness and importance of community and family. It is through beautiful works like *A Pie is for Sharing* that readers, young and old alike, can be reminded of and inspired by the brilliance of tangible actions that mirror God's goodness.

However, Ryken's outline of the good, true, and beautiful, does not suggest that God takes pleasure only in goodness. "Art," Ryken states, "is an incarnation of the truth. It penetrates the surface of things to portray them as they really are."[5] He uses the tabernacle as an example to describe this truth. The purpose of the tabernacle was in service to the truth of who God is and how He relates to His people. The stories filling our children's imaginations should point to this truth in some capacity. Trillia J. Newbell's *God's Very Good Idea* is an excellent example of this truth. Not only do Newbell and illustrator Catalina Echeverri share the truth of God's plan throughout the gospel story, but they also show the deep richness of the diversity of God's people. They show that God created and Jesus came to rescue all types of people. Newbell graciously invites us to this ageless celebration and encourages the next generation of believers get excited about being in the church and a part of this beautiful family.

Ryken continues, "Art communicates truth in various ways. Sometimes it tells a story, and the story is true to human experience—it is an incarnation of the human condition."[6] This truth, and the goodness of the human condition, can also be found in the people who cross a child's path. Matt de la Peña and Christian Robinson's book *Last Stop on Market Street* explores a world of poverty, service, and city life filled with kindness, empathy, and joy.

The story follows CJ and his grandmother as they go on their weekly bus ride across town to the local soup kitchen. CJ complains that they never take a car and always have to go to a poorer part of town. His grandmother responds to each critique and question by pointing to the beauty and joy all around them in the little, ordinary things—ultimately pointing to the great good in loving one's neighbor. With a little poetry, the reader is encouraged toward empathy and kindness through the wisdom and love of CJ's grandmother. This is a taste of God's standard for excellence, His character, and how His relationship with His children plays out in everyday human connection.

The final, pivotal piece is beauty. Ryken writes,

> God is a great lover of beauty, as we can see from the collection of his work that hangs in the gallery of the universe. Form is as important to him as function. Thus it was not enough for the tabernacle to be laid out in the right way; it also had to be beautiful.[7]

This beauty is not just one cookie-cutter experience. Just as all of creation is unique and diverse, so too should be the beauty we introduce to our children.

Dianna Aston and Sylvia Long's Nature Books are an example of God's gallery. *A Butterfly is Patient* is a journey through the life cycle of a butterfly, full of detailed, scientific illustrations and poetic descriptions of the different stages of the process. Aston and Long open the door to scientific discovery in this introduction to caterpillars and butterflies and give the reader an up close and personal look at the magnificent details of God's creation—details that might normally fly past without a second glance. Works like *A Butterfly is Patient* open the world up wider for the reader and give his imagination permission to soar. Aston and Long's work shows young readers that just as God is infinitely creative, they can be, too. God's creation didn't stop growing or moving after works like *The Chronicles of Narnia* or *Goodnight Moon*. We must constantly be reminded of God's great gallery as it forms and changes throughout time and space.

Just as beauty is displayed in natural creation, it should also be explored in the beauty of God's people. What better way to show a child that they are valuable than a story of imagination and wonder like Kelly Dipucchio and Raissa Figueroa's *Oona*? This sweet story follows a beautiful Black mermaid named Oona and her pet otter named Otto as they seek treasure and adventure. When they face trouble on their journey, they must work together to find a solution and uncover the beauty of the ocean. Not only are readers caught up in the natural magnificence of God's oceans, but they are also reminded that every person made in God's image is unique, valued, and beautiful.

But the authors of classic literature were not exempt from depicting ugliness. Nor are their modern counterparts. Ryken states,

> This does not mean that goodness, truth, and beauty are always easy to define (especially beauty). Nor does it mean that Christian artists never portray anything ugly. We have truth to tell about the ugliness of a fallen world. Indeed, Christianity offers the best explanation for that ugliness in its doctrine of depravity: the world has been spoiled by sin.[8]

I would argue that only focusing on one age of art versus another and making claims that modern works are of less value than classic works leaves our children with a small view of the world and an even smaller definition of depravity. Just as the Gospels point to the Old Testament's telling of the goodness of God, the beauty of His promises, and the true story of the ways God's people brought ugliness to the world, so too should we in modernity look back at ages past and celebrate the quality work it produced. The New Testament doesn't stay stagnant. It's alive and moving, even today. The art and literature we introduce to our children should also move and breathe.

Modernity hasn't stopped any commitment to forming hearts and minds and helping children understand what it means to be human and, to return to Ty Fischer's point, how to cultivate taste and desires for the good, the true, and the beautiful. Artists are still creating new works of children's literature, because God's creativity has not run out. New wine is still being made, and just as the best wine in the wine cellar has aged to its highest quality, so too should new works of art and literature be given the chance to ferment.

Comparing apples to oranges will never serve you well. Apples may make a better pie, but that doesn't diminish an orange's quality and importance as a fruit. Your fruit salad will thank you for taking the time to search for the best fruit combinations. So too will your child's imagination—as well as her sense of the value of others, her desire to live in community, and her understanding of God's goodness, truth, and beauty—be richer if you provide her with the best of both classic and modern literature.

Baby Wren and the Great Gift
Sally Lloyd-Jones | *Illustrated by Jen Corace*

I love anything by Sally Lloyd-Jones, but I think this is my favorite. This sweet story follows a tiny wren as she explores the world of her canyon home. She struggles with feeling like she cannot contribute to the greatness of the world, but in the end finds she has her own unique gift that brings glory to God just like her friends.

The Dark
Lemony Snicket | *Illustrated by Jon Klassen*

Jon Klassen is one of my favorite illustrators, and this story is just a small sample of his goodness. Lemony Snicket, best known for his *Series of Unfortunate Events*, shines in this story about how to get over the fear of the dark. This poetic tale follows a young boy named Laszlo. The dark lives in Laszlo's house, but it usually stays in the basement—until it doesn't. Laszlo learns that some things that seem scary are actually meant for good.

Captain Starfish
Davina Bell | *Illustrated by Allison Colpoys*

This lovely story follows dear Alfie as he learns how to celebrate being introverted and work past his anxiety. Full of sweet illustrations and words of kindness, readers will walk away with an understanding of how to balance feelings and of what bravery truly means. I think this story captures all three criteria of a good modern classic.

Hello, My Name is Ruby
Philip C. Stead

Ruby is the sweetest little bird on a mission to make some friends. This story follows her as she meets many different types of birds and personalities. She learns how to navigate new creatures and ask questions. I know this is another book about a bird, but the illustrations and storyline tick all the boxes for a timeless book. Philip C. Stead (as well as his wife—and frequent collaborator—Erin Stead) is a classic author and illustrator in the making. One of my favorites.

The Boy, the Mole, the Fox, and the Horse
Charlie Mackesy

This book is a work of art. Not only are the black-and-white ink drawings gorgeous, but the poetic language invites readers to ask questions about the world and about themselves. The story follows a little boy as he befriends a mole, a fox, and a horse and learns how to work through difficult times toward kindness and love. They have hard conversations as friends and help model how to speak truth in love to those around them. Charlie Mackesy leaves the reader with simple but profound truth nuggets to take into everyday life.

ENDNOTES

1   G. Tyler Fischer, ed., *Teaching Beauty: A Vision for Music and Art in Christian Education* (Baltimore, MD: Square Halo Books, 2016), p. 71.
2   Philip Graham Ryken, *Art for God's Sake: A Call to Recover the Arts* (Phillipsburg, NJ: P&R Publishing, 2006), p. 37.
3   Ibid.
4   Ryken, *Art for God's Sake*, p. 39.
5   Ibid.
6   Ryken, p. 40.
7   Ryken, p. 42.
8   Ryken, p. 44.

WORTH A THOUSAND WORDS

CONTEMPORARY PICTURE BOOKS

CAROLYN LEILOGLOU

Many of us have a tendency to romanticize the past. White picket fences, neatly dressed children, and mothers in aprons making chocolate chip cookies—surely those people were practically perfect in every way. And we often apply this attitude to the books we give our children. Maybe you've heard people say that only older picture books are safe. Contemporary picture books, they say, aren't well-written. Or they violate Christian morals in a way older books don't. But this rosy view of the past glosses over the very real sins of earlier generations. Indeed every generation, regardless of how enlightened it considers itself, has at least one speck it its eye.

Books are meant to be a conversation—the Great Conversation, as it is often called—and that conversation can't just be one-sided. Contemporary picture books should come alongside older ones as part of the conversation. Older books can be beautiful, but I want you to see that contemporary picture books, too, are good. If we wish to raise kids who shape the culture we live in, we cannot ignore contemporary picture books. We must give our children examples of authors who speak into the present with humor, truth, and grace.

I notice three particular strengths in contemporary picture books: art, poetry of language, and engaging nonfiction.

Today's picture books give us the opportunity to introduce our children to a wide range of artistic styles. While there is much to admire in the detailed oil and watercolor paintings of older picture books, there has never been such variety and talent among picture book artists as today. Mediums such as collage, watercolor, and digital art all add to the visual feast we can present to our children.

But more importantly, the role of the illustrator has changed. In times past, the illustrations, while beautiful, simply gave a visual for what the words described. Today's illustrators are expected to add nuance to the text. Sometimes that means adding details that are not mentioned directly (as in *Accident!* by Andrea Tsurumi), showing details that contradict or tell a different story than the text (*Beautiful*, by Stacy McAnulty and Joanne Lew-Vriethoff), giving life to metaphor or imagination (*Sleep Like a Tiger*, by Mary Logue and Pamela Zagarenski), adding details that allow the child to know more than a character does (*Sam and Dave Dig a Hole*, by Mac Barnett and Jon Klassen), or even telling part of the story just through visuals (*Waiting*, by Kevin Henkes).

The contemporary author and illustrator engage in a kind of dance, each with their own part, neither stepping on one another's toes. And the end result is something greater than either the words or the pictures alone.

Contemporary picture books are typically quite short—often less than five hundred words—but that doesn't mean they sacrifice poetic or creative use of language. Many people bemoan the loss of the beautiful, lengthy sentences of older books, citing shortening attention spans as the culprit. Yet the brevity of contemporary picture books often lends to their beauty. Each word must earn its place, and the best picture book writers are as choosy as poets in their word selection. Jim Averbeck's *In a Blue Room* and Brendan Wenzel's *The Stone Sat Still* both make beautiful use of poetic language, while *Spoon*, by Amy Krouse Rosenthal, plays with creative language.

Another area that has truly blossomed in contemporary picture books is nonfiction. When I was young, nonfiction books were fairly dull. If you weren't already interested in the topic, the book wasn't likely to change your mind. Today's nonfiction picture books are proving that anything can be interesting if presented in the right way.

Gone are the days of boring biographies. Modern picture book creators know that every life is a story, and they zero in on the interesting tidbits that make a life worth considering and a person worth cheering for. Expository nonfiction books—like the many fantastic books by Jess Keating, Steve Jenkins, and Barb Rosenstock—are poised to capture readers with surprising facts and stunning illustrations.

Of course, contemporary picture books have their failings as well as their strengths: there are more books published today than ever before, and that includes picture books. With such a vast number of books, wide differences in quality are more present than ever. And with such a wealth to choose from, how can we find the best ones? I have a few suggestions.

Look for art you enjoy. This won't be the same for everyone. But the books you choose to have on your shelves will influence your children's tastes. Make sure you find them beautiful.

Choose books with read-aloud-ability. Try to find language that tastes delicious, be it seasoned with beautiful phrases, word play, metaphors, or silliness. Hearing the same books again and again is great for kids developmentally, so a picture book that isn't torturous for a parent to read multiple times in a row is a great picture book.

Select books with diverse characters. Books show us the similarities we share with others and help us appreciate our differences rather than fear them. Reading these kinds of picture books helps kids to see themselves in stories, and it is one way to teach our kids to love their neighbors. This doesn't mean each book you buy will have diverse characters. After all, some wonderful books feature animals or even inanimate objects, and there are many classic picture books that may not feature diverse characters but that are certainly still worth reading. But it does mean you are aware of your overall shelf when purchasing books or bringing them home from the library.

Seek books with messages you agree with. The best books have a message that naturally emerges from the story, rather than one that is heavy-handed or overly moralistic. It's good to be choosy when buying the books you and your child will be reading over and over.

Whatever books you choose, don't miss the chances to snuggle with your child and enjoy reading together. After all, picture books aren't just for kids. They're for everyone.

My Papi Has a Motorcycle
Isabel Quintero | *Illustrated by Zeke Peña*

My Papi Has a Motorcycle is a beautiful story of the love between a father and daughter and the time they share riding his motorcycle around their neighborhood. It celebrates culture, family, community, and hard work. Laced with Spanish words and Latin food and culture, this book embodies a beautiful, specific picture of home and community.

Van Gogh Paints the Night Sky: Vincent Can't Sleep
Barb Rosenstock | *Illustrated by Mary Grandpré*

By choosing one thread—insomnia—Rosenstock pulls readers into the story of van Gogh's life. Her carefully crafted writing makes use of metaphor and echoing images, like church steeples and the night sky, to give the story shape. The illustrations make it seem as though van Gogh has entered his paintings. Van Gogh lived a difficult and complicated life, but Rosenstock keeps this first introduction appropriate for younger kids.

After the Fall
Dan Santat | *Illustrated by Dan Santat*

Dan Santat won the 2014 Caldecott Medal for his book *The Adventures of Beekle: The Unimaginary Friend,* but in my opinion, *After the Fall* is an even bigger masterpiece. This continuation of Humpty Dumpty's story deals with not letting fear win. It's a beautiful example of how much the illustrations can add to a simple text—the cereal aisle is especially brilliant. And the stunning ending, which I won't give away, relies on the interplay between the text and illustrations.

The Rabbit Listened
Cori Doerrfeld | *Illustrated by Cori Doerrfeld*

At just 296 words, *The Rabbit Listened* is deceptively simple. But it is a thoughtful treatise on how to be a friend to someone who is struggling. Taylor, a curly-headed child in pajamas, builds something amazing, but it gets destroyed. A progression of different animals try to tell Taylor how to respond. Only the rabbit listens, showing how a true friend can help in times of crisis just by being present.

A House That Once Was
Julie Fogliano | *Illustrated by Lane Smith*

Fogliano is a master wordsmith, and she manages to make her text poetic and lyrical without being sing-songy. This book speaks to the dual audience of picture books by simultaneously evoking nostalgia in parents and sparking imagination in kids. The multimedia illustrations lend a sense of mystery to the story. By the end, *A House That Once Was* draws the reader to see their own home in a new light.

GROWING HOLY IMAGINATION

MIDDLE GRADE FICTION

JOY STRAWBRIDGE

I care for two five-month-old boys on the weekdays near my Nashville neighborhood. As I prop up their side-by-side bottles, I try to tell them true things: *You are the good guys. You are so good! We are so glad you're here. You make everything better. You make everything fun! What do you have to tell us? How can I help you? You are my little friends. I am so happy to see you.*

There isn't much time in a child's life when they can hear and process language but don't yet have the developmental skill to return the favor. And so, I pack my two little friends with as many good words as I can—my words, good music, and board books—while they're still using their voices in symphonic hollers for milk and mattresses. That way, when their words do come, they'll have good ones to choose from.

Having served as a preschool, elementary, middle, and high school teacher at different points in my life, this is the thing that stands out to me the most: children say what they hear. They make their high notes sound like sparkly ice princesses. They borrow the words that made them laugh from the Friday family superhero movie. My students talk to me the way their parents talk to them. Then once they can read, they spend their lives repeating after their peers. Imitation, I often remind myself, is the highest form of love. Knowing this, how can we— as writers, educators, parents, or aunts and uncles who share our favorite stories and hide wrapped books under the tree—put a heart for adventure and the highest caliber of language, beauty, and empathy into the minds and mouths of the little saints we love?

Through some of the best words, worthy of our imitation, middle grade fiction, in particular, has the power to nourish empathy and adventure in readers. Neon squares of distraction, self-obsession disguised as insight, deets dished about our neighbors, news foretelling imminent doom—let's leave these slices of literature for readers with facial hair and savings accounts. Chapter books that reinvent the possible, carried by kindred spirit characters, should be the entire food pyramid of the snow day that is childhood: fast-accumulating, soon-melting; it twinkles.

As we grow up, our perspective widens, wonders, narrows, and focuses. The books recommended here, for middle grade readers, fit between widening and wondering. In our conversations, my fourth-grade students would wonder if the place I ate dinner the night before was near their sister's ballet studio, off Main Street; in the next breath, they would share a great deal of concern about the social implications of bringing a new backpack mid-year. The confluence of knowing more and caring more makes this stage soft soil for growing empathy and adventure through the best books.

The books in this chapter are meant especially for readers who have graduated from *My Father's Dragon*, *Henry and Mudge*, and Ramona's belly-laughable episodes but who may not be ready to reach for the last half of the *Harry Potter* series. Middle grade fiction, as a genre, serves readers ages 8–12; it is my secret, perhaps unpopular, opinion that the books written for readers ages 8–12 are the pinnacle of literature. Picture how delightful, how tedious, how glittery it can be to talk to a child, particularly one who knows their multiplication facts, but who needs to be reminded who the current president is. Phone-less, they look out windows when they're bored. They sport sneakers and tutus and cat-ear headbands worn unironically; some of their playmates are still imaginary. They deserve our best. As readers, their imaginations are hydrated by valiant quests, animals stories, and the adventures of other nine-year-olds who wonder why life isn't fair. They only actually finish books about the real world (or the real-seeming one).

One of my favorite writing teachers once gave my classmates and me writing exercises that she said "could make the world feel more write-able." It is my hope that these kinds of books make middle grade readers see the world as more explore-able, their classmates and family members more compassion-able—that they present our world as a remarkably beautiful place to live. Because of the real and imagined. Because of what is here, and what isn't, yet. The visible and the invisible.

As we raise a generation of readers surrounded by the best stories we can mine for them, as we shape and hydrate holy imaginations, we do so inviting in The Great Imaginer—our Maker and Storyteller—to never be absent from our adventures.

I wonder about the friendships, the conversations, the lives led, and the work done by those among us who have spent their snow days strengthening their capacity to discover and to care, through reading the best chapter books. Imagine the fruit from lives of little believers trained by ink and paper that goodness is growing in and around them. Through them. Imagine classrooms and breakfast tables, playgrounds with friends they haven't met yet, school buses, church pews, and soon: dorm rooms, news rooms, court rooms, kitchen tables. Imagine the way they'll talk to those around them, they way they'll love their self-identified enemies, the worlds they will build for still smaller saints who model them.

It starts with a good book.

The Phantom Tollbooth
Norton Juster | *Illustrated by Jules Feiffer*

Milo longs to be wherever he isn't. But after he embarks on a magical adventure—featuring a large package, a ringing dog, and a zippy car just his size—Milo becomes a kind and hilarious hero. If you come for a character-building adventure, you'll stay for the brilliant wordplay. The best books for children, of course, are also good books for grown-ups. Milo visits Expectations, Conclusions (an island you can only reach by jumping), as well as Dictionopolis and Digitopolis, the warring kingdoms with fighting brothers for kings. Books that break words with their crackling intelligence and wit are tough to summarize—find a copy and one long sitting. Somewhere you can laugh at top volume.

Number the Stars
Lois Lowry

There is a particular kind of love I've felt for writers like Lois Lowry. After a recess spat or a long morning featuring a hard math test, my students and I could open *Number the Stars* and sit together around the Johansens' table for dinner; hide with those we were protecting; hold our breath when angry soldiers kicked at our front door. The book opens in 1940s Denmark, with a friendly race between best friends, Annemarie and Ellen, who are stopped by a Nazi soldier as they come home from school. We feel Annemarie's joy, bravery, uncertainty, and the love that wings its way off the pages of this novel. The fourth-grade girls in my classes often reread the book as soon as we finished it. Ellen, Annemarie, and Kirsti felt like honored guests in our classroom.

The Long Winter
Laura Ingalls Wilder

Laura Ingalls is one of the patron saints of middle grade empathy and adventure. In the sixth Little House story, Laura and her family persevere with less and less as they nearly starve during seven long months of blizzards. As she describes the world she and her family inhabited, Wilder puts us in her own cold, tattered boots, and we see her family's gratitude in the face of shocking lack.

Of the books in the Ingalls family saga, this one in particular allowed my students and me the chance to pause and critique. As we discussed the story, I wanted my students to enjoy the characters in this classic without deifying them, and to resist the temptation to excuse hatred and un-biblical attitudes toward the stranger by saying, "It was a different time." Loving the good work of the past, without blindly accepting every word that comes from those older than we are, is important work. We must read with open arms and discerning hearts. With gospel eyes.

The Facts and Fictions of Minna Pratt
Patricia MacLachlan

For older middle grade readers, Minna Pratt is a lesser known but quintessentially modern coming-of-age heroine. Minna feels out of place, longs for a normal family, and ultimately wants to succeed in playing the cello by finding her vibrato. With a cast of quirky, pre-phone tweens and bothersome little brothers (who sing newspaper headlines aloud on the bus), this story embodies the heart, hilarity, and almost-not-yet itchiness of being eleven.

From the Mixed-Up Files of Mrs. Basil E. Frankweiler
E.L. Konigsburg

E.L. Konigsburg is a master middle grade storyteller. Her characters feel like real-life friends, whose sagas captivate your mind and heart long after the last page. In this story, siblings Claudia and Jamie run away from their northeastern suburb to the Metropolitan Museum of Art in New York City, where they camp out: bathing in the fountain, narrowly avoiding security guards, and discovering a classical art mystery along the way. Has there ever been a young reader who didn't imagine running away? This story invites the reader to imagine the independence and adventure required to eat and sleep in a famous museum. An exciting read-aloud, this story is a museum mystery, an art-history primer, and a coming-of-age novel all in one.

WHAT'S THE USE OF A BOOK WITHOUT PICTURES?

ILLUSTRATED CHAPTER BOOKS

CAROLYN CLARE GIVENS

I used to be scared of "big books." That's humorous to me now, when I look at my living room wall covered with bookshelves full of books or think back to my teenage years, when I constantly buried my nose in novels hundreds of pages long.

But as an elementary student, dense pages of text intimidated me. I was far more likely to pick up an early reader or a "picture storybook," as I like to call the now-disappeared genre of picture books with long blocks of text on an illustrated spread that were a staple of my childhood. Most of all, I loved the middle grade books that interspersed pen-and-ink illustrations among the pages of text with an illustrator's interpretation of a writer's scene and a glimpse into the world behind the words. Those books provided me an on-ramp to the story, a picture for my mind's eye to start with when it tried to image the tale.

For me, it took moving to another country with a limited English library and reading *Anne of Green Gables* to turn me into an avid reader of "big books" at age ten. But I've since discovered that I was not alone in my aversion to pages of text without a break. The famous Alice (of Wonderland) herself found them useless. Jeffrey Garn Howard writes:

> *Alice's Adventures in Wonderland* begins with Alice sitting "by her sister on the bank and having nothing to do" except peek over and see what her sister is reading. Upon discovering that the book is just a lot of prose, she declares "What is the use of a book ... without pictures or conversations?" Alice's reference to the practical significance of images implies that human

communication is at its basis multimodal, and reliance on a single mode, such as writing, detracts from a work's potential influence.[1]

Howard here introduces a key concept with the idea of *multimodal communication*. As we train our children in literacy, we begin with board books and picture books—highly visual codices that rely very little on written text. Slowly, we transition them through visual literacy, to auditory literacy when we read aloud, and on to verbal literacy, the ability to read and write. In all of these, our goal is for our children to comprehend and engage with stories, in the hope of creating lifelong learners. David Rapp writes, "Lifelong learning, after all, requires sustained interest in and success with understanding what others have written, making connections among the texts we read, and applying that knowledge in our everyday lives."[2]

The drawback of our traditional formal system for training in literacy is that formal education tends to weigh importance to verbal literacy (reading and writing) at the expense of other forms of communication and to the detriment of those whose learning styles are not primarily verbal. Even for a highly verbal learner like me, the gap between visual literacy and verbal literacy was too broad to cross without assistance. I needed an illustrator to open the eyes of my imagination to the world of the story.

Joe Sutphin, an illustrator of children's novels, describes the role of these illustrations this way:

When you're reading a novel, you create this mind's eye—this picture in your head of these characters, who they are, what they look like, where these environments are, what's happening. And then, in a novel, you'll suddenly reach a page where there's art. And that's the illustrator's opportunity to inform your mind's eye. You get this little glimpse of what someone else is telling you, "It all actually looks like this."[3]

The list of illustrators whose work falls in this category is long, but chief among them must be Garth Williams. I can recognize Garth Williams's style anywhere and have often picked up new-to-me books simply because I saw his work on the cover. Sarah Larson of the *New Yorker* calls Williams's illustrations "an indelible part of twentieth-century American childhood."[4] She notes that he illustrated more than eighty books in his life. "Beloved children's books are often re-illustrated, sometimes badly; too often, the visual subtlety of earlier illustrations is lost. . . . Happily, Williams's work has stayed in print, and for the books he illustrated, many of them classics, the illustrations are integral and essential."[5]

It's this essential quality that strikes me about Garth Williams's illustrations. I've probably read the *Little House on the Prairie* books a hundred times, and the images—of the tiny shanty on the wide-open prairie, or the girls playing catch with a pig's bladder, or Mary's new dress made by Ma for her college years—are vividly a part of the story for me. I find the same thing when I pick up my well-loved copy of *A Cricket in Times Square* and take a look at Tucker Mouse and Harry Cat and Chester Cricket feasting on a sardine-tin table in the drainpipe they call home. The pictures are not an addition or afterthought: they are another portal into the world.

Williams, though, is not alone in his recognizable and vivid style. On the opposite end of the spectrum, visually, are the illustrations of Quentin Blake, who may be best known for his work on Roald Dahl's *The BFG, Matilda, The Twits*, and more. In an article on him for the *Guardian*, Fiona Sturges highlights the simplicity of his style:

> Blake is, he says, a fast worker. He once described his style as "deceptively slapdash," though "if you know anything about it, [you know] it isn't slapdash," he adds. "I had a very nice student who once said 'You're like Fred Astaire, you make it look easy.'"[6]

The lines of Blake's illustrations are simple and strong. On his website, a caption with one of his illustrations reads "'The Twits' was first published in 1980, with illustrations Quentin had drawn using a very hard nib—perfect for capturing the spiky quality of Mr. Twit's beard. Quentin also experimented with the grim spikiness of the Twits' house and garden in this drawing, though it was not included in the final set for the book."[7] It's this "spiky quality" that draws me to Blake's illustrations. They're funny, and a little weird, but the Miss Honey of Blake's illustration in *Matilda* brings to life Dahl's description, "Some curious warmth that was almost tangible shone out of Miss Honey's face when she spoke to a confused and homesick newcomer to class."[8] As a young and intimidated reader, the pictures of Miss Honey welcomed me into Matilda's story as much as the words about her.

There are contemporary illustrators whose work plays this role of portal to the story as well. I think of Brett Helquist, who is best known for illustrating Lemony Snicket's *A Series of Unfortunate Events*. In that series, the author includes Helquist by name in his "Letters to the Editor," making recommendations of items he should study in preparation for the upcoming books. Helquist thus becomes a part of the fictional world as well as a doorway into it. In Blue Balliett's

Chasing Vermeer, Helquist's illustrations hold one of the puzzles that the reader is challenged to solve in the book.

Joe Sutphin, illustrator of the New York Times bestseller *Word of Mouse,* writes:

> I'm always attempting to give the reader a visual memory of things they are reading, that they begin to recall as they keep reading where there is not art … Once I've given the reader a visual depiction of a character … it makes an imprint on the reader's memory. They might read the following chapter where I have no illustrations placed, yet they begin to see the visuals I provided … within the new textual information they are reading.[9]

In more recent years, graphic novels or graphic narratives have become much more common, both in the publishing industry and in the classroom. Often, teachers use them to help struggling readers bridge the gap from visual to verbal literacy. But graphic novels are a further iteration of multimodal communication in print. Elizabeth E.G. Friese describes her first encounter with reading a graphic novel this way:

> With a graphic narrative, to read both the words and the pictures, I had to consciously slow down, over and over again. I had to relearn to read, approaching each page differently and developing an appreciation for the way words and pictures worked together. Instead of an inferior type of reading, I realized that graphic narratives represent a more sophisticated, multimodal form of reading than alphabet-only texts.[10]

Long before *Maus* and *Persepolis* raised the profile of the graphic narrative from fanboy comics to serious literature and opened the door for learning multimodal communication through print in the classroom, illustrators of middle grade novels were already doing the work of transitioning young readers between modes of communication and comprehension, teaching them that the world of words is not so scary after all, not if you've got mouse by your side or a spider in your corner.

The Misadventured Summer of Tumbleweed Thompson
Glenn McCarty | *Illustrated by Joe Sutphin*

Glenn McCarty's young scallywag, Tumbleweed Thompson, is perfectly captured by Joe Sutphin's illustrations. The adventures that young Eugene Appleton has that summer that Tumbleweed and his father stop in Rattlesnake Junction will be the legends he tells his grandchildren. From gambling with smugglers on a river boat to escaping from them on horseback, the adventures of Eugene and Tumbleweed never let up and keep you laughing all the way along. Joe Sutphin's illustrations are scattered throughout the text, sometimes laid out in two-page spreads. He captures the rough and tumble of the Old West town and the lazy summer days of a boy's life within it. I want to hand this book to every ten-year-old boy I know—and to most of the girls, too.

Chasing Vermeer
Blue Balliett | *Illustrated by Brett Helquist*

Blue Balliett's first children's art mystery novel brings together two classmates to solve the mystery of the theft of a Vermeer painting. An adventure from start to finish, *Chasing Vermeer* also opens the door to a wide world of art, mathematics, history, and more. The book itself is full of puzzles for children to solve. Helquist's illustrations bring to life the shy Petra and the pattern-loving Calder. Included in the illustrations is another set of puzzles, another mystery for an engaged young reader to solve, and clues that tie into the main mysteries of the novel. Balliett's novel is full of the tropes of any mystery, without the violence sometimes present in those written for an older audience.

The Cricket in Times Square
George Selden | *Illustrated by Garth Williams*

When Chester Cricket accidentally travels from the countryside to the Times Square subway station in New York, city-wise Tucker Mouse and Harry Cat take him under their protection and show him the lay of the land. Chester is cared for by Mario, the boy whose family runs the newsstand. When the business faces financial trouble, Chester's keen ear for music and his ability to play perfectly from memory set the stage for concerts by the cricket to save the newsstand. Williams's illustrations bring to life the wily Tucker Mouse, the suave Harry Cat, and the innocent Chester Cricket, along with the spaces of the newsstand and the city subway. You will never find more personality in a mouse's eyes than you see in Tucker's, as he and Chester share a bite of liverwurst on their first night as friends.

Matilda
Roald Dahl | *Illustrated by Quentin Blake*

Matilda Wormwood is a genius with incredibly stupid, selfish parents. She thinks circles around them at home, playing practical jokes, but when she goes to school, young Matilda is faced for the first time with truly bad people, including her headmistress, Ms. Trunchbull. Fortunately, her teacher Miss Honey is there to help her cultivate her genius—and to support her when she discovers some rather surprising telekinetic abilities. Quentin Blake's strong illustrations bring out the horribleness of the villains and the beauty of the heroines with the same simple lines. He captures Miss Honey's sweetness and Mr. Wormwood's weasley-ness and Matilda's innocence equally well.

Homer Price
Robert McCloskey | *Illustrated by Robert McCloskey*

I have told the story of Homer Price and the doughnuts—in which a wealthy lady helps make a massive amount of doughnut batter and then the doughnut machine won't shut off and makes hundreds of doughnuts, into one of which they realize the wealthy lady's diamond bracelet is baked—more times than I can count. I'm always baffled when I discover that people don't know it, because it's one of the funniest stories of my childhood. That chapter of McCloskey's book is just one of the entertaining escapades Homer Price finds himself in. McCloskey illustrated his own book, so his images are always spot on.

ENDNOTES

1   Jeffrey Garn Howard, "'What Use is a Book … Without Pictures?': Images and Words in Lewis Carroll's *ALICE'S ADVENTURES IN WONDERLAND*," *The Explicator*, Volume 73, Issue 1 (2015).

2   David N. Rapp, "Comic Books' Latest Plot Twist: Enhancing Literacy Instruction," *The Phi Delta Kappan*, Vol. 3, No. 4 (2011–2012), pp. 64–67.

3   Joe Sutphin, *Informing the Mind's Eye*, produced by Josh Stephens (Vimeo, 2018), https://vimeo.com/306420816.

4   Sarah Larson, "Garth Williams, Illustrator of American Childhood," *The New Yorker*, June 3, 2016, https://www.newyorker.com/books/page-turner/garth-williams-illustrator-of-american-childhood.

5   Ibid.

6   Fiona Sturges, "Quentin Blake: 'Spend time with children? Good God, no'," *The Guardian*, February 29, 2020, https://www.theguardian.com/books/2020/feb/29/inside-the-magical-world-of-quentin-blake.

7   "The Twits' house and garden," QuentinBlake.com, accessed October 25, 2020, https://www.quentinblake.com/gallery/twits%E2%80%99-house-and-garden.

8   Roald Dahl, *Matilda* (New York: Puffin Books, 1990), p. 67.

9   Joe Sutphin, email message to author, October 28, 2020.

10   Elizabeth E.G. Friese, "Visual Narratives: Reading and Writing Through the Pages of Graphic Life Stories," *Knowledge Quest*, Volume 1, Issue 3 (2013): p. 24.

NAVIGATING THE IN-BETWEEN

MIDDLE SCHOOL

LAURA PETERSON

I don't know any adult for whom the words "middle school" inspire cozy, comforting memories. Of all the years in life when we might feel lost, alone, and at sea with our emotions and our very selves, I think these years are some of the worst. Even the very idea of middle school is hard to pin down; school systems vary in how they define this age, and developmental markers are all over the place. The publishing world splits the group in half, with "middle grade" books being those largely marketed to eight- through twelve-year-olds, and "young adult" books those marketed to thirteen- through eighteen-year-olds.

But for the purposes of this chapter, let's define middle school readers as those between the ages of eleven and fifteen. Still, how do you lump together a group that includes both kids who have barely reached puberty and those who are just a year away from their learners' permit? It's a stressful time, crammed with formational experiences. Think back to those years in your own life for a moment. Did you have conflicts with friends? Arguments with your parents? Embarrassing moments where you just wanted the earth to swallow you up? All of us can probably recall those experiences. Now take a moment to think about some of the favorite books you read in your childhood. Which characters made you laugh or cry or feel brave? What stories interested you the most? I'll hazard a guess that many of the characters and plot lines you just recalled came from stories you first encountered when you were in middle school.

Middle school is a time of growing independence and intellectual skills, meaning that kids this age are reaching for more complex and challenging books, and are primed to be emotionally impacted by their content. It's a sweet spot for formational stories, which is probably why I love middle school books so much.

I've often heard authors say that they want to write particularly for this age group because they remember what a tough time it was for them. They want readers to feel like someone is on their side, to know that they are not alone. It's no wonder, then, that there are so many excellent books written for middle schoolers! But where to start? Obviously no two readers are alike, and genre interests (mystery or fantasy?) and format preferences (graphic novel or 352-page tome?) can vary widely. When I think back to my own middle school self, or consider the kids this age who come into my library today, a pattern starts to emerge. I think the books that middle schoolers are most drawn to (and deeply need!) fit into three broad categories.

The first category I'll call Everyday Books. These are stories that portray middle school kids going about their daily lives and encountering the standard challenges and experiences that come with growing up: school days, summer camp, relationships with friends and family. What's great about these types of books is that they present opportunities for kids to both see themselves and their own experiences reflected back at them, and to see others' lives and experiences that they may be less familiar with. Educator Emily Style introduced this idea of "mirror" and "window" books in the 1980s. To choose an example from that time, let's consider Gordon Korman's hilarious *Bruno & Boots* series, published from 1978 through 1995. This set of books about a group of boys at a Canadian boarding school who can't seem to stay out of trouble with their headmaster, Mr. Sturgeon ("The Fish"), was foreign and fascinating to middle-school me, a shy rule-follower who didn't talk to boys; these stories functioned as "window" books. They were a safe peek into a different way of living. To a reader who actually did attend a boarding school, however, or who had a crew of friends he liked to clown around with, these would be "mirror" books, reminders that he wasn't alone in his daily experiences.

Kids of all experiences and backgrounds need both window and mirror books. Scripture tells us that we are each God's workmanship (Eph. 2:10), each made in the image of God (Gen. 1:27). If part of our reason for reading is to understand our world better, then the diversity of that world should be reflected in our reading choices. I'm especially glad for the recent increase in great books featuring non-white characters, like Jason Reynolds's *Track* series.

The four-book series features a group of Black middle schoolers in their first year on the competitive Defenders track team, all struggling with some aspect of friendship or home life or school, as all middle schoolers do. Jerry Craft's 2019 graphic novel *New Kid* is another Everyday Book that I recommend often; it follows a full school year through the eyes of seventh-grader Jordan Banks, one of the few kids of color at a prestigious private school. Readers who feel out of place at school, who live in single-parent homes, whose lives are touched by violence, or who unexpectedly find out they are soon to be an older sibling will find "mirror" elements in these stories, moments when they hear "you're not alone." And for readers who don't fall into any of those categories, picking up one of these books will be a window, an opportunity to grow in empathy and understanding of the different experiences that make an everyday middle school life.

Another type of book that I think middle schoolers need and are drawn to is what I'll call the Adventure Book. Who doesn't love a good adventure story? Middle school years are a prime time for kids to grow a bit apart from their parents and encounter their own unique life experiences—say, by flying alone on a plane and crash-landing with little means of survival (Gary Paulsen's *Hatchet*). Of course, there are also silly adventures (Tom Angleberger's *Fake Mustache*) and fantastical journeys—like attending a prestigious wizarding school (J.K. Rowling's *Harry Potter* series), or traveling through space and time to rescue your father (Madeleine L'Engle's *A Wrinkle in Time*). Both eleven-year-old Harry and thirteen-year-old Meg in the stories I just mentioned are old enough for the reader to not get too distracted by the occasional absence of responsible adults—and along with Harry and Meg, to start to push back at the idea that adults are always the responsible type (enter Lord Voldemort and the Man with the Red Eyes).

The presence of fully-realized villains who aren't just caricatures is one way that fantasy and adventure stories for middle schoolers start to draw apart from more simplistic fairy tales written for younger readers. Happily, middle school kids are also of an age to really start to grasp the truth of Neil Gaiman's well-known paraphrase of G.K. Chesterton in *Coraline*: "Fairy tales are more than true—not because they tell us dragons exist, but because they tell us dragons can be beaten." Adventure Books for this age often pin the fate of a society or even a whole world on the shoulders of an eleven- to fifteen-year-old, and the reader is swept up in watching them rise to the challenge, cheering for them to beat that dragon. N.D. Wilson's *100 Cupboards* trilogy is one of my favorites that fills this space. In the first book we are introduced to twelve-year-old Henry York, a somewhat lost, scared, scrawny kid. Two books later, Henry has come through such a transformation that it makes perfect sense for him to lead a small army of faeries and bring a world back from the edge of ruin. Most middle schoolers aren't facing an evil witch and generational curses, but they do have to make choices each day to stand up for what they believe and to act true to themselves. Henry's journey gives them a model for how to conduct that fight.

The third category that I think middle school readers gravitate toward is my personal favorite: the Heart Book. Keep a good stock of tissues in your house if you have a child who leans toward Heart Books, because these are the tearjerkers. Stories in this category are built primarily on the interior, emotional journeys of their characters. Of course, a well-written Everyday Book or Adventure Book might also include these elements, but in a Heart Book the emotions are just a bit more intense. Think about Katherine Paterson's *Bridge to Terabithia* or *Jacob Have I Loved*. These books are crucial for middle schoolers who are often coming to terms with big feelings: navigating cliques and friend groups, dealing with the physical changes of adolescence, trying to figure out their place in the world. These are sometimes the books that elicit an "it was boring, nothing happened" review from readers who like a lot of action in their stories. But I've found that even these kids will come around on a good Heart Book if it has a hook that draws them in.

Most Heart Books seem to feature girls, but one author who is great at depicting the big emotional ups and downs of a middle school boy's life is Gary D. Schmidt. The "hooks" in his novels vary from hiking to cricket to Shakespeare to the drawings of John James Audubon, but somehow each seems to fit perfectly with the often heavy subject matter: absent parents, the death of a sibling, abuse, world turmoil. Schmidt can also reach back in time and still find resonances with today's readers: his books *The Wednesday Wars* and companion novel *Okay For Now* are set in the late 1960s during the Vietnam War, but they are also popular read-alouds in many middle school classrooms. Both these books are written in the first person, and the protagonists do a fair bit of talking directly to the reader, which is a perfect recipe for developing deep empathy for what the characters are experiencing—especially within their complicated families.

Family emotions get me reaching for the tissues every time: the very first Heart Book I remember loving is Julie Andrews Edwards's *Mandy*, about a ten-year-old orphan girl who deeply longs for a home, a place of her very own. By chance one day she stumbles across a little cottage in the woods and claims it as her refuge. The cottage is part of a larger estate, and when Mandy escapes to the cottage in the middle of a storm and ends up very ill, the Fitzgeralds, the estate owners, open their home to her to allow her to recover. Mandy's emotional battle to protect her heart as she comes to love the Fitzgeralds is heartbreaking, but the chapter when they ask her if she'd like to come live with them as their daughter brings me to joyful tears every time. Unlike in real life, it's a fairly swift resolution to a big jumble of feelings, but I think that catharsis of journeying through these emotions and then seeing them understood and resolved is a big help to readers who feel stuck in the middle of a jumble of feelings themselves.

Of course, right now you're probably thinking of great books that don't fit nicely into the groups I've described, and of course you may know a middle schooler who doesn't seem to resonate with any of them. And despite a full chapter of discussing these types of stories as crucial for middle school readers, I want to emphasize my firm belief that I don't see these stories as merely "stepping stones" on the way to books written for or marketed to teenagers and adults. Especially for older readers who first connected deeply with words and stories as middle schoolers, returning to what brought them laughter or encouragement in that time is a gift. A good middle school book is chock-full of empathy along with a laugh or two, opens the reader's eyes to new ideas or experiences, and hopefully inspires them to live forward with bravery and with care, both for themselves and others. Those seem to be pretty good aims for a mature reading life, so it's with that goal that I make this wish—may we all be more like middle schoolers.

Banner in the Sky
James Ramsey Ullman

This historical fiction tale is loosely based on the first ascent of the Matterhorn, and it ticks all my favorite "adventure book for middle schoolers" boxes: physical and mental challenges, conflicts around independence and choices, a young person deciding who they want to be in life. It's set in the Swiss Alps in 1865, a period often considered the "golden age" of mountaineering. Our teenage hero, Rudi Matt, is the son of Josef Matt, a renowned climbing guide who perished on the Citadel, the tallest mountain in the range and the only one deemed "unclimbable" by the rest of the village guides. Climbing is in Rudi's blood, and despite his mother's fears for his safety and her insistence that he give up going to the mountains, Rudi knows that the Citadel is his destiny. Themes of dedication, sacrifice, community, learning from mistakes—this one's got all the good stuff.

The Penderwicks Series
Jeanne Birdsall

From the first summer adventure in the Berkshires to the closing chapters of the final book, the four Penderwick sisters change and grow and love each other deeply, and generously welcome new family members and friends along the way. They are fiercely loyal and wonderfully creative, and Birdsall somehow accomplishes the task of giving them all distinct personalities, interests, and elements of personal growth in a relatively small number of pages. This is a set that belongs in conversations with *Anne of Green Gables* and *The Saturdays*, a timeless history of a close-knit family with plenty of spunk.

Orbiting Jupiter
Gary D. Schmidt

Like the other Gary Schmidt books I've mentioned in this chapter, this one is complex and deep and tough, but oh-so-beautiful. Told through the eyes of twelve-year-old Jack Hurd, the book opens with Jack and his parents welcoming Joseph Brook, a fourteen-year-old foster kid. Joseph is quiet and jumpy, and his caseworker fills the Hurds in on his complicated story. At the heart of it is Jupiter, Joseph's three-month-old daughter whom he's never met. Nothing about Joseph's story is easy to read, although Schmidt writes about the difficult material in a wholly age-appropriate way for older middle schoolers. My heart broke for these characters as the story unfolded, but I think the best kind of tale is one that can make a reader cry with both sadness and gladness in the space of a few pages.

Amal Unbound
Aisha Saeed

Slight shifts in fortune can devastate the most vulnerable, a truth that is evidenced in this story of twelve-year-old Amal, a good student who has hopes of becoming a teacher in her Pakistani village one day. But as the oldest daughter in her family, Amal is the one who is asked to sacrifice her education when her mother is slow to recover from a difficult pregnancy. Frustrated and feeling unheard, Amal makes a spur-of-the-moment choice during a confrontation with her village's powerful landlord, and the consequences are dire. Amal's strong sense of justice is not easily swayed, and she fights to make a better future for herself and her village.

All's Faire in Middle School
Victoria Jamieson

Eleven-year-old Imogene is jumping into her first year of middle school, but it's a massive transition; she is much more accustomed to being homeschooled and helping her family in their roles as permanent cast members at the Florida Renaissance Faire. Imogene tries to make friends, but she's not finding middle school all that she hoped it would be. Her trials at home and struggles with friend groups will be familiar "mirror" plot lines for many readers, and the renaissance faire setting is a fun and unique window into a less-common middle school experience.

THERE AND BACK AGAIN

GRAPHIC NOVELS

COREY LATTA

Graphic novels are portal texts—they give us passage from the lexical to the visual. Through the artists' renditions of the writers' words, graphic novels lift us from the mundanities of our world and situate us in a sensory experience of the imaginative. I liken this portal experience to what Tolkien described as the phenomenon of escape. In his seminal essay on the nature and functions of fairy stories, Tolkien expounds on the effect that escape fairy stories have on the reader. Against those who would accuse fairy stories of promoting escapism— an irresponsible flight from the "real world"—Tolkien gives this defense:

> Evidently we are faced by a misuse of words, and also by a confusion of thought. Why should a man be scorned if, finding himself in prison, he tries to get out and go home? Or if, when he cannot do so, he thinks and talks about other topics than jailers and prison-walls? The world outside has not become less real because the prisoner cannot see it.[1]

While Tolkien is here discussing the functions of fairy stories, there are enough similarities to graphic novels to draw productive parallels. Tolkien positions life as something one might want to transcend. We could hardly blame someone who feels life as a confine of imperfection and pain for wanting to escape his imprisonment. Fairy stories offer us such an escape. The writing in a fairy story sponsors transcendence, and the otherworldly elements of these stories pair that transcendence with a destination. Graphic novels operate in much

the same way, with the obvious exception that so much of what facilitates escape
is visual in nature.

Graphic novels offer children and adolescent readers a kind of escape
through immersion. Whereas a purely literary text transports readers through
the constructive power of the imagination, a graphic novel, with its aesthetic
composition and reliance on the illustrative, invites the reader into a sensory
experience unachievable through a purely lexical experience.

To stay with Tolkien, and to use one of my favorite examples of the kind
of escape a graphic novel mediates, let's consider the illustrated edition of
The Hobbit.[2] Published more than fifty years after the beloved novel's original
release in 1937, the graphic version demonstrates just the kind of escape Tolkien
describes in his "On Fairy Stories." Through its paneled visualization, the graphic
adaptation opens a door for the reader to journey along with Bilbo and his
dwarven company as they quest to the Lonely Mountain. Of course, so much of
that ability lies in Tolkien's language, in the accessibility of the characters, and
in the well-formed nature of the story. That same story, however, offers a more
multi-faceted experience when adapted to the form of the graphic novel.

In an illustrated adaptation of Tolkien's classic, the reader's constructive
imagination is baptized in a spectrum of color and visual rendering. In the
graphic novel version, a descriptive line like "At the twanging of the bows and
the shrilling of the trumpets the dragon's wrath blazed to its height, till he was
blind and mad with it" is accompanied by an orange-bathed panel depicting
the monstrous Smaug as he exhales a sulphury wrath on the helpless citizens of
Lake-town. The reader's experience of escape is artistically compounded, visually
enhanced, and multisensory in nature.

Escape implies a *to* as well as a *from*. So much of what constitutes what we
escape to has to do with a work's thematic makeup. The distinctive visual nature
of graphic novels only compliments the thematic. So when we look at, say, a work
like Frank Miller's heralded *Born Again*,[3] a graphic novel intended for a more mature audience, we can appreciate the ways the prose and the illustrative panels
work artfully to convey complex theological themes.

Born Again[4]—a graphic novel about Marvel's vigilante superhero, Daredevil—
weaves the visual with the thematically sacred. The experience of escape here
is one to a theologically charged world. *Born Again's* reliance on religious tropes
serves as an interpretive key given to the reader that unlocks the world to which
readers can escape. So much of this particular experience of escape is tied to the
character of Daredevil. Inherent to who Daredevil is—and how readers are asked

to understand him—is the inner tension between a sinner's rage and a saint's redemption, between offering brutal justice and accepting tender mercy, between a sense of tormented exile and that of solaced rest. All these elements are transmitted through frames of the sacred and pictures of the profane.

Specifically, the world to which readers of *Born Again* escape is distinctly Catholic. The graphic novel patterns Matt Murdoch's battered story after the passion and resurrection of Christ. Specific symbolism that situates Matt in a larger Christian narrative abound. For example, the splash pages in the first three chapters—titled respectively "Apocalypse," "Purgatory," and "Pariah"— depict Matt lying down. In "Purgatory" and "Pariah," he's in the fetal position. The posture is one of defeat, one of death. In "Born Again," an injured Matt lies in a crucifix position in a Catholic mission, caressed by and cared for by Sister Maggie—a nun depicted as Matt's mother, who assumes the role of Mary, holding the crucified body of Jesus. Matt finds himself in a recreated Pietà. And in the fifth chapter, "Saved," we find Matt combatively posed in a stance of strength and ferocity, a posture of resurrection.

Miller's story clings to these Catholic symbols because they're vital to who Daredevil is. They're as fundamental to his persona as they are representative of what his grander story is about. At its heart, *Born Again* is a story of redemption and return. In Christian thought, redemption is salvific recovery from guilt and sin, pain and violence, hate and vengeance. Redemption traditionally means being saved from some form of damnation or condemnation. The idea of return is closely tied to redemption in Christian thought. Scripturally, return means coming back to God. The theme of return is always tied to exile and separation from God.

Daredevil's appropriation of redemption and return in a Catholic context isn't allegorical in that strict allegory requires a one-to-one correlation between one narrative and another. The religious elements in this story are more nuanced, more layered. These religious tropes originate in an essential aspect of his character—his lost relationship with his father. Matt Murdoch's story begins before he lost his sight and gained a super alter ego. It begins with his father, Jack, who alone raises Matt in the crime-ridden New York neighborhood, Hell's Kitchen. Jack's character is brawny and tough, protective and fierce.

Matt's relationship with his father is the single most influential force in his life, and he grows up with a love and awe made more intense by his father's death. When Jack, a boxer with a reputation in Hell's Kitchen for his in-ring resilience and brutality, is killed by gangsters for refusing to throw a fight, Matt is left alone, fatherless, and angry. Matt enters into a fatherless exile. His life becomes a revenge quest, an exilic separation from peace. After years of intense training, a fatherless blind Matt, with overly developed senses and extraordinary combat abilities, dons the horns to fight organized crime as Daredevil. This return is for the redemptive good of Matt's community. Much like Bilbo's quest to the Lonely Mountain and return to the Shire, Matt's journey to becoming Daredevil culminates in a return home. The reader's escape isn't only to this familiar arc of the hero's journey, but rather to a visual and lexical composite of the hero's journey.

Escape as facilitated by graphic novels can bring the reader back to the world from which she escapes. When the subject matter is nonfiction, graphic novels can act as reflexive portals, transporting the reader "there and back again." In a beautifully illustrated account, the graphic novel version of *The Diary of Anne Frank*[5] recounts and reframes the harrowing account of Anne Frank, the young Jewish girl who, from 1942 to 1944, lived in hiding from the Nazis during the occupation of the Netherlands. Anne Frank was eventually found out and died in the Bergen-Belsen concentration camp in 1945.

The power of Anne Frank's diary lies partly in its depiction of reality as she knew it. Readers are taken right back to the all too real world of unparalleled evil. But the graphic novel edition of Anne Frank's diary creates a door within a door to that harsh reality. We find visual depictions not only of her external world but also of imaginative renditions of her interior world.[6] We are visually taken through the plot and into her consciousness. That Tolkienian function of escape carries us from our world back through the doorway of Anne Frank's life and into an artistic rendering of her conflicted inner world.

This high art of escape, while certainly innate to any good story, is more remarkably achieved through the multisensory nature of the graphic novel. The world from which we escape is no less real to us when we enter these visual portals. Indeed, we might find that once we've returned to these graphic novels through which we've escaped that we've brought some of the colors of their imaginative worlds back into our own.

Scarlett Hart: Monster Hunter
Marcus Sedgwick | *Illustrated by Thomas Taylor*

Scarlett Hart, the orphaned daughter of two famous monster hunters, wants to continue in the family legacy. The problem is the Royal Academy for the Pursuit and Eradication of Zoological Eccentricities says she's too young. But that won't stop Scarlett. Her determination, along with a faithful butler and an especially clever mind, will help her battle a sudden emergence of monsters. This book is just fun. Sharp illustrations and a story about fighting for your destiny make this an exciting, compelling story.

Rapunzel's Revenge
Shannan Hale and Dean Hale | *Illustrated by Nathan Hale*

This revisionist take on Rapunzel's story puts the princess in the role of avenging heroine. After escaping her tower-prison, Rapunzel discovers a hostile world that she must navigate to rescue her real mother and catch her kidnapping would-be mother. Rapunzel partners with Jack the Giant Killer in a western-style adventure. As retellings of fairytales go, this is one of my favorites. It adds a dramatic, more relationally motivated element to the classic plot. Vibrant, action-oriented illustrations give the familiar Rapunzel a more relevant makeover.

King Arthur and the Knights of the Round Table
M.C. Hall | *Illustrated by C.E. Richards*

If you're looking for a classic good versus evil story, this is it. This is a world of wizardry, magic, and dragons. King Arthur and the Knights of the Round Table are Camelot's one defense against evil. This classic, mythic tale framed in graphic-novel format includes prompts for discussion and written reflection, making this text interactive. As a lifelong fan of King Arthur and world of Camelot, I found this graphic adaption nostalgic but refreshingly new.

Mighty Jack
Ben Hatke | *Illustrated by Ben Hatke*

This graphic novel is the first of three volumes about a kid named Jack. While his mom works two jobs in the summer, Jack has to watch his little sister, Maddy, who is autistic and non-verbal. But one fateful day, Maddy talks. She talks Jack into selling their mom's car for a box of magic seeds. The rest is an adventure. This retelling of "Jack and the Beanstalk" combines fantasy with elements of real-world issues, like growing up with single mom who works two jobs and a sister who has autism. The illustrations are fun and lively, and the story makes for a compelling rendition of a classic children's tale.

Giants Beware!
Jorge Aguirre | *Illustrated by Rafael Rosado*

Claudette lives in a quiet, quaint, pleasant village. The problem is that there aren't any giants in it! And Claudette's greatest desire is to slay a giant. This wonderfully told graphic novel captures Claudette's quest to slay a giant. Accompanied by her best friend and brother, Claudette sets out to find a giant. But what will her parents think? *Giants Beware!* raises interesting questions about the maturing power of adventure versus parental wishes for children to be safe. It's also a classic journey narrative that brings readers along on a trip about friendship, courage, and self-discovery.

ENDNOTES

1   J.R.R. Tolkien, "On Fairy Stories," in *Tree and Leaf* (London: HarperCollins, 1964), p. 60.
2   J.R.R. Tolkien, *The Hobbit: An Illustrated Edition of the Fantasy Classic*, adapted by Charles Dixon, illus. David Wenzel (New York: Del Rey, 2012).
3   Frank Miller, *Born Again*, illus. David Mazzucchelli (New York: Marvel, 2010).
4   *Editors' note:* This book is intended for a more mature audience—upper high school and beyond—as it refers to some difficult subjects like drug use and prostitution. We encourage you to preview this book to determine whether or not it's a good fit for your young reader.
5   Anne Frank, *Anne Frank's Diary: The Graphic Adaptation*, adapted by Ari Folman, illus. David Polonsky (New York: Pantheon Books, 2018).
6   *Editors' note:* While the original text of *The Diary of Anne Frank* contains some exploration of sexuality, the graphic novel places an emphasis on this that may require some discussion. We encourage you to preview this book.

A BETTER WORLD

CHRISTIAN LEITHART

The first time I was away from my entire family—miles away, with no parents, no siblings, and no contact—I was thirteen or fourteen and was backpacking in the Bitterroots with a group from church. We drove into the wilderness, hiked for an hour or two (pack mules alongside), and set up camp in a clearing thick with mosquitoes. You could have sold DEET for thirty bucks an ounce. Our counselors forbade the words "um" and "like" and made us do pushups if either word slipped out. One counselor said he'd give a prize to any two boys brave enough to build a shelter with their own hands and sleep in the woods, away from the rest of the group, with no sleeping bags, blankets, or fire. I paired up with someone, and we built a structure that wouldn't have held a tame gerbil. We spent the night back to back, shivering and blue. At first light, around two dozen boys dragged themselves back to camp, battered, but triumphant. The prize, split between twenty-four of us, turned out to be a bag of beef jerky.

That was a great trip.

The most frustrating thing about being a child is constantly being reminded of your limitations. Not tall enough, not strong enough, not careful enough, not tough enough. Those agonizing days drag on and on until, one day, you're given a shot at independence. A trip in the woods! Mosquitoes! Pushups! Sleepless nights! At last, I am become a Man. As it turned out, the trip was merely a taste of adulthood. Sure, I had camped in the middle of the woods without my family, but I was still fully dependent. My parents paid my way. Grown-ups shepherded me. When I trudged out of the woods with sticks in my hair, someone had to drive me home.

It's easy to see why I escaped into books and movies. My own life was chaotic and confusing; nothing resolved cleanly. The stories I read, on the other hand, were *satisfying*—vivid worlds, talented characters, story arcs that came to rest. Reading gave me a certain kind of independence because I could identify with characters who faced life-or-death problems and overcame them. I escaped into fat novels—the fatter, the better. I didn't select them based on their age-appropriateness. I was just looking for faraway lands, magic, and talking animals. I wasn't aware there was such a thing as "young adult fiction." To be honest, I'm glad I didn't.

In 1963, Flannery O'Connor wrote an essay called "Total Effect and the Eighth Grade," in which she took issue with some of the novels assigned in school to teenage readers. It wasn't the number of swear words that bothered her. If you know Flannery, you know that she wasn't squeamish about content. What concerns her in the essay is whether a teenager (an eighth-grader) can be expected to handle a modern novel.

O'Connor points out two characteristics of modern novels that set them apart from older narrative writing. The first is that modern novels are more complex. The author takes pains to remove himself from his story, leaving "the reader to make his own way amid experiences dramatically rendered and symbolically ordered."[1] In other words, the level of subtlety in modern fiction means that the new stories are actually harder for teens to grasp than the old ones, even though they may find the subject matter more to their liking. Much better, O'Connor says, to start with old books and work your way forwards, building up your literary strength as you go.

The other reason O'Connor gives for removing modern novels from the curriculum is something called "total effect." Many modern books are filled with self-destructive behavior and uninhibited passions. Typically, modern authors *understand* that. They justify the content by appealing to "total effect": the whole picture viewed from a distance, so much more than the colors of the paint. This makes for beguiling reading. It immerses the reader, making him feel as the characters feel. Their horror horrifies him. Their lust makes him feel lustful. The best modern novelists arouse these passions, then arrange them into a new experience, "which *is not in itself* sensuous or simply of the moment"[2] (my emphasis). Every detail serves the whole. The story eventually resolves into a complete, truthful picture of life (as it appears to the author) and is often just as didactic as any of the old tales.

But a teenager can't experience this total effect. He simply hasn't lived and read enough. An adulterous fling, described in vivid detail, eventually devolves into ruin; a teen will only remember the titillating descriptions of the affair, which he has read so many times he has them all but memorized. He may try to appeal to "total effect" in his arguments with his parents ("I know there's a lot of profanity and gore, Dad, but it's actually a really good movie!"), but the fact is that the images will stick longer than the complete picture.

This brings us to the problem with young adult fiction. Young adult (or YA) fiction began as a marketing term: certain books appealed to readers who were young, but were not exactly children (*The Outsiders*). In the past twenty years or so, an industry has grown up to match the marketing, an entire genre of books aimed exclusively at teenage readers. It will come as no surprise that YA fiction almost exclusively panders to teenage obsessions: violence, sex, vanity, etc. Even when one of these YA books has a subtle lesson to teach (*The Hunger Games*), the "total effect" is lost in the thrill of romance, violence, and self-expression. Those who sell YA know this. It's the lifeblood of their market. If I, in my teenage years, had lapped up novels designed for my immature tastes, I may have never tasted anything else. I would have had all the easy, unearned adulthood I wanted: independence, sex, and self-expression galore. The more YA books are published the less chance a teenager has of developing good taste. And children must learn good taste because it does not come naturally.

The five books I recommend below are not the greatest in English literature, but I hope that the books will avoid the worst qualities of Young Adult Fiction. I didn't select these books based on their "total effect" or any overarching lesson they teach (though they are all healthy), but because each of them contains vivid *scenes* that admirably portray adulthood, independence, irony, friendship, and responsibility—things that many teens might not even know they crave. I hope these glimpses of a better world will grip teenage minds, sink into the imaginations, and equip young souls for life. I hope these are the stories they remember when they're shivering in a hut built of sticks in the woods.

True Grit
Charles Portis

Charles Portis may not be a household name, though two film adaptations of his most well-known novel have done something to fix that. *True Grit* is the story of a young woman, Mattie Ross, who heads into the Western wilderness with a hired gun named Rooster Cogburn and a Texas Ranger named LaBeouf (pronounced La-Beef). Mattie is book-smart but unlearned in the ways of the world. The story is told from her point of view, which means a lot of five-dollar words and circumlocution. She is capable and, most importantly, independent. The story highlights her independence by contrasting her with multiple rough adult men, most of whom possess "grit" in one form or another. They have what it takes. In the end, Mattie proves she does, too.

But this is no "believe in yourself" fantasy. Mattie is frightened, horrified, and even injured in her quest. She survives by leaning heavily on her companions and on her own upbringing. Her entire quest is motivated by her love for her father, and there is more than a tinge of Mattie's desire to prove herself worthy of his memory. She also quotes liberally from the Bible, as do all the characters—as though Portis strung various Proverbs together to form his plot. This is not a story of a teenager torching what remains of tradition and parental authority. The independence Mattie builds for herself stands on a firm foundation.

The Illustrated Man
Ray Bradbury

As a teen, I loved irony, that gap between expectations and events, between appearance and reality. I especially loved the idea of the world operating outside our control, yet somehow mysteriously resolving events and tying lives together. I knew that life was beyond *my* control, and it comforted me to know that everyone was in the same boat.

Fahrenheit 451 is Ray Bradbury's most famous novel and is often assigned in school. Its complexity makes it tough sledding for teens. I confess to being completely confused during much of the book my first time through. His short stories, on the other hand, are much easier to grasp, and they're packed with irony. They're full of scientists murdered by their own inventions, gardens in the middle of ruins, nature twined around destruction. *The Illustrated Man* is the first collection I read and the one I would recommend to teens.

Holes
Louis Sachar

Many young adult books focus on friendship, but the vast majority of them are about friendship between girls. Those that are about male friendship tend to either focus on one boy's admiration for another boy (John Knowles's *A Separate Peace*) or tell a different kind of story entirely. This shouldn't be surprising, considering the fact that, between boys, the stronger the friendship, the less they tend to think about it. Enough about us, they seem to say. Let's get on with the adventure.

Holes is the story of Stanley Yelnats, who is plagued by a generations-old family curse. Over the course of the story, he grows up. His hands get calluses. He finds out just how long he can go without water. And he and another boy named Zero grow from strangers to business partners to friends literally leaning on one another to survive. The strength of the relationship lies in its gradual, almost invisible, growth.

The Queen's Thief Series
Megan Whalen Turner

This is one of those rare young adult series that does not have a teenage protagonist. In fact, the protagonist shifts with every book of the series. Without giving too much away, the books deal directly or indirectly with questions of authority and respect. For the good of others, characters have to shoulder responsibility they don't want and aren't accustomed to. The responsibility always comes at great cost to themselves, sometimes even to their own identities. When a new monarch assumes the throne in a Megan Whalen Turner story, he or she is henceforth referred to by the name of their country. (I suppose it would be like Harry going by the name "Hogwarts.") Any blow to a teenager's self-absorption is a welcome one. This series is a gut-puncher.

To Kill a Mockingbird
Harper Lee

It's only in retrospect that a person feels a lost childhood. It's fitting, then, that Harper Lee's classic is told in the first person, from the perspective of an adult, looking over the map and tracing the path she followed in her youth. Perhaps I don't need to recommend this one, as almost every American child reads the book in school, thrilling with Scout as she runs from the imaginary bogeyman, wondering alongside her at Atticus's secret mastery of the rifle, and feeling baffled as she was baffled by an innocent man suffering at the hands of a justice system that does not deliver true justice. But this book captures so well the giddy feeling that teenagers feel as they teeter on the brink of adulthood. My wife told me this was the first children's book she read in which everything did not turn out all right in the end. It troubled her as it troubled Scout. But life moves on whether you are ready or not, as every adult knows and every teen soon realizes.

ENDNOTES

1   Flannery O'Connor, "Total Effect and the Eighth Grade," in *Mystery and Manners* (New York: Farrar, Straus and Giroux, 1957), p. 139.

2   O'Connor, "Total Effect," p. 139.

CONNECTING THROUGH TIME AND SPACE

AN INTERVIEW BETWEEN SARAH ETTER AND LESLIE BUSTARD

A curious thing happens when you are a teacher. You come to guide young hearts and minds toward what is good and true and beautiful. But then one day, you discover your student has learned more than you taught her and has crossed over from student to kindred spirit. The following is a record of a delightful, laughter-filled conversation I had around my kitchen table with a lovely young woman I have known since she was eight years old and was her literature and writer teacher in eighth grade. We talked about classic books in the high school years, and I began with the question:

Which book first made you recognize "Oh, I love books, and I love words . . .?"
The book that made me love words was *Jane Eyre*. Through it, I learned to see the difference between a good story and a well-told story. The way Charlotte Brontë frames the characters matters just as much as what is happening to them and among them.

In eighth grade all you wanted to talk about was *Jane Eyre*.
I was obsessed. It was my favorite book from seventh to tenth grade. *Till We Have Faces* replaced *Jane Eyre* when I read it in tenth grade. But *Jane Eyre* is probably still my second favorite book. Jane is always going to be my hero, even though she is a deeply flawed character. I can learn from her mistakes as well as

from her strengths.

I wonder at this book because it was written an era where Charlotte Brontë was not sitting at a computer, editing every sentence. To an extent, this is authentic, unedited Charlotte Brontë. That is marvelous to me—that she was able to write organically in this profound and beautiful way.

How does *Jane Eyre* contrast with other books you were reading at the time?

I had been reading a lot of histories. In the classical education I experienced, I read fantastic and amazing stories, such as *Three Hundred Spartans*, which is as exciting as *Jane Eyre*. But it is not artistic. Herodotus was not trying to put together beautiful prose.

When I read *Jane Eyre*, I encountered an author who wanted to arrange a story in a beautiful way and not just tell the facts of something. This is how God tells stories; He gives us more than data. The Bible is not a list of facts. In a way, *Jane Eyre* helped me better understand the reason why the Bible is written the way it is.

Why are beauty and profundity important to our world today?

They are very relevant to Christians today. How can we have discussions with people when even the most basic terms like beauty, truth, and goodness are not on the table? Not only do we have different definitions, some people even refuse to have definitions. That is difficult.

Classics address the reality of the world. Flannery O'Connor didn't write dystopian works like Ray Bradbury or George Orwell, but she wrote about the most grotesque things in the most grotesque ways. And she said that her preferred medium of horror is *horror as a mercy*, because "horror that awakens the soul to the danger it is in is no horror but actually a mercy."[1] Some non-Christian writers are portraying this depravity in their dystopian works; it is important that Christians use stories as a way to communicate the depth of human depravity as well.

Also, classics help us communicate the beauty and depth of love, which transcends time. The fact that Jane Eyre, Pyramus and Thisbe, and Romeo and Juliet are still these stories that make us feel deeply proves that there is something universal in the human spirit. I think stories are the best way to bring to the table the idea that something connects us in our humanity—we hold some things in common, and not because of evolution. Something connects the human spirit.

You can start the conversation using literature. And you can dive into the horrific reality of *1984* and *Fahrenheit 451* and agree with others that humanity is heading in this direction. But good news! We have this thing of love connecting us. And *Jane Eyre* becomes relevant again—it isn't just a story to sit on a shelf collecting dust.

As we think about choosing books to read to those in the upper high school age bracket, it sounds like you are saying there is a training and discipleship that comes through reading literature. What criteria would you look for when choosing books for this age group?

That is a complicated question, because what it is really asking is what makes a book good? And when picking books for a high schooler to read—when she might not be reading anything else, and she might not keep reading after graduation—one must really evaluate how one chooses books. Those decisions may need to be based on more than just how beautifully the books are written.

I would put an author's technical ability (slightly) to the side and focus more on which questions the author is answering that are relevant to humanity. That's what profundity is—an attempt to answer hard questions. Because one day we are going to be thirty, forty, fifty years of age and older, and the one thing we can know about our life is that we are going to ask questions like why do we suffer? Why are we here? What is my purpose?

I would care more about authors who are going to answer those questions than I would about authors who have a command over their pen. That's where *Jane Eyre* becomes really wonderful, because in the end I care more about Jane Eyre herself because of the questions she answers than I do how graceful Charlotte Brontë's writing is.

How can we get beyond dissecting a book and instead learn to appreciate the words or the beautiful sentences? How can we help each other pay attention to beauty?

I think being read aloud to really helps us pay attention to words and to beauty.

My senior year of high school, my class was reading *To the Lighthouse*, by Virginia Woolf. The class had a huge discussion on feminism; it was very heated, and people were mad. The teacher came into it and, without passing any judgment, said, "I am just going to read this out loud to you all." And as he read, we all started tearing up and getting into the story. It also helps when teachers point out what they find beautiful and what excites them in the stories they are teaching.

I may disagree with what a writer is saying, but in the case with Virginia Woolf, the sentences were beautiful to listen to. This is why literature is one of the most effective tools of communication and why I think Jesus used parables. It's hard to be angry at something when it is so beautiful.

So many classics have been adapted for the screen now—such as *Emma* by Jane Austen. Why would I read *Emma* if I could watch the movie? I can get a lot out of the six-hour version of it. What do I get from reading the book?

This question tells a lot about what we are looking for as viewers and as consumers: we want to minimize the effort and maximize the benefit. We want to take in something with the least amount of trouble. But who defines the benefit? The author is the one who is guiding us to the benefit. The reader can demand all she wants from the writer and the book, but in the end, she is called to a submission to the author and to the piece.

I do love films. They one of my great loves. There is so much value in the movies. But with a book, we are given the experience to share minds. Nothing in your physical world changes when you read; everything is internal. And a good author can command your mind to do what he wants; the author dictates what a reader is thinking about in the moment. How powerful! Movies can only show you something external, and you can only take it in.

As a culture we could be more gracious with artists and not be so self-centered. We can learn to submit to the experience.

Why is it better to be led by an author into someone's world instead of just watching it in a movie?

High schoolers are growing into new self-knowledge. They are learning that they are not the center of the world, and that the world is complex. They are also learning that even though they have more independence, what they do affects people.

The most important thing in life, other than knowing Christ, is how we think of people. If I can see in my friend or neighbor or cousin the complexity of one of Jane Austen's characters, I might be much more kind and have more understanding and depth of relationships with others. I think books can help us with this because we are participating with them.

For example, in Dostoevsky's *Crime and Punishment* the reader is in the mind of a murderer for about four hundred pages, and when she reaches the other side, she has a richer understanding of human sin and a deeper understanding of God's grace.

In *Till We Have Faces,* one of the main characters is quite unlikeable, but you are in her brain, and it's a captivating experience—it's like a car wreck that you can't stop. But then by the end of the book, you get a deeper understanding of being human. Reading can make us more relational.

Which books did not make your five book recommendations and why do you love them?

Great Gatsby, Fahrenheit 451, Brave New World, and *1984.* They are great reads that I value, but I'm not emotionally attached the way I am to Flannery O'Connor's stories, which are so jarring. I get disturbed and emotionally involved with her stories.

These all have the common theme of "things are pretty bad." The conversations about philosophy are unavoidable. Each book has an agenda; the authors know what they want us to think, and their books are their persuasive arguments. This is an interesting place to be as a reader: "Do I agree or not?"

For Christians, these books should be illuminating reads. And they should help us see why there is literally one solution to the problem, and it is Christ. But in our age, we think we can find our own solutions. *Brave New World* is so crushing! You think you are going to be happy but really you are not! *Amusing Ourselves to Death* by Neil Postman is good to read along with these.

How are these books different from the books you did choose?

Mine are a little more solution-oriented; they give some sort of answer for why things are messed up. Even *Emma* does, in a lighthearted way. And, in the end, there is good news. You get a sense that God is full of grace. They are all just written by good writers, and they make me want to read them out loud.

Any final thoughts?

Walt Whitman said at the end of his poem "O Me! O Life!" that there is a powerful play that continues on, and we may contribute a verse to it. As much as I feel passionate about contributing a verse, I find I have just as much passion for studying and reading the powerful play and other people's verses.

If we had to reconstruct history through art alone, the literary canon would be the great story of history. Connecting to people through time and space, like reciting creeds in church, means I am participating in something that people have done before. I love this.

Till We Have Faces
C.S. Lewis

This was life-changing for me the first time I read it, and it continues to be life-changing whenever I revisit it. The plot retells the Cupid and Psyche myth from the perspective of Psyche's jealous sister. Orual discovers through her lifetime that her attempts to love and cherish people are really more devouring than they are loving, but still, like so many of us, she blames the gods for her destructive loneliness. Ultimately, Lewis engages the question of suffering and God's existence. Even though Christianity itself makes no appearance in this story, Orual's journey mirrors a stark universal reality of human affliction and shortcoming.

Crime and Punishment
Fyodor Dostoevsky

Raskolnikov, the book's anti-hero, presents an enticing and experimental worldview to the audience and carries it out through murder and deceit. From inside Raskolnikov's perspective, the reader is forced to ask the same questions he asks, and ultimately to experience firsthand his descent into crippling insanity. Readers don't just hear about hedonism or utilitarianism from a distance, they are engrossed in scenes of murder, visions, and despair in tangible ways. Conversely, the reader also experiences Raskolnikov's long and painful journey to redemption. This is the type of novel that can be reread at every new stage of life, reminding us of both the harrowing reality of sin and the shocking goodness of God's grace.

Frankenstein
Mary Shelley

This is a portal into modern science fiction and is perhaps the most imminently relevant book on my list. Dr. Frankenstein's experiment with human life is disturbing and thought-provoking, forcing readers to ask the culturally imperative question of whether science, power, and philosophy ought to have any limitation. How does the power of life and death affect the human psyche, and is it a power we should ever have? Mary Shelley's shocking narration of murder, betrayal, and desperation keeps the reader terrified of and for the characters. This horror masterpiece continues to demand deep thinking from its audience.

Emma
Jane Austen

In contrast to the other books on this list, *Emma* is a social comedy about pride, control, and love. Clearly, *Emma* still resonates with young audiences, as it has been remade into numerous hit TV shows and movies. Although it can be difficult to read for those who relate to her impulse to assess, invade, and control, and for those who find her hypocrisy with social status unsettling and embarrassing, *Emma* is nonetheless convicting. Having to endure humiliation alongside Emma is, for many people, a transformative experience. Though many attempts at cautionary romance tales have been done in literature, Jane Austen remains unmatched in the literary canon with her masterful, graceful, and witty writing.

East of Eden
John Steinbeck

East of Eden is ambitious, consuming, and—at least for me—impossible to put down. The story features unexpected turns and unimaginable loss in characters that feel like real people. Beyond the emotional pull of the story, the writing is profound and interesting. The portrayal of human suffering is under girded by the characters' unique and complex approach to the life they have been given. Not only is *East of Eden* a must-read for literature lovers, it is a must-read for anyone striving to view the world around them with understanding and depth.

ENDNOTES
1   Jonathan Rogers, *The Terrible Speed of Mercy: A Spiritual Biography of Flannery O'Connor* (Nashville: Thomas Nelson, 2012), p. 97.

BOOKS THAT SING

RHYTHM & RHYME

AMY KNORR

This is not going to be an essay about the importance of rhyme in early literacy development. Oh, I could tell you how reading books with rich rhymes and enjoyable rhythms increases phonological and phonemic awareness in preschool and early elementary-aged children. I could expound on the ways that rhythm and rhyme can improve memory and cognitive development. I could demonstrate how rhyming leads children to a greater understanding of language patterns. I could show you how all these things lead to increased literacy, and then I could remind you how important literacy is to the social and emotional development of a child. But what I really want to tell you is just how much I adore reading books that sing.

I have this image in my mind when I think about my favorite books: I can see each book lined up on library or bookstore shelf just quivering with anticipation, ready to be cracked open, ready to offer its song into the world again and again. It might be but a whisper of a song meant to woo in stillness, or it might be a rip-roaring, all-night party of a song sure to make its audience belly-laugh by the second line, but I am certain each book does have a song. Some songs, it is true, made their way into their books before they were fully formed, but the best of books sing in your head long after the cover has been shut and the book put back on the shelf. In "The Figure a Poem Makes," Robert Frost wrote that a poem begins in delight and ends in wisdom. The same is true of the picture book read aloud. Begun in a delight of sound and meter, it ends in wisdom, if only the wisdom of realizing afresh that laughter is truly the best medicine.

We have always been a read-aloud family. From the time the children were but pink, wailing lumps, we made reading aloud a part of our nighttime rhythm. For years, a constant parade of picture books danced from library bag to reading chair and back again, only to be replenished with a new batch fresh from the library shelves. Our favorite day of the week was Library Day. We would walk up to the library and, after story time, I would sit on the floor in the fiction section and start skimming every book, starting with the As and moving as far as I could in the time allotted by my children's attention span. When a book hinted at a song worth hearing, it went into the bag until not one more book would fit. I could usually tell within the first page or two if the book had true musical potential. The cover would draw me in, either by illustration or by title. As I flipped through the first few pages, I would taste the words, nibbling at the corners of the story just a bit. Delight is like birthday cake. You want to savor it, and part of savoring it for me was enjoying the full flavor of the words with my children. I met *Jazz Baby* on the floor of that just-up-the-street library in just this way. In fact, I remember the song of Lisa Wheeler's book being so captivating that it pulled my children over into my lap and, right then and there, we enjoyed the whole story together.

> Brother's hands tap. Sister's hands snap.
> Itty-bitty Baby's hands clap-clap-clap!
> Grandpa toot-toots. Granny sings scat.
> Bitty-boppin' Baby goes rat-tat-tat!
> Mama sings high, Daddy sings low.
> Snazzy-jazzy Baby says "Go, Man, Go!"[1]

Delight indeed! I dare you to try to read it without a little bop in your voice and a snazzy jazzy move tickling your shoulders. The words taste like summer as they spill into the air like so many late afternoon rays of sun, and you are pulled into the dance as the music winds in and around you. *Jazz Baby* is the perfect example of a book that sings, and not only because it is actually about a song.

On the floor of that library, our family met book after delightful book, and *Jazz Baby* was nearly the only one that was filled with a literal song. There was Sandra Boynton's *The Going To Bed Book*, a quiet, rhythmic lullaby with just the right amount of repetition and anticipation for the surprising exercise page. I anticipated the giggles at how silly it was for those animals to bathe first and then go up for exercise as much as I anticipated the page itself.

Sometimes, anticipation is the melody that shapes a book. Deborah Guarino's *Is Your Mama a Llama?* is full of this anticipation (as well as ridiculous hilarity) as the little llama explores the types of animals all his friends have as mothers. The expectation of calling out the mother animal before I turned the page often produced bouncing and quivering in the children grinning on my lap. It is also quite difficult to read the words "Is your mama a llama?" repeatedly without at least cracking a smile. Trills of delight wriggle out from between the pages of books like this one, and from other classic books like *Chicka Chicka Boom Boom* (will there really be enough room?), *The Seven Silly Eaters* (poor Mrs. Peters and her seven persnickety eaters!), and *Silly Sally* (perhaps we should all try going to town walking backwards upside-down). These stories on their own hold the promise of fun, but the fact that they are wrapped in the harmony of rhythm and rhyme carries the delight from the pages of the book into daytime pretend and nighttime dreams.

After reading such stories, it was not unusual to hear peals of laughter coming from the general direction of the playroom following the question of parental identity being put to each stuffed animal in turn—all with the singsong cadence gifted by the story lyrics. Even as an adult, with hands deep in dishwater or ears full of conference-call drone, I could feel the tug of a grin as the cadence of "Silly Sally, backwards, upside down" danced through my afternoon.

Of course, there is something pleasing in the resonance of a good rhyme, but even stories that do not follow a particular rhyme do play the tune of their own music. Some books just have a rhythm and repetition that draw in the listener, building the giggle potential with every page turn. *The Napping House* by Audrey Wood is such a book. The potential for disaster grows with each new plot twist until the disaster is upon you, and yet there is laughter and sunshine rather than anger and thunderclouds. A wise ending, indeed. Sometimes these kinds of wise books sing quietly, the words on a page gently, lyrically adding note upon note until the full weight of beauty opens before you. Libby Gleeson's words in *Half a World Away* are like that, softly building with a gentle, understated rhythm until you turn the last page and are left holding the magical power of friendship in your own beating heart.

> When Amy was in the sandbox
> and Louie was on the swing,
> she called to him across the yard
> with the special word her mother taught her.
> "Coo-ee, Lou-ee!"
> Louie always came to play.[2]

The cadence of this special word sung out across the yard, and then across the miles, leads the reader into places of childhood sorrow that follow us into adulthood—the sorrow that turns bitter with no rhythm to lead us until we find our new song. Rhythm and rhyme. Rhyme and rhythm. Together or alone, these picture book standbys work to move the story along the measures of Frost's continuum from delight toward wisdom.

As my children grew and the lovely *Goodnight Moon* was no longer their bedtime book of choice, it was good to discover that there are books out there that still have melodies to offer us. There are still books that croon us to sleep, books that weave beauty in notes so exquisite that our throats ache, and books that sing laughter into our very souls. The grace and spaciousness of these stories open to us new ways of holding mirth, beauty, or even sorrow. These books continue to sing, sometimes gently warbling refrains of delight when life no longer feels quite as delightful as it did in the days of llamas and the tree-climbing, chicka-chicka-booming alphabets. These are the books that captivate us with their tender melodies of wisdom; they enthrall us with their powerful arias and become forever friends.

Barnyard Dance
Sandra Boynton | *Illustrated by Sandra Boynton*

Boynton has written and illustrated over sixty children's books since 1974. She has also produced six albums of children's music, which she terms renegade music. *Barnyard Dance* is perfect for getting the wiggles (and the giggles) out. Bow to the horse and cow and don't forget to twirl with the pig if you know how. You will prance and skitter and promenade. Don't be surprised if you find yourself reading this one on repeat.

Bear Snores On
Karma Wilson | *Illustrated by Jane Chapman*

Bear Snores On is the first in a series of delightful books about Bear and his friends and their escapades. Karma Wilson believes in growing friendship and empathy, and her books sing of these important qualities. Her books are loaded with rich vocabulary, rhyme, and rhythm. They engage readers' feelings and offer a few surprises on the way.

Crossing Bok Chitto
Tim Tingle | *Illustrated by Jeanne Rorex Bridges*

In gentle words, Choctaw storyteller Tim Tingle tells the story of a river, a law, a slave auction, and a Choctaw girl who led seven slaves across to freedom, "not too fast, not too slow, eyes to the ground, away you go." This haunting tale of freedom, faith, and friendship is worth sitting still for the quiet telling. This book is decorated with multiple awards, from the Native American Youth Services Literature Award to the Jane Adams Peace Award Honor Book notation.

Martin Rising
Andrea Davis Pinkney | *Illustrated by Brian Pinkney*

Andrea Davis Pinkney is a Coretta Scott King Award winner. This important walk with Martin Luther King through his life and beyond is told in poems that act as a timeline, as stepping stones from beginning to end. The words on the back cover sing out, "Can a Dream ever die? A burst of sun replies: His life well lived for peace and good. Martin's spirit—still alive! And with love, we all shall rise."

All He Knew
Helen Frost

Helen Frost has written half a dozen novels in verse, each more beautiful than the last. When picture books no longer spill from overstuffed library bags, it's easy to believe that rhythm and rhyme fall by the wayside. But Frost's intentional and beautifully complex rhythms prove otherwise. Her use of verse gives life to each character in her novels, telling the story with enough white space that the reader is drawn into the story, painting the beautiful and heartbreaking images into the margins of the score. The emotions of this story, set during WWII, about a deaf boy and the sister who loved him blend into a harmony of righteous rage, deep compassion, delicate hope, and enduring faithfulness that will captivate the reader.

ENDNOTES
1   Lisa Wheeler, *Jazz Baby*, illus. R. Gregory Christie (Orlando, FL: Harcourt, 2007).
2   Libby Gleeson, *Half a World Away*, illus. Freya Blackwood (New York: Scholastic, 2006).

IMAGINATION BOOT CAMP

FAIRY TALES

KATY BOWSER HUTSON

My family went to the beach in Florida recently. After a year of quarantine, we jumped at the chance to stay in a friend's house, be in a new space, and run around on the beach, even though it was winter. We played in the sand. We splashed in the waves, wearing wetsuits to make the February water bearable. On the last day, we piled in the car, exhausted from fun and from throwing ourselves against the enormity of the ocean, our calves sore from navigating shifting sand. We noticed our salty lips as we drove back to the house for hot baths.

The kids were that rare kind of quiet that happens when they are wonderfully spent. As I drove, my husband mused, "I wonder why the ocean is salty." The thought hung in the air. Then Story, our ten-year-old daughter began, with a dash of bardic flair, "Well, you see, there were two brothers, one rich, and one poor. It was Christmas Eve, and the poor brother didn't have a bite in the house." Her six-year-old brother jumped in. "The younger brother asked the older brother for some food for Christmas." An argument ensued as Story and Del negotiated over who would get to tell the tale. In the end, Story got to tell the main points, and Del was allowed to add color commentary.

They told their dad of a bargain between brothers, a man who met the younger brother en route to Dead Man's Hall, who then counseled him to bargain for the magic hand-mill behind the door—with the caveat that the magic mill's owner must know how to make it stop once it had ground out the requested riches. The younger brother escaped from under his brother's thumb and got the better of him, finally selling the mill for great riches to a traveling skipper. The skipper commanded salt from the magic mill and, in order that he might rest from his perilous travels overseas, ran away to sea before anyone could take the mill from him. But the captain, in his greed and fear, had not asked how to stop the mill. As Story and Del ended the tale, the ship sank beneath the weight of the salt. The mill lies at the bottom of the ocean, grinding on to this day.

My husband sat in the front seat and grinned. "Why the Sea is Salt," a Norwegian fairy tale first published in the 1840s, was now knit into our story. Our kids know it's an old story. We can speculate how the story came to be: somebody's dad in Norway was playing with them at the beach sometime, probably, pulling in his fishing nets, and a child asked, "I wonder why the sea is salty." Or maybe the dad asked, and the child told the story. The fact remains: the sea is salty, and it is wondrous and worth wondering about. Like hymns and other great works that survive centuries, fairy tales remind us we are part of something bigger. Something magical.

I read "Why The Sea Is Salty" to my children a couple of weeks ago at the beginning of our school day. (We homeschool.) I've considered whether to officially include fairy tales as part of our school time. When something is added to our official school day, the kids get suspicious. It becomes obligatory. But fairy tales don't come with any baggage. I don't require a narration, and I don't test. Generally. Okay, this time I did. On a whim, I asked my kids to write a fairy tale; my son had to narrate his for me to write down, and my daughter had to write one. There were two requirements for this fairy tale: it had to explain something inexplicable in the world, and it had to have a twist of magic.

It was effortless for them. Because kids get magic, and kids get wonder.

Our family is not a "books only" family, but books do comprise a large part of our story diet. Books dominate a good bit of square footage (and floor space, and counter space) in our home. We read *The Chronicles of Narnia* again this year. We are finishing up *The Hobbit* again and hoping this time the six-year-old and ten-year-old will be up for *The Lord of the Rings*. We love *The Blue Fairy Book* and Grimms' fairy tales. We love D'Aulaires' *Book of Norse Myths* and *Greek Myths*. I'm finally giving J.R.R. Tolkien's *The Simarillion* a shot. Emily Wilson's translation of *The Odyssey* I really dig. (You see me blurring the line between fairy tales and myths. I know. I think it's blurry.)

We are not purists or traditionalists. My daughter also devoured Chris Colfer's *Land of Stories* series, which are fun and mischievous takes on Grimms' and others that Colfer conceived of in childhood. I am thoroughly enjoying

Neil Gaiman's *Norse Mythology*.

We read fairy tales because they enrich our imaginations. And that is a big deal. I do not believe that fairy tales are tinsel, simply decorating our lives. I do believe that the strength and content of a person's imagination is of life and death importance. Fairy tales prepare us for life.

A few weeks ago we were all at home when Story called from the living room, "Mama, there are a bunch of cars out front and police yelling, and they just pulled guns out." We yelled to the kids to run to our bedroom and made them lie low behind our bed. We told them everything we could about what we knew—that God watches over us, and that we have very strong brick walls bullets can't go through. We prayed for the police officers, and we prayed for whomever they were chasing. We heard helicopters overhead, and the kids were scared. We were scared.

After a while Kenny and I crawled to the front window to see what was going on, and the situation was in hand. Two people were handcuffed. The police had identified a stolen car, and there had been a chase all over town. The culprits had gotten lost in our neighborhood, and the whole situation had come to a head in front of our house.

After talking it out some, we had rest time. We typically separate the kids so that they settle down, but they asked if they could be together, and we kept doors open between us. They looked out the front window where the whole event had happened. They told the story. They came up with scenarios. "What if I had gone out there in Dad's army helmet from when he was a kid and my bubble gun?" (They laughed.) "What would they have done?" "What if the bad guys took the car because theirs was all rusty? What if this one looked so fast and good?"

In Bessel van der Kolk's wonderful work on trauma, *The Body Keeps the Score*, he tells about visiting friends in New York City shortly after September 11. The morning the first tower fell, the parents had run to their child's kindergarten and brought their child home. During van der Kolk's visit, the child showed him a picture he had drawn of the burning tower, the plane, and the people falling. But van der Kolk had a question about the dark circle the child had drawn below the tower. "It's a trampoline, so next time they won't get hurt," the boy said. This child's imagination was helping him through trauma by imagining a scenario where things could be better next time.[1]

The ability to imagine that we could respond with creativity—that we can do something good to help something awful, that it could be better—is the kind of hopeful thinking that allows us to move through trauma without despairing. Dr. van der Kolk later says of people frozen in a moment of suffering: "Trauma has shut down their inner compass and robbed them of the imagination they need to create something better."[2]

Fairy tales do not simply amuse and distract. They arm us. They enrich the arsenals of our imaginations. What does Bilbo do when the dwarves are imprisoned by the elves? What does Saint George do when the dragon captures the well? What do Jill, Eustace, and Puddleglum do when the Green Lady enchants Prince Rilian? What do we do in the face of brokenness and evil? Is there any help for us? Sometimes, fairy tales show us that cleverness, bravery, or even conniving will get us out.

I predict the objection, "But we do not live in a world of magic and fairy tales." To which I strongly disagree. We have forgotten how to look.

Consider this thought of G.K. Chesterton's:

When we are very young children we do not need fairy tales: we only need tales. Mere life is interesting enough. A child of seven is excited by being told that Tommy opened a door and saw a dragon. But a child of three is excited by being told that Tommy opened a door. Boys like romantic tales; but babies like realistic tales—because they find them romantic. In fact, a baby is about the only person, I should think, to whom a modern realistic novel could be read without boring him. This proves that even nursery tales only echo an almost pre-natal leap of interest and amazement. These tales say that apples were golden only to refresh the forgotten moment when we found that they were green. They make rivers run with wine only to make us remember, for one wild moment, that they run with water.[3]

Fairy tales shake us up; they make us see the world with clean eyes. Imagining a world with dragons reminds me that we live in a world with birds: creatures with jeweled bodies flying everywhere. Magic forests and Ents remind me that we have trees, soaking up and breathing life into our world. Conversely, the major flooding in Nashville this week reminds me of the peril of Saruman's evil in hastily tearing up old-growth trees.

There is a wonderful TED Talk on the genius of babies, wherein psychologist Alison Gopnik compares their brain chemistry to what happens in an adult's brain when they travel, when they experience romantic love, and when they have had caffeine. She likens babyhood, with all its highs and lows, to "being in love in Paris for the first time after you've had three double espressos."[4] Don't fairy tales help us recover some of this? To see the world's wonders anew?

One of the most formative things I've heard on books versus movies taught me something about the value of reading fairy tales. When I attended a L'Abri conference as a new mom, I heard Jerram Barrs speak on the seventh *Harry Potter* book. A mom asked when he thought it was okay to let her children read or watch *Harry Potter,* or *The Lord of the Rings*, or other epic fairy tales. Jerram replied that he read *The Lord of the Ring*s to his grandchildren when they were very young. But he would not let them see Peter Jackson's movie of the same story until much later. Children, he explained, know very well that there is evil. But they do not need Peter Jackson's apprehension of evil as he, a grown man, understands it. Let them understand a Ringwraith with a child's scope of darkness and grapple with it in their own understanding of light and dark.

Fairy tales are light and darkness boot camp.

Children are trying to make sense of the world. It does not make sense without wonder, without heroes, without supernatural beings, or a grand rescue. Frederick Buechner nails this with his book *Telling the Truth: The Gospel as Comedy, Tragedy, and Fairy Tale.* God is telling the biggest, best, most magical story. We grownups have made tentative sense of things. We've made enough peace with mysteries to put them on the shelf and be "productive." Which is necessary, but perilous. That's why God gives the world children. They are still skeptical enough to wonder. Their inability to rein in their curiosity waylays curated lessons. They are still wandering off paths into dark, magical woods.

Fairy tales give children a magic saltshaker to season their days; they give them a lexicon of courage and wonder. We grownups know that our children have beanstalks and giants ahead, and that's why we need fairy tales, too. Let's read them together.

The Fairy Books
Andrew Lang

Fairy tales are always evolving in the hands of readers and tellers. Lang's collections provide a sturdy body of stories from which a reader can build. We live in a time full of umpteen reimaginings of fairy tales, full of twists, takes, and critiques of the originals. Some are wonderful, and some are not. In order to truly partake and consider, though, a reader has to know the original story.

Lang's many classic collections of fairy tales, titled by color, are a wonderful way to dig into both better- and lesser-known fairy tales. *The Blue Fairy Book,* for example, has excellent retellings of the classics "Little Red Riding Hood," "Beauty and the Beast," and "Sleeping Beauty." But do you know "The Goose Girl," "Blue Beard," or "Felicia and the Pot of Pinks"?

Jack and The Fire Dragon
Gail E. Haley | *Illustrated by Gail E. Haley*

Haley's Appalachian fairy tales are favorites in our house. With fairy tales and folktales rooted in oral traditions and Appalachian dialect, Haley's vibrant linocuts pop with color and detail. In *Jack and the Fire Dragon*, brave and mischievous Jack must outwit shapeshifter Fire Dragaman, dodge his fireballs, and rescue Jenny from his cave. A fascinating historical note is that Haley's story is set on Brown's Mountain in North Carolina, where inexplicable lights have been seen at night.

Haley has an entire collection of "Jack" stories as well, *Mountain Jack Tales*. The "Jack" tradition is really fun to follow in folk and fairy tales. Try checking out five different versions of Jack and the Beanstalk and see what you get.

Odd and the Frost Giants
Neil Gaiman | *Illustrated by Chris Riddell*

This delightful story—a light nine chapters—makes for a fantastic family read-aloud, especially since Chris Riddell's delightful illustrations grace every single page spread. My family read it as a palate cleanser between longer books. Our protagonist is a boy named Odd, whom Gaiman draws from an Icelandic story tradition about a hero named *Örvar-Oddr*, or "Arrow-Odd."

The boy Odd has a limp, no friends, and an abusive stepfather. When he wanders into the woods, he encounters the Norse gods Odin, Thor, and Loki, who are imprisoned in animal forms. The gods' actions are true to their mythical characters, with the joy of Gaiman's playful tone putting words in their mouths.

The Girl Who Drank the Moon
Kelly Barnhill

This modern Newbery winner is especially wonderful for older children. Barnhill's fairy tale world tells of a hopeless village swathed in a permanent fog. The quasi-religious leadership demand that the villagers sacrifice one of their babies to a witch in the woods every year to protect the village from her wrath. We get to know a girl, a witch, a boy, a swamp monster, and an undersized dragon. The author weaves her bittersweet tale deftly, pulling tensions tight and mingling sorrow with sweetness and levity. See if you can predict what will happen next as the characters come to realize the true natures of their world and one another.

The Journey Trilogy
Aaron Becker

My children's imaginations have been sparked by Aaron Becker's wordless books so often that I had to include them. *Journey* begins with a girl, sitting on the stoop of her house. In the cross-section illustration of her city street, we can see that everyone in her house is busy working, or playing on a screen, or talking on a phone. But no one can play.

In her gray room, the girl sees a red crayon. She draws a door on her wall, goes through, and enters a magic forest. As you can imagine, adventure, including peril and a kindred spirit, awaits. The magic grows and deepens in *Quest* and *Return*. These are books that grow as you grow. I love to wander through this world, letting my imagination wander free in this welcoming place.

ENDNOTES
1   Bessel van der Kolk, MD, *The Body Keeps the Score: Brain, Mind, and Body in the Healing of Trauma* (New York: Penguin Books, 2014), pp. 51–52.
2   Van der Kolk, *Body Keeps the Score*, p. 98.
3   G.K. Chesterton, *Orthodoxy: The Romance of Faith* (New York: Double Day, 1908), pp. 53–54.
4   Alison Gopnik, "What Do Babies Think?", *TED*, July 2011, https://www.ted.com/talks/alison_gopnik_what_do_babies_think?language=en.

FAITH AND THE POETIC IMAGINATION

POETRY

MISSY ANDREWS

To many modern readers, the word "poetry" calls up singsong versification, or abstruse obfuscation. It is no surprise, then, that so many dislike it. In her "Poetry," Marianne Moore empathizes: "I too dislike it: there are / things important beyond / all this fiddle. / Reading it, however, with a perfect contempt / for it, one / discovers that there is in / it after all, a place for the genuine."[1] Perhaps it is due to this element of authenticity that poetry was once considered the highest form of imaginative literature, surpassing its cousin the novel in the faithful art of imitation. No one likes bad poetry, but a good poem gleams like a gemstone, throwing light.

The poet Jay Parini suggests that a poem proceeds by way of images, bowing to certain conventions to become something like a verbal object.[2] Poetry traffics in animated pictures. Hang them on the walls of your mind. Carry them with you. Ponder them like worry stones; wear them soft with your fingers, feeling. Poems refine what novels portray. They are the substance of universal ideas, reassociated with their roots.

Ideas reference forms, which, as Plato observed, by nature exist in the abstract. This word, abstract, hearkens to its Latin parts: *ab*, meaning away from, and *tractare*, meaning to pull. Something abstract, then, has been quite literally pulled away from its concrete foundation. The poet, then, involves himself in something of a reunification project. He reimagines these abstract ideas in context, and as he does so, he lends you his spectacles. "Look," he says, "See what I see?" And if you read carefully enough, the world stands still. The common thing he figures suddenly springs forth in all its uncommon grandeur. With a gasp, you wonder: "I've never seen that before." And the gift is complete. You see.

Sight seems, historically, to be a preoccupation of poets. Nineteenth-century poet Percy Bysshe Shelley calls poets "the unacknowledged legislators of the world," arguing that poetry "is a mirror that makes beautiful that which is distorted."[3] A poem, he explains, is a powerful prescription that, when peered through, corrects the reader's vision of the fallen world to reveal its innate beauty. The poet, in offering his poetic lens, images the world for his readers.

Shelley was not alone in his perception of the ocular power of poetry. His contemporary Matthew Arnold called it "at bottom a criticism of life; that the greatness of a poet lies in his powerful and beautiful application of ideas to life— to the question, How to live."[4] This is a far cry from the inane verse of a greeting card. So too does it fly in the face of the obtuse. Poetry, Arnold argues, elucidates truth to suggest action.

Nineteenth-century English poet Robert Browning goes even further in his dramatic poem "Paracelsus": "God is the perfect poet who in His person acts His own creations." Browning recognizes the historic incarnation as a poetic act in which the abstract, unseeable Spirit of the Son took on the concrete form of human flesh to become, as the Apostle John called Him, the Living Word (John 1:14). Jesus, suggests Browning, was a walking poem.

Browning's definition of poetry fingers the numinous mystery present in poetry, and perhaps it is this feature that proves it not merely useful, but rather indispensable—especially for the Christian parent and educator. Since poetry works most potently in figures, it enjoins that faculty of man which is most necessary in the pursuit of faith. It exercises "in-sight," that inner vision that is the stuff of imagination.

While the modern mind associates the imaginative faculty with "unreality," the Bible suggests that figured things are often more real than things material. The Apostle Paul argues: "So we fix our eyes not on what is seen, but on what is unseen, since what is seen is temporary, but what is unseen is eternal" (2 Cor. 4:18 NIV). If this is so, how is one to perceive the unseen reality of the gospel but with the figurative faculty that is the imagination? How is one to perceive the invisible truths without poetics?

Paul might as well have been arguing with the modern materialists of the twenty-first century when he explained: "The god of this age has blinded the minds of unbelievers, so that they cannot see the light of the gospel that displays the glory of Christ, who is the image of God" (2 Cor. 4:4 NIV). It would seem unbelievers have an underdeveloped imaginative faculty. They cannot perceive the meaning behind matter because they assume the existence of nothing but matter. The poet Mary Oliver puts it this way: "Only if there are angels in your head will you / ever, possibly, see one."[5] If we believe truth exists only in matter, how are we to perceive the realities of the spirit?

Poetry, therefore, like the incarnation, proves God's mercy toward matter-bound man. Christ Himself asserts the reality of metaphor in His very person: "If you have seen me, you have seen the Father" (John 14:9 CEV). He amplifies this argument like the proverbial loaves and fish: "I am the bread of life" (John 6:35); "I am the door" (John 10:9); "I am the way, the truth, and the life" (John 14:6); "I am the light of the world" (John 8:12). The literalist cannot comprehend His meaning, which appeals via metaphor to the poetic faculty. Jesus reveals His true identity through association.

It follows then that any education that omits a study of poetry misses a ripe opportunity to cultivate the field of the mind to receive the mustard seed of the Kingdom. Consider Hebrews 11:1: "Faith is the substance of things hoped for, the evidence of things not seen" (KJV). Faith, which anticipates things that will be, employs the imagination to foster expectant hope. If poetry exercises the imagination, it strengthens the inner eye to see things that are materially imperceptible. Poetry makes abstract things tangible. In so doing, it validates the existence of immaterial reality through imaginative, *verbal* figures, in much the same way that math demonstrates abstract truths through imaginative, *numerical* figures.

Poetry, like mathematics, is a figurative language which proves the invisible truths of the world through demonstration. Like math, poetry must be learned. It must be practiced. While everyone is born with the ability to imagine, some take to it more intuitively than others. The cultivation of the imaginative faculty is progressive, and this is where an apology for poetry leaves the heady realms of academic rhetoric to find its feet in the activity of daily education. Just how is a parent or educator to teach the subject of poetry at the various grades—to properly till the imaginative soil?

Any approach to poetry must begin with the playfulness of language—which is by nature abstract and representative. Words embody sounds and senses. Let them be read aloud, chanted and sung and enacted in nursery poems. Children should be given strong doses of these to develop a taste for words on their tongues. Let them memorize rhymes and verses, making friends of the delightful figures that people them. Any child deprived, for example, of A.A. Milne's John, dressed in rubber boots and a raincoat, splashing in puddles, is a child impoverished indeed! Let them splash with him and discover "Happiness":

John had
Great Big
Waterproof
Boots on;
John had a
Great Big
Waterproof
Hat;
John had a
Great Big
Waterproof
Mackintosh—
And that,
(Said John)
Is
That.[6]

As children encounter the figure of John playing with gleeful abandon, they experience his joy vicariously through the language and movement of the poem. As they make friends figuratively with John, they make friends with words, keeping forever a room in themselves where such play may be enacted.

This room is repurposed as the child grows. The art that hangs on the walls of their mind multiplies as they turn to more mature figures for inspiration, companionship, and wisdom. Introduce them to some of your friends: Paul Revere, riding through the countryside at midnight, calling his countrymen to arms,[7] the homely and faithful Village Blacksmith, "toiling, rejoicing, sorrowing, . . . at the flaming forge of life,"[8] the relatable and proud Casey at the Bat,[9] striking out before the Mudville crowd, and E.R. Sill's Fool,[10] who is wise enough to pray for mercy. Give them broad associations, a catalogue of acquaintances with whom to greet their world.

By the time your readers reach high school, they'll be ready to meet not only the figures, but also their authors. Let them know Homer and Virgil, Milton and Donne, Shelley and Wordsworth, Herbert and Hopkins. Furnish them with a multitude of eyes so that, in time, they might see themselves. Surround them with a chorus of voices. Let them hear in those voices the eternal questions of man and know they are not alone in their private inquiries. Having stood with Shelley at the foot of Ozymandias' wrecked likeness,[11] pondering mortality and time; with Donne, confronting proud Death with his own, ultimate mortality;[12] and with Herbert, humbled by Love's welcoming table service,[13] they will know they walk in company with a great cloud of witnesses.

These witnesses invite you, as you read with your children, to recover your own imagination. Pick up Pooh and shake off the dust! Remember how to play. Recall your first looks and loves, the nursery that wrought you and the voices that soothed. Map your own imaginative landscape, and find that it teems and chatters, informing your present experience. Borrow a poet's spectacles, and re-imagine the marred world, full of "God's Grandeur":

The world is charged with the grandeur of God.
It will flame out, like shining from shook foil;
It gathers to a greatness, like the ooze of oil
Crushed. Why do men then now not reck his rod?
Generations have trod, have trod, have trod;
And all is seared with trade; bleared, smeared with toil;
And wears man's smudge and shares man's smell: the soil
Is bare now, nor can foot feel, being shod.

And for all this, nature is never spent;
There lives the dearest freshness deep down things;
And though the last lights off the black West went
Oh, morning, at the brown brink eastward, springs—
Because the Holy Ghost over the bent
World broods with warm breast and with ah! bright wings.[14]

When you return the spectacles, thank the poet for the loan, for his eyes, for the enlarged and benedight vision. And thank God; we never outgrow poetry.

When We Were Very Young and *Now We Are Six*
A.A. Milne | *Illustrated by Ernest Shepherd*

Published in 1924 and 1927 respectively, these are some of the most iconic children's poems ever written. Evocative and playful, melodic and sensitive, they color my own childhood imagination. When my children were young, I'd brew a cup of tea, gather them on my knee, and sing these poems aloud. Bouncing and clapping, frowning then smiling, we danced through the collections, romping with Christopher Robin and his friends. Silly poems like "The King's Breakfast" and "Disobedience" evoked certain smiles. "Daffadowndilly" figured a fairy world, enchanted, and "Vespers," childlike piety: "Hush, hush, whisper who dares. Christopher Robin is saying his prayers."

A Poke in the I and *A Kick in the Head*
Paul Janeczko | *Illustrated by Chris Raschka*

These imaginative collections present the sense and subject of poetry through creative concrete poems and artistic renderings of various poetic forms. This primer, rather than merely presenting poetry as an art, demonstrates it. You'll find the poems and the forms they represent accessible, as playful and funny as they are clever and clear. Your young readers will be inspired by this kick in the head and poke in the eye! They (and you) might never see poetry the same way again.

Poetry for Young People Series

Published by Sterling Children's Books and with academic contributors like Gary Schmidt, Edmund Wilson, James Engel, and Frances Schoonmaker Bolin, each of these beautifully illustrated volumes introduces young students to carefully curated works of famous poets. Artists like Emily Dickinson, Robert Frost, William Shakespeare, Henry Wadsworth Longfellow, and many others are addressed by volume. Readers learn to recognize their artistic styles and voices. I'd start with the volume on Emily Dickinson: "There is no frigate like a book to take us lands away, nor any courser like a page of prancing poetry . . ."

The Harp and Laurel Wreath
Edited by Laura M. Berquist

A classical educator, Miss Berquist employs the three classical stages of learning—Grammar, Logic, and Rhetoric—as the organizing principle of her anthology. Lines for dictation follow the grammar and logic selections. Brief study questions and their answers are included in the rhetoric selections, which are prefaced by a brief glossary of poetic terminology. Those schooling classi- cally will appreciate this author/editor's commitment to pedagogy as well as the Christian temperament that guides her selections. Readers of all kinds will enjoy this introduction to narrative and lyric poems alike as they traverse history and poetic forms chosen to delight, instruct, and inspire.

A Sacrifice of Praise
Edited by James H. Trott

With introductions to every period from Anglo Saxon to the twentieth century, this anthology sets Christian poetry centerstage though thirteen centuries. Readers must come away acknowledging the centrality of Christianity to the Western experience. The selections serve to demonstrate, as Trott argues, the unified vision of Christ that has poured forth from the church throughout the ages in unrestrained praise. This chorus of voices has been intentionally and chronologically arranged. Trott's readings are honest; none of the contributing poets would gainsay the inclusion of their work in this project. Likewise, the work is ecumenical. Trott majors in the majors of Christianity here, describing his parameters in creating this anthology as poetic unity, length, distinctiveness, diversity, and his own personal taste. For this last, we most thank him. The reader's own tastes will likely improve as a result of Trott's broad palette.

ENDNOTES
1   Marianne Moore, "Poetry," in *Complete Poems* (New York: Penguin Books, 1967), p. 36.

2   Jay Parini, *An Invitation to Poetry* (London: Pearson, 1986), p. 4.

3   Percy Bysshe Shelley, "A Defense of Poetry," 1840, Poetry Foundation, accessed October 9, 2021, https://www.poetryfoundation.org/articles/69388/a-defence-of-poetry.

4   Matthew Arnold, "Wordsworth," from *Selected Poems of William Wordsworth,* ed. Harrison Ross Steeves (New York: Harcourt, Brace and Company, 1922), p. 12.

5   Mary Oliver, "The World I Live In," from *Devotions: The Selected Poems of Mary Oliver* (New York: Penguin Press, 2017), p. 5.

6   A.A. Milne, "Happiness," from *The Complete Tales and Poems of Winnie the Pooh* (New York: Dutton Children's Books, 1966), p. 356.

7   Henry Wadsworth Longfellow, "Paul Revere's Ride," 1860.

8   Henry Wadsworth Longfellow, "The Village Blacksmith," 1840.

9   Ernest Lawrence Thayer, "Casey at the Bat," 1888.

10 Edward Roland Sill, "The Fool's Prayer," 1879.

11 Percy Bysshe Shelley, "Ozymandias," 1818.

12 John Donne, "Death Be Not Proud," 1633.

13 George Herbert, "Love III," 1633.

14 Gerard Manley Hopkins, *Poems and Prose* (London: Penguin Books, 1953), p. 27.

CRACKS IN CREATION

SUFFERING

ASHLEY ARTAVIA NOVALIS

When we were young, my sister and I couldn't wait for our weekly trips to the public library. While our mother worked on the library's computers, we set off to work of our own. Wandering through the rows of books, starting in historical fiction and then rounding the corner through fantasy and adventure, I took careful inventory before making my week's selection. And each week, I ended my search in the same spot.

After I had chosen a few new books for the week, I would circle back to the bookshelf closest to a large, round window facing the main road. My finger would scan a few rows up from the bottom and land on a gold-foil spine that read *The Easter Story*. This beautifully illustrated book by Brian Wildsmith tells the story of Jesus' last week of life on Earth from the perspective of a little donkey that carries him around Jerusalem. I checked out *The Easter Story* every chance I had. As a sensitive and creative child, I was captivated by the colors and details of Wildsmith's illustrations and moved by watching the donkey observe the final days of this good man's life (I had never learned the story of Jesus' death, so I was especially amazed). I resonated with the little donkey, encountering this terrible thing happening to this fascinating person in a strange, unknown world. Tracing my fingers across the gold foil parts of each picture, I would turn to the page of Jesus being put to death on the cross and cry.

Thinking back, I'm sympathetic toward that young, eager reader. The story of Jesus' death means something much different to me now, but at the time, I was a child making sense of the hard things in the world around me, and this story of injustice, death, and betrayal gave me an avenue to do that. From an early age, I was aware of the profound impact storytelling could have.

Having spent nearly a decade working with children across professional and social settings, books have been some of my greatest resources. I have particularly come to value stories that depict suffering and hardship in deeply honest or creative ways. I've seen these kinds of books generate meaningful discussions, encourage empathy, and provide safe, creative spaces to process pain.

Understandably, we sometimes hesitate to introduce books with heavy topics to children, or we desire to limit their exposure to stories about loss, death, fear, or poverty. We would love to be able to protect them from some of the darker realities of this world. While age-appropriateness is certainly important here, stories of adversity are a meaningful part of a child's library and not as far from the child's imagination as we would think. From the time children learn to sing about Humpty Dumpty falling off the wall and how none of his friends were able to help him, they are acutely aware that there are cracks in creation. Beautiful children's stories do not hide that truth or offer cheap fixes. Instead, these stories give room for children to explore the heaviness of pain and the goodness of hope. The Christian Scriptures also give us examples of honest stories that don't shy away from brokenness. They present us with opportunities to work through the tension of the beauty of creation and its fall—to wrestle with the permeating effects of sin and the reality of hope. Good stories of adversity give children a framework that helps them make sense of the world around them.

From picture books to young adult series, stories of adversity are not limited to a single genre or age level, and even the term "adversity" could refer to anything from divorce to deep sadness, from bullying to homelessness, injustice, disease, or abuse. Often the Christian tradition generalizes these kinds of life experiences as "suffering" or "brokenness"; I use all of these terms interchangeably here. My goal is not necessarily to make a case for which specific elements make a good book on suffering, but to show what a good story that includes suffering *does* for the child—how it can teach, encourage, guide, and enrich a child's mind and life for years to come.

In the last few years, childhood development icons like Fred Rogers and Margaret McFarland have resurfaced in the spotlight. This well-deserved recognition, along with decades of research in the childhood development field, has brought us to a place where the importance of social-emotional learning is increasingly on the minds of those who love, teach, or serve children. In *Mister Rogers' Neighborhood*, the child's mind was at the center of every decision:

the way Mister Rogers entered the room, stared into the camera, or paused to listen.

In the memorable episode about the assassination of Robert F. Kennedy, there is a noticeable shift in the neighborhood. Daniel Tiger and Lady Elaine have a sincere conversation about what "assassination" means, and how the characters in the neighborhood are all coping differently with the scary news. "When you feel sad, sometimes you don't feel like a picnic," Lady Elaine reassures Daniel Tiger when he just wants to stay home.[1] Another somber moment happens when Lady Elaine explains to X the Owl that thinking about doing a bad thing, like shooting someone or getting very, very angry about something, is different than doing it. This episode is a masterclass in how families can help children grieve and serves as a prime example of one of Mister Rogers's key philosophies behind the neighborhood: "Anything that's human is mentionable, and anything that is mentionable can be more manageable."[2]

In the same way, good stories of adversity provide a language for suffering. Children experience emotions deeply; just like adults, they have many ways of naturally expressing those emotions. Unlike most adults, however, they are still in the process of developing the ability to express themselves through words. This relationship between language and emotion is a key component in social-emotional health, and children's books are an abundant resource here. This can be learned through metaphors (Harry feeling "as though he too were hurtling through space" after watching someone he loves being murdered in *Harry Potter and the Half-Blood Prince*[3]), illustrations (a monster following a boy around in *Jonathan James and the Whatif Monster*[4]), or mindfulness of the body (Digory's "lump in his throat and tears in his eyes" in *The Magician's Nephew*[5]).

Play—often referred to as the work of children—is crucial in developing and practicing this kind of language. I would suggest that reading is a type of play that encourages imagination, requires participation, and creates a playground (in the pages of a book) for rehearsing their growing emotional vocabulary. And in providing children with the ability to put words to their big emotions, we offer a way to begin to manage them. When Digory, on the journey given to him by Aslan in *The Magician's Nephew*, is preoccupied with thoughts of his sick mother, he blurts out, "But please, please—won't you—can't you give me something that will cure Mother?" Aslan responds, "My son, my son. I know. Grief is great."[6] Digory's worry and grief is not solved in his conversation with Aslan, but through this acknowledgement and shared language of suffering, he becomes more certain he can complete his journey with "new strength and courage."[7]

This scene shows us another way stories of adversity teach children: they provide a way forward, a means of hope. This isn't to say that every story with hardship or evil must have a happy ending where each conflict is neatly resolved. On the contrary, those kinds of easy fixes can lead to unhelpful or misguided conclusions about the realities of our world, thus minimizing the effects of suffering. True hope doesn't overlook suffering; it perseveres in the presence of it.

In some stories, this hope is obvious, like a man once dead coming back to life or peace being restored to a kingdom. Other times, hope comes through more subtle images, like the flags hanging through the streets at the end of the Second World War in Lois Lowry's *Number the Stars*. The reader is left with questions unanswered, and this is where hard conversations about the world begin: where are all the people who had to flee for safety? How will the Jews be treated now that the war is over? Will their country be able to rebuild, and will life be like it was before?

We are often tempted to avoid these conversations with children because we want to keep thoughts of the evil in our world away from the child's imagination. But the child's imagination is one of the first avenues through which they process those evils and think through those unanswered questions. By providing hope and a way forward amidst adversity, good books add to the child's imagination the idea that, as G.K. Chesterton writes, "these limitless terrors [have] a limit, that these shapeless enemies have enemies . . . that there is something in the universe more mystical than darkness, and stronger than strong fear."[8]

Good stories of adversity also build self-awareness, develop understanding for others, and give opportunity for empathy and neighborly love. Stories that reflect hardships or pain that a child can personally relate to can help build crucial identity and belonging, while seeing another's perspective of suffering grows a child's ability to sympathize with an experience unlike theirs. Dr. Rudine Sims Bishop asserts that the best books go even further and ask for participation from the reader.[9] Rather than simply looking into another's world, a child is invited to enter in, to feel as another would feel, and, I would add, to respond in neighborly love. Though this essay is far from a comprehensive list of the benefits of including stories with adversity in a child's library, the most meaningful stories that I have read share these common threads: they provide language for suffering, give a picture of hope, and encourage empathy for one's neighbor.

The Christian Scriptures themselves demonstrate this framework for responding to the cracks in creation. Through the psalms, we're given ample language for suffering: from "My tears have been my food day and night"

(Ps. 42:3) to "Why, O Lord, do you stand far away?" (Ps. 10:1), God constantly provides a way forward for His people, a hope for the future through the promise of all being made new. We are given individual stories of suffering throughout biblical history that we can see ourselves reflected in or use to understand others. Finally, the reader of the Scriptures is challenged to "weep with those who weep" (Rom. 12:15) and "to love your neighbor as yourself" (Mark 12:31). And God enters into our pain with us: in the story of God, the response to all the suffering, violence, doubt, and death is the incarnation of Jesus.

As participants in the incarnation and those given the sacred task of stewarding the imagination of children toward goodness, truth, and beauty, we gain much when we invest in stories of adversity that help children make sense of the world around them.

Amelia's Road
Linda Jacobs Altman | *Illustrated by Enrique O. Sanchez*

Amelia and her family are migrant farm workers who travel from place to place to find work during harvest seasons. The reader follows Amelia as she thinks about the most difficult parts of not having one place to call home, and as she finds a small, special way to cope with wanting a place that's all her own. The author uses this fictional story to shed light on some realities that migrant children face when their families have to travel for work. This story gives children a glimpse into a world that may be very different from their own, while also sharing relatable themes like loneliness, missing an old home, moving, or trying to hold on to hope in a situation beyond your control.

The Librarian of Basra
Jeanette Winter | *Illustrated by Jeanette Winter*

This beautiful true story takes place during the war in Iraq. Alia Muhammad Baker is the librarian in her city of Basra, and when war threatens the safety of the books that she loves, the community jumps to action. The illustrations are stunning and sobering, portraying the true emotions of war and adding depth to the reader's understanding of Alia's hardship. Winter achieves an important and delicate balance of honestly portraying the effects of war while refraining from violent descriptions. This book is sure to inspire conversation about community coming together in the midst of conflict to protect the history and traditions they value.

The Wingfeather Saga
Andrew Peterson | *Illustrated by Joe Sutphin*

While stories of adversity in the genres of nonfiction or historical fiction can have more obvious applications, works of fantasy certainly deserve to be highlighted. Magical worlds like *The Chronicles of Narnia* or the *Harry Potter* series provide extraordinary settings for children to process ordinary experiences. Andrew Peterson's *The Wingfeather Saga* is an enchanting, well-crafted example of this. Readers join the Igiby siblings on an adventure to escape the terrible Fangs of Dang while seeking a lost kingdom. The four books in the series happen in a world that is "quite miserable indeed," and our characters experience real danger, cruel injustice, and heartbreaking loss. With plenty of humor and creativity, Peterson tells a brilliant story of enduring hope in what seems like overwhelming darkness.

Shouting at the Rain
Lynda Mullaly Hunt

If there were a book I could hand out to every preteen girl I know, it would be *Shouting at the Rain* by Lynda Mullaly Hunt. The story is told from the perspective of Delsie, a creative and witty young girl who lives in Cape Cod with her Grammie. Delsie has to learn what true friendship means and how to cope with her unconventional family. Through her honest writing, Hunt provides a language for suffering, as Delsie and her friends process trauma, anxiety, and betrayal. What I find most inspiring about Hunt's writing is the dignity and respect with which she (very accurately) describes the middle school experience. While some books minimize teenage drama as insignificant, Hunt recognizes the real emotional and mental anguish that conflict between friends can cause children and provides a beautiful way for the reader to express that.

The Bridge Home
Padma Venkatraman

In *The Bridge Home*, two sisters who live in an Indian village run away from home in search of a better life. This book depicts characters searching for hope in the midst of deep suffering, and it provides a look into a world that is likely unfamiliar to most readers. The love, loss, and resilience reflected in this heartbreaking tale make this book a great one to read alongside your child. Its heavy themes of child homelessness, death, poverty, and abuse provide great topics of conversation to help your child process as they read. Venkatraman was inspired to write this book by children she met while growing up in India and through it she aims to stir up empathy and good works in readers.

ENDNOTES

1   *Mister Rogers' Neighborhood,* season 1, "The Mister Rogers' Neighborhood Assassination Special," aired June 7, 1968, on PBS, https://archive.org/details/youtube-juwdeDzjVCQ.
2   *Won't You Be My Neighbor?,* directed by Morgan Neville (2018; Focus Features), DVD.
3   J.K. Rowling, *Harry Potter and the Half-Blood Prince* (New York: Scholastic, 2005), p. 597.
4   Michelle Nelson-Schmidt, *Jonathan James and the Whatif Monster* (Tulsa: Kane Miller, 2012).
5   C.S. Lewis, *The Magician's Nephew* (New York: HarperCollins, 1955), p. 168.
6   Ibid.
7   Lewis, p. 169.
8   G.K. Chesterton, *Tremendous Trifles* (New York: Dodd, Mead and Company, 1909), p. 130.
9   Rudine Sims Bishop, "Mirrors, Windows, and Sliding Glass Doors," *Perspectives: Choosing and Using Books for the Classroom,* Volume 6, No. 3, Summer, 1990.

REMEMBERING TO SEE

HISTORY

LESLIE BUSTARD

"History is *His* Story," Mrs. Byrd declared as she wrote the sentence up on the chalkboard. That day in seventh grade, Mrs. Byrd opened up the study of history in my heart and mind as something that mattered because God was at the center of it all.

I loved learning about Egyptian pyramids and Roman aqueducts, as well as stories of real people and their adventures. Cultural details concerning architecture and clothes also grabbed my attention. In high school, I loved to see how art and ideas were connected. And intertwined through my discoveries of historical events and people was evidence that God was shaping His Story throughout time—from Genesis to the resurrection of Jesus, to the present, with God's future plans still ahead.

I have since taught history to middle schoolers, and I have loved reading about people and past events to my own children. Before visiting Plymouth Plantation and Williamsburg, our family read *Three Young Pilgrims* by Cheryl Harness and *Homes in the Wilderness* by William Bradford. Before wandering around Sterling Castle and Iona in Scotland, we read *Castle* by David Macauley and *A Medieval Feast* by Aliki. These times together still rank as some of my favorite family memories, and the stories we shared beforehand deepened our appreciation for the places we visited.

But not everyone enjoys history as I do. So why would I encourage you to add these stories into your family culture, especially if your child may already be learning history in school?

In 1916, Henry Ford was quoted in *The Chicago Tribune* as saying, "History is more or less bunk" and that "it's tradition. We don't want tradition. We want to live in the present, and the only history that is worth a tinker's damn is the history that we make today."

But C.S. Lewis countered thoughtfully in his essay "Learning in War Time":

> We need intimate knowledge of the past. Not that the past has any magic about it, but because we cannot study the future, and yet need something to set against the present, to remind us that the basic assumptions have been quite different in different periods and that much which seems certain to the uneducated is merely temporary fashion.[1]

C.S. Lewis reminds us that to read the present wisely one needs to view the past well—without the present-day mindset clouding our attempts at interpretation. The seventeenth-century English philosopher Thomas Hobbes's view extends Lewis's thesis. He states, "For the principle and proper work of history [is] to instruct and enable men, by the knowledge of actions past, to bear themselves prudently in the present and providentially towards the future."[2]

Despite how cliché it may sound, the maxim "Those who do not learn from the past are condemned to repeat it," still rings true. Attending to and remembering the past will help us cultivate wise, faithful adults and citizens. This is more than enough reason to read history.

Reading biographies and autobiographies, books about battles and buildings, stories about explorers and makers—these are also ways of encouraging curiosity and discovery in our children, whether they encounter these stories at home or in the classroom. It is too easy to allow children's minds and preferences to be formed by the Pied Piper of mainstream marketing. Each stage of development and each generation can easily get stuck in the "pre-packaged bubble of the new"[3] and misguided by the anxieties and demands of the present age.

As we guide our children in reading and studying history, the following three ideas can offer us direction. First, those who pay close attention to the stories of history will learn what it means to be a broken image-bearer of God—knowing this should make us humble interpreters of the men and women we read about. Second, young history learners are starting on the path of *remembering*, which is foundational to growing in wisdom and love. Third, studying history enlarges students' imaginations, offering them people from the past that can inspire them.

If history is a way of seeing His Story, our minds need to be formed by His word. In Genesis, we learn that God made humans in His image and called them to mirror Him by caring for the land, cultivating places, multiplying, and being creative. Then Adam disobeyed the one "do not" directive from God and brought sin and brokenness to humanity and the world. With this truth in mind, we should look humbly at stories of civilizations building and making culture, warring and tearing down.

What we see in them is what it looks like to be made in God's image, but fallen—able to create, but also sinful and capable of spreading destruction. When we approach both history and the present age with humility and an awareness of our own brokenness, we can come to understand that just as our past heroes did both right *and* wrong, our present-day heroes will do the same.

The work of *remembering* (in contrast to merely memorizing people and dates, although memorizing names and dates has its proper place in education) is one way we plant the seeds of wisdom in our children.

After God called Moses to rescue the Hebrews from slavery in Egypt and led them to the Promised Land, God created a culture of remembering His saving work through songs, festivals, and rituals. He told the first generation to create memorials, to learn and obey His laws, and to recite the stories of His faithfulness to their children. By doing so, the people passed on the shared memory of God's work to the next generation . . . and then to the next. This was God's way of forming a people for Himself, set apart from the rest of the cultures around them.

Remembering was meant to be the tie that bound the Hebrews to God. By remembering their past, they could walk forward into the future that God had promised them. God gave Moses' successor Joshua, who led the Hebrews through the Jordan River, a directive to choose one man from each of the twelve tribes to take stones out of the river and place them in the area where they lodged, making a sign for them all. Joshua said,

> When your children ask in time to come, "What do those stones mean to you?" then you shall tell them that the waters of the Jordan were cut off before the ark of the covenant of the Lord . . . So these shall be to the people of Israel a memorial forever. (Joshua 4:5–7)

The work of remembering is part of the life of the church as well. Sabbath keeping, gathering for worship, preaching the Word, and taking communion are ways that Christians young and old retell the work of God in saving His people through Jesus. They are thus a means of grace in the formation of His body, the church. But memory keeping is not just for church-time.

Cindy Rollins elaborates on the goodness of remembering, stating that the early stage of education

> is the time we have to download our collective memory to our children so that they are tethered to the past and not adrift in the universe. The value is not in the skills they pick up or the facts they accumulate; the value is not in memorizing but in remembering.[4]

This type of remembering is more than the memorization of dates and events (which cannot form hearts that love God and neighbor). It requires us to pay attention to the people, words, and stories that came before us, knowing that if we listen close enough, we have much to learn from them.

Thus we offer to our younger children picture books, true stories, fables, and historical fiction to fill their minds and pique their interest. As they grow older, they can dig deeper and discuss the whys of what they have learned and read philosophers, authors, historians, and original documents that can enlarge the realities of the past. As we read, we give them a starting point to a life of remembering.

Lastly, studying the people of the past—those heroes and heroines that fill our imaginations—can inspire and give vision to our children. When we learn about people who accomplished the seemingly impossible, we can see our own potential to overcome hardship or to pursue a difficult calling. When we see how God used ordinary people to do good, we can be encouraged that our ordinary lives matter.

Hidden Figures, the story of Katherine Johnson and Dorothy Vaughan, may give a young girl interested in science and math the encouragement she needs to follow a path fitted to her giftings—despite the difficulties she may face. Reading *The Faithful Spy* (a dynamic biography of Dietrich Bonhoeffer) or the classic *The Hiding Place*, about Corrie Ten Boom and her family, can show a middle school reader how one's faith in Jesus Christ, love for family, and love for country can inspire a Christian to make difficult sacrifices.

Learning about the steadfast courage of Christian men and women of the past—such as Phillis Wheatley, William Wilberforce, Frederick Douglass, and Queen Liliʻuokalani—incarnates for young readers the way God uses His people to bring about His justice and goodness in the world.

When my own daughters were young, one of my favorite library discoveries was the biography picture book section on the children's floor—here shelves and shelves of interesting and creatively illustrated books about real people were located. We found books about John and Abigail Adams, John James Audubon , and Helen Keller. *Teedie: The Story of Young Teddy Roosevelt* by Don Brown started our infatuation with President Theodore Roosevelt. *Duke Ellington: The Prince and His Orchestra* is still a book we remember. We admired the courage and words of Marion Anderson and Langston Hughes; we discovered books about pirates,[5] pilots,[6] and political dissidents.[7] Because the library had a large selection of David Adler's picture book biographies we read many of them, including *A Picture Book of George Washington* and *A Picture Book of Florence Nightingale*.

As our family grew, reading historical novels, picture books, and nonfiction occurred almost effortlessly as we added what interested us to our library book bag. With these wonderful books in hand, we discussed with our children the real stories behind them, asking why the men and women who inspired us could be both heroic and un-heroic, helping them see what it meant to be a broken image-bearer of God, and remembering the past so that we could do our part in God's great story.

When one of our daughters became president of her college house, The House of Sojourner Truth, she helped introduce the ladies in her house to their namesake by reading them a picture book: *My Name is Truth: The Life of Sojourner Truth*, by Ann Turner. By remembering this story from the past, she invited her housemates to look beyond their current moment and remember who they are: broken image-bearers called to live out their place in God's story with the conviction, courage, and grace they saw reflected in Sojourner Truth.

Pyramid
David Macauley | *Illustrated by David Macauley*

This classic illustrated book is a series of fine pen-and-ink drawings that explore, step-by-step, the building of a pyramid. As with Macauley's *Castle, Cathedral,* and *City* books, a rudimentary story ties the whole book together. Through these books the reader learns how things were made and about the culture of the people who made them. The craftsmanship in the illustrations will captivate your children for hours. *Pyramid* is a great place to begin developing a child's curiosity about the grand story of history.

Peril and Peace
Mindy Withrow and Brandon Withrow

The first in a series of five books on the history of the church, *Peril and Peace* explores the first six hundred years of the followers of "The Way." This series blends history with fictional writing and can be read aloud or enjoyed by upper elementary students on their own. Connecting the New Testament writings to this early history will help your students connect the dots between God's work back then and His work in the world today.

I realize it is cheating a bit to include book recommendations within book recommendations, but since we are talking about church history, I can't resist at least mentioning these three books about God's work with His people throughout history: *Church History ABCs*, *Reformation History ABCs*, and *Bible History ABCs*, written by our friend Stephen J. Nichols and illustrated by my husband.

Joan of Arc
Diane Stanley | *Illustrated by Diane Stanley*

Beautifully illustrated in a faux-illuminated manuscript style, this story is about the young woman who led the armies of France to victory during the Hundred Years' War. Diane Stanley also has many other wonderful historical picture books that are worth investigating on a wide range of historical figures including Cleopatra, Da Vinci, Peter the Great, Elizabeth I, and more.

The Groundbreaking, Chance-Taking Life of George Washington Carver and Science & Invention in America
Cheryl Harness | *Illustrated by Cheryl Harness*

George Washington Carver discovered many uses for peanuts, and this wonderfully illustrated book gives the reader plenty to discover as well. After learning about George Washington Carver, keep exploring American history through Cheryl Harness's other lush and informative books.

A Hobbit, A Wardrobe, and a Great War
Joseph Loconte

Joseph Loconte is an amazing historian and an entertaining speaker (and one of our daughters' favorite history professors when they attended The King's College in New York City). This book is for high school students and older. To study how the Great War impacted the writings of Tolkien and Lewis, this book dives deeply into the history, ideas, and cultural influences of the time.

One of my favorite things about studying history is learning about the stories of how people and places were influenced by the major events of the past. This book pushes all the right buttons for me.

ENDNOTES

1   C.S. Lewis, "Learning in War-Time," in *The Weight of Glory* (New York: HarperCollins, 1949), p. 58.

2   Thomas Hobbes quoted in *Breaking Bread With the Dead: A Reader's Guide to a More Tranquil Mind*, by Alan Jacobs (New York: Penguin Books, 2020), p. 18.

3   Tony Tost quoted in Jacobs, *Breaking Bread*, p. 17.

4   Cindy Rollins, "I Remember Words," *CiRCE Institute*, June 12, 2013, https://www.circeinstitute.org/blog/i-remember-words.

5   Jane Yolen, *The Ballad of the Pirate Queens*, illus. David Shannon (New York: Voyager Books, 1998).

6   Nikki Grimes, *Talkin' About Bessie: The Story of Aviator Elizabeth Coleman*, illus. E.B. Lewis (New York: Orchard Books, 2002).

7   Alan Schroeder, *Minty: A Story of Young Harriet Tubman*, illus. Jerry Pinkney (New York: Dial Press, 1996).

THE HEARTBEAT OF HUMANITY

VIRTUE

PAHTYANA MOORE

Train up a child in the way he should go;
even when he is old he will not depart from it.
—Proverbs 22:6

As the daughter of an author and avid bibliophile, books from around the world adorned the bookshelves, nightstands, kitchen tables, and armchairs wherever we lived. I understood from an early age that books were a doorway to the outside world and often found an escape through them. I dreamt of reading to my own children one day the adventures of *Ali Baba and the Forty Thieves*, *King Arthur and His Knights of the Round Table*, "The Nightingale" by Hans Christian Andersen, and other international classics. As life would have it, I found that when I did have my own children I was not only reading these classics to them, but I was doing so while living in an international community in Nairobi, Kenya.

Our neighbors in the compound where we lived hailed from Germany, India, Ethiopia, the Philippines, Brazil, Canada, and Great Britain, among other places. And what a tight-knit community it was. I was continually astonished at the level of investment and generosity my little girls were shown by this community. Some of our neighbors would bring gifts for all the children on the compound when they returned from work trips or visits back home. For birthdays and holidays my girls enjoyed receiving beaded sandals from Ethiopia, brightly painted wooden dolls from Germany, ornate scarves and purses from India. If I sent the girls outside to go play, I would inevitably find them happily ensconced at a neighbor's apartment, learning to make potato latkes or chapatis from scratch and thoroughly soaking up their neighbors' abundant hospitality. I often felt like we had stepped into one of my childhood books and were living the very stories I had read.

As we have continued to travel and live internationally over the years, it has been with great joy that I have witnessed my girls modeling an innate hospitality towards others of all cultures. Whether this is displayed in airport play areas during long layovers, or on bustling street corners as we stop to pick up a local trinket, they seem keen to find the similarities with whomever is there and by so doing, emulate their heavenly Father's heart for humanity.

As we take a closer look at the myths, fables, and folktales of various cultures, we see a common theme woven throughout: that of humanity longing to fully engage in the Great Story they have been drawn into and the understanding that the straightest pathway toward that is through acting virtuously. The "moral of the story" at the end of each culture's fables leaves a lasting declaration of that culture's hope and investment in future generations. This creates a kind of North Star that is imparted to those who would follow in the footsteps of their ancestors and gives us a peek into what each culture values. We see the wisdom learned and handed down from one generation to the next, and this wisdom illuminates for us the priorities of that culture. In all the things learned throughout life, what has been included in the culture's canon of stories? By looking at the stories that have woven their way into the minds and hearts of a particular culture's ambassadors over generations, we come to know what is at the heart of that culture.

Whether these stories were imparted by a parent, to those sitting on a sofa in the comfort and stability of a brick-and-mortar home, or whether they were imparted by a *griot* (West African traditional storyteller) to those sitting on a dirt floor, in front of a smoldering village fire, the heart in these moments is the same. Prepare the next generation for what they will undoubtedly face. Embed in their hearts and minds the treasures of their people so that they will not only carry on the priorities of their people, but they will live lives rich with the wisdom of all who have come before them.

While the wisdom of the world is perhaps something that we as Christians tend to steer away from, seeking first and foremost the wisdom of God, there is still something significant in it. There is a key to be found in the perspectives of other cultures. It is not a key that will give us all we need to live lives that glorify God—only His wisdom is able to do that. But it is a key that gives us invaluable insight into what makes us all human—what unites us in our common needs, common hopes, common pitfalls. But what is this connecting point? The answer can be found in one, simple word: virtue.

Virtue is not a word that is tossed around often in these modern times, but it informs our humanity just the same, regardless of culture. The word refers to moral excellence, goodness, and righteousness. Those who are virtuous conform their lives and conduct to moral and ethical principles. Virtue serves as the avenue by which we reflect the character of God in our everyday lives and impact all who cross our path. A life of virtue is our strongest and surest witness of His presence in our hearts, and the pursuit of virtue has been a constant presence in every society from the beginning of time. Without the practice of virtue, we cannot hope to understand who God is in a practical sense or who we are meant to be as those made in His image. We also cannot hope to share His heart with the world unless the practice of virtue is evident in our lives or the lives of the children we raise and send out.

God has created every single one of us with the ability to find and be reconciled to Him and with the freewill to do so. As human beings, we desire to not only engage with right and wrong, but to engage the challenges found in circumstances that wake us up and draw out our depth, and this is the beginning of the pathway to Him. There are towering brambles and thorn-laden hedges aplenty between us and the castle of destiny that we're riding hard toward. And many do not find their way. But in our innate desire to rise in response to good and evil, to lean on the foundational wisdom that has been passed down to us, we stumble upon the thread that connects every human being, what ties every culture together.

So when children peek into these cultures and see characters from diverse backgrounds choosing to engage the virtuous in their own unique ways, this creates a connection and paves the way for future understanding, respect, and dignity. Children who grow up with this rich, fundamental recognition become adults who are capable of seeing others the way God sees them. As Rachel Naomi Remen writes, "When we know ourselves to be connected to all others, acting compassionately is simply the natural thing to do."[1]

So, how can we in our snug corners of the world gain access to these children's tales told perhaps at dusk in a remote, dusty village outside Calcutta? At a family dinner table in Italy? On a walk to fetch water in Addis Ababa? In makeshift refugee camps in northwestern Kenya? We look to the stories that other cultures have carried with them and to stories that give new and insightful peeks into places and peoples unknown.

Let us share with our children stories that embody the heart of humanity in one way or another. Whether traditional or modern, these stories will highlight a unique collection of virtues and paint a picture of their significance in delightful, powerful, and heart-warming scenarios. They will draw out the merits of mankind and give readers something to aspire to—a cause to fight, a beauty to pursue, an evil to vanquish. The heroes and heroines of these stories embody the virtues in various ways and not only accomplish what they set out to do but become who they were meant to become along the way. Within these books lies wisdom that translates into any culture and ties us together.

Young readers who are privileged to read these tales will find an open doorway leading into the wide, wide world from the comfort of their own homes. These stories seek to enlighten and invest in young minds, planting virtuous seeds of compassion, determination, dignity, generosity, purity of heart, and a deep regard for humanity. While these tales may not be overtly Christian, they powerfully display the heart and character of God in the virtues they highlight. They contain virtues hidden snugly within those storylines, as if God Himself was hiding little treasure troves of His character in every culture for us to find and emulate. Drawing readers into their unique cultural perspective, these stories demonstrate how all of us as children of God can walk out His character in our everyday actions and impact the world around us. Through the avenues of the virtues, we can carry His heart for humanity wherever we go, and we can be quick to recognize His heart in others.

––––––––––––––––––––––––––––––––––––––

The Adventures of Mali & Keela
Jonathan Collins | *Illustrated by Jenny Cooper*

Published by The Virtues Project, an international initiative that encourages virtuous living in any culture, *The Adventures of Mali & Keela* introduces readers to virtues such as determination, kindness, truthfulness, and respect—to name just a few—in a multi-cultural context. With delightful illustrations and relatable characters, these stories are meant to be read aloud to young listeners and include age-appropriate definitions at the end of each story.

Mufaro's Beautiful Daughters
John Steptoe | *Illustrated by John Steptoe*

This award-winning book gives a unique spin on where true beauty is found. It is the tale of two beautiful but vastly different sisters as they embark on a journey to the king's palace, where one will be chosen as queen. With stunning illustrations inspired by the Zimbabwe landscape, the story opens with village life and ends with both sisters being presented to the king. However, the journey between those two destinations reveals more about their respective characters than anyone expects. This classic explores issues of purity of heart, loving the unlovely, selflessness, and what makes a true queen. Winner of the Caldecott Medal and the Coretta Scott King Award for Illustrators, this gem draws readers into lush African life and tells an impressive tale of true virtue.

A Map into the World
Kao Kalia Yang | *Illustrated by Seo Kim*

This is the inspiring story of a young girl who hails from the Hmong people group in Southeast Asia. When Paj's neighbor Bob loses his wife, she finds a creative way to connect with him and to offer him sympathy through an unexpected gift. This story explores the themes of life and death, empathy, and cross-cultural and multi-generational community. It shows how a child's simple yet inspiring perspective of the world can bring hope to someone. What also makes this story special is that Bob is not just a character in the book—he is the author's real-life neighbor and a widower. From an acclaimed Hmong-American author, this debut picture book is a sweet depiction of how universal the issues of the human heart are and how, with a little creativity, anyone can make a difference.

My Name is Not Refugee
Kate Milner

This award-winning book takes the young reader into the world of a little boy as he tries to make sense of the world that is suddenly changing around him. His mother explains every step of their journey—what they will see and hear, what they will leave behind, what will be strange and new. Through each step the reader is presented with a simple question that invites them to engage on a personal level and look at how they would respond if they were in his situation. With quiet and intriguing illustrations, this story helps readers understand a little more of the refugee journey from a child's viewpoint. *My Name is Not Refugee* closes with a powerful reminder that a person's current circumstances do not determine who they are.

Usborne Illustrated Fables from Around the World
Sam Baer, Susanna Davidson, Rosie Dickins, and Rosie Hore

With delightfully immersive illustrations from Usborne's signature artists, this one-of-a-kind collection of classic fables covers age-old tales, from the Japanese folktale "The Fox Maiden" to "The Wall of Asgard" from Norse mythology. This beautiful compilation spans the globe and gives young readers a unique peek into the most beloved fables from eighteen different cultures. In these venerable tales, readers are privy to the wisdom and perspectives of generations of people from India, Korea, Egypt, Ghana, Ireland, China, and more.

ENDNOTES
1   Rachel Naomi Remen quoted in Sue Hart and Victoria Kindle Hodson, *The Compassionate Classroom: Relationship Based Teaching and Learning* (Encinitas, CA: PuddleDancer Press, 2004), p. 59.

THE WELLS OF SOUL AND MEMORY

WRITING FOR CHILDREN

AN INTERVIEW BETWEEN MITALI PERKINS AND CAROLYN LEILOGLOU

Over the last several years, Mitali Perkins has become one of my favorite authors. She writes resonant young adult novels, chapter books deeply rooted in place, and picture books that shine a light on the immigrant child's experience of belonging to multiple cultures. She's also written a book for adults about rereading classic children's literature titled *Steeped in Stories: Timeless Children's Novels to Refresh Our Tired Souls*.

I first learned about Mitali and her books through an article she wrote for *Christianity Today* in which she shares how the novels she read as a child prepared her heart to later receive the gospel.[1] And I have no doubt that some of her own books will bear similar fruit in her readers. I'm thrilled to be able to share this brief interview with her here.

What drew you to writing for children, and what is your vision as a writer?

Books I read as a child changed and shaped my heart, mind, and soul for life. I kept returning to children's books to be refreshed and empowered even when I became an adult. I was pursuing a career in alleviating the suffering of children through political science and public policy, but bit by bit it dawned on me that my "hobby" of writing stories for children could also fulfill that goal. My first novel (*The Sunita Experiment*) won a contest and was published quickly, but my second novel (*Monsoon Summer*) was rejected by twenty-two publishers before it was published twelve years later.

During that period of time, in prayer, I didn't give up on that story. I submitted, revised, got a rejection, revised, submitted, revised, and got another rejection, and so on, but through that process my craft was improving. My desire to do the work was also increasing. Slowly, gradually, I began to see that writing for young people could be my full-time vocation, because as Frederick Buechner put it, "The place God calls you to is the place where your deep gladness and the world's deep hunger meet."[2] And here I am.

You have written in other places about the way classic children's books primed your heart to later receive the gospel. Are there ways you try to have a similar effect in your own books?

I pray my writing might infuse a child's heart with courage, hope, love, faith, and any of the other virtues, but I don't start a book with that goal in mind. So much of writing is mystery—every book is a curious relationship between reader, writer, and the story itself. What the reader takes out of it may not be at all what the writer intended. What the writer puts into it may not even be what the writer intended. As creatives, we draw deeply from the wells of soul and memory without even knowing what's there. I'm often surprised by what emerges in my writing as I let go of control and rigidity of agenda. My comfort is that as I seek to live in a state of grace and pursue goodness, maybe some of that will seep into my stories. I certainly hope so.

You write for the general market, yet several of your books have what I would call an "encounter with Jesus" moment. How do you keep these feeling like an invitation rather than a sermon?

The reader has to know a character so well that when such an encounter takes place it feels natural and right in the moment. It's all about creating believable characters, good dialogue, a compelling plot, and an immersive setting. In short, I want to keep improving my craft so that any spiritual, emotional, relational, or physical experience I include in a novel rings true.

How does your Bengali heritage, as well as the fact you lived in several countries as a child, influence your writing?

The well of my memory includes all of that multicultural beauty, so my stories draw deeply from those experiences. That's what God has given me; I'm grateful.

What are some of your favorite children's books?

In my book, *Steeped in Stories*, I wrote about my five favorite children's books: *A Little Princess, Little Women, Anne of Green Gables, The Hobbit*, and *The Chronicles of Narnia*.

Please tell us some other South Asian authors or books you'd recommend, both to help kids feel seen and to help them see the world through new eyes.

Many, many writers are creating stories with South Asian content. Your public librarian will be able to steer you to lists and recommendations. Another good source of such books is the South Asia Book Award. Specifically, check out the work of Uma Krishnaswami, Padma Venkatraman, Kashmira Sheth, Chitra Divakaruni, and Aisha Saeed.

Thank you so much, Mitali, for talking with us about your books!

I've come up with a short list of some of my own favorite books by South Asian authors for a variety of ages, including one of Mitali's, of course—though I was tempted to include several of her's because she has written everything from picture books through young adult novels!

The Library Bus
Bahram Rahman | *Illustrated by Gabrielle Grimard*

This story follows Pari on her first day helping Mama on the only library bus in Kabul, Afghanistan. Mama drives to villages and camps where she teaches girls and lends books. She tells Pari how her father taught her to read when it was still illegal to teach girls. Sharing this book is bittersweet given current events in Afghanistan, where the fate of girls' rights and education is still unknown. Nevertheless, this is a great resource for talking to kids about life for children in other countries and how change happens.

My First Day
Phung Nguyen Quang | *Illustrated by Huynh Kim Lien*

This may be the most unique first day of school story you will ever read. This beautiful picture book follows a boy paddling a boat to school in the Mekong River Delta in Vietnam. It's full of poetic writing and lush illustrations that lend a touch of magic to the world. Young readers may not even realize the boy is headed to school until he gets there and they see all the other children paddling their boats to school. This is a great way to introduce children to a new culture through a kid doing something they do but in a very different way.

Meet Yasmin!
Saadia Faruqi | *Illustrated by Hatem Aly*

Yasmin is a spunky girl who gets caught up in her imagination, where everyday events are an adventure. Creative problem solving and supportive, loving parents help Yasmin navigate her world. Kids will appreciate Yasmin as a girl very much like them, while also learning a few Urdu words and a little about Pakistani culture. This is a great book for young readers just beginning chapter books.

Midsummer's Mayhem
Rajani LaRocca

LaRocca weaves together a fascinating retelling of Shakespeare's *A Midsummer Night's Dream* with the story of Mimi, an aspiring young baker, the youngest of four kids in an Indian-American family. Mimi longs to be as talented as her older siblings, and a baking contest at the mysterious new bakery in town seems to be just the thing. This middle grade novel is clever and magical and works well as a retelling without falling into predictability.

Forward Me Back to You
Mitali Perkins

Sixteen-year-old Katina is dealing with the aftermath of an attempted sexual assault. Eighteen-year old Robin/Ravi, an Indian-born boy adopted by white parents, is grappling with his identity. When Katina and Robin find themselves in the same youth group, a mission trip to India serving exploited girls seems like to perfect opportunity for each of them to conquer their deepest need. *Forward Me Back to You* is a beautiful story of faith, friendship, and family.

ENDNOTES

1   Mitali Perkins, "Testimony: When God Writes Your Life Story," *Christianity Today*, December 31, 2015, https://www.christianitytoday.com/ct/2016/january-february/jesus-christ-haunted-hindu-testimony.html.

2   Frederick Buechner, *Wishful Thinking: A Seeker's ABC* (New York: HarperCollins, 1973), p. 119.

FINDING JOY IN
THE EVERYDAY

QUOTIDIAN BOOKS

MARGIE HAACK

When I was a child, the very first book I read when I graduated from picture books was *Bambi*. I had not seen the Disney movie. I knew nothing of the story except from the short, illustrated, tattered copy of the Little Golden Book we owned, so I was shocked to learn that *Bambi* was a novel-length story found in our very own school library. As I read, I was gripped by the desire to see Bambi and Faline living safely in a forest near a meadow where they could eat and play. I longed for them to be safe from the hunters and free from the bully deer who wanted to harm Bambi and take Faline from him. To my great relief, this is what happened. Bambi and Faline were restored to the kind of everyday life any deer could ever want. It was so satisfying.

Both iconic stories and Scripture[1] demonstrate that an ordinary day in an ordinary life is a place where the pleasures and rituals of a normal life can be celebrated. One of the problems of our modern Western culture is our insatiable desire for the extraordinary. The spectacular. The impossible. We do need miracles and heroes who do the impossible, but too often the compelling and healing nature of the ordinary is undervalued and replaced in favor of the sensational.

A friend once pointed out that even the amazing adventures and powers of Superman were all focused on restoring the safety of ordinary life to the citizens of Metropolis. The people were filled with relief when given the chance to return to their normal activities.

It is interesting that when Jesus was on earth, He did that actual thing again and again in His encounters with people. He sent them back to their ordinary lives to be a testimony to the sacredness of the everyday. In one case, a man was so besieged by demons he could not be kept from harming himself. People tried to keep him chained up, but he always broke free and roamed the countryside, injured and naked. He had such strength that people were afraid of him. But the day he met Jesus his life was completely changed. Jesus restored his mind and body to what he was meant to be. For the first time his heart could rest. He could eat and sleep like a normal person. After so much suffering—now that he was free from such terrifying evil—he naturally wanted to go with the person who healed him. In fact, he begged Jesus, "Let me go with you." But as Jesus left, He said, "No. You need to stay home. Return to your life."

After suffering so much and for so long he was not going to become the sensational headline of Jesus' healing ministry. He was going to reenter the place where all the normal routines of his life had been stolen from him. He would now have the chance to enjoy the pleasures of an everyday life free from his former nightmare existence (Mark 5:1–20).

Some version of celebrating the ordinary is found in many books written for children. The calming illustrations of the classic book *Goodnight Moon* demonstrate this by helping a child review the familiar pieces of his little life as he prepares to release the day and fall asleep for the night. Going to bed is a daily ritual of his life, just as it is for every person. He is reassured that even the moon and the mice say "Goodnight" to the day. Margaret Wise Brown's quiet examination and Clement Hurd's creative illustrations make the ordinary wonderfully appealing.

Of course, an ordinary day is also the place where things go awry. A happy ending is not the complete story of life on earth. As children mature, they learn that not everything ends happily. This is the reality of life in a broken world. When we experience a season of struggle, often what we want most is to be free of the drama and the suffering. We want the ordinary restored. We want the pleasure of returning to what is normal—to a familiar place of peace and safety. The best remedy for this longing might be the actual experience of something quite common, like the simple pleasure of fresh-baked bread and a bowl of soup. Or the warmth of a soft, dry bed on a stormy night. Or even receiving a simple hug from a friend who has listened to us. Such things can inspire us to continue living into the next moment and on into the next day without giving up. This is the theme of many beloved children's books.

A person's daily life can be very different from the one I happen to know, but the yearning for a sunny day when all things go well is a universal longing found in every human heart. A story has the power to take us to another people, country, or experience far from our own where we learn that, though their days may be different from ours, we value the same things.

Whether the story is as simple as *Goodnight Moon* or as complicated and familiar as *The Chronicles of Narnia,* we find joy in being led to a place where we safely celebrate the common goodness of the everyday. In *The Lion, the Witch and the Wardrobe,* we don't wait long for the children to reach the Beavers' home, where they are welcomed to a supper of fresh fish that came sizzling out of the pan, and

> a great and gloriously sticky marmalade roll, steaming hot . . . at the same time the kettle was moved on to the fire, so that when they had finished the marmalade roll the tea was made and ready to be poured out. And when each person had got his (or her) cup of tea, each person shoved back his (or her) stool so as to be able to lean against the wall and gave a long sigh of contentment.[2]

Of course, the context of this delightful supper came in the midst of a very dangerous time for Narnia. This is the reality of living in our world and is true for all our lives. As Christians we firmly believe that complete restoration will come, but perhaps not until the next life. While we wait here for our final home, all our stories of restoring the normal are only partial, and yet they remain precious. So we welcome those times, those places and people who give us courage, respite, and hope for the future.

Bunny Cakes
Rosemary Wells | *Illustrated by Rosemary Wells*

Who doesn't love birthdays and cake? The delightful humor and charming illustrations of this common celebration lead us to a sweet ending. Ruby intends to make a wonderful cake for her grandma's birthday, but she runs into all sorts of obstacles. All she needs is a few ordinary ingredients, but sending her brother Max to the grocer with a list is an unexpected challenge: Max has an idea of what he wants to add the unique cake he is making, but he cannot make the grocer understand what he needs. Solving this dilemma with a creative solution is the delightful climax of the story. When at last the two bunnies are done, Max has created an earthworm cake and Ruby's is "just beautiful." Grandma doesn't know which to eat first.

Fry Bread
Kevin Noble Maillard | *Illustrated by Juana Martinez-Neal*

Each day, bread nourishes and comforts people of every culture and nation around the world. Bread can seem so common that we might overlook the delight it gives. In the American Southwest, over 150 years ago, Navajo were the first to make fry bread, after the deprivation of land and indigenous crops of corn forced them to find new ways of using government rations. Out of that hardship was born a new kind of bread—Fry Bread. Warm, delicious, piled high on a plate accompanied by honey, beans, and cheese, fry bread became more than an everyday staple. It brought families together at powwows and festivals. In this book, we are pulled into the creation of fry bread and its power to bring friends and family together any time—but especially in time for an ordinary weekday supper.

Dr. De Soto
William Steig | *Illustrated by William Steig*

On an ordinary day in their dental practice, two mice face a practical problem: how to treat a fox who on *his* ordinary day would happily eat a mouse. Despite their policy to not treat predatory animals, they decide, out of compassion, to treat the fox who is in terrible pain. In the end they outsmart the fox, who thinks he can do both: be treated for his "rotten bicuspid" and have a snack as well. What was a crisis for the dentist and his assistant becomes a way of finding a creative solution that restores their safety. In response to a happy ending, they celebrate by kissing and taking the day off.

A Baby Sister for Francis
Russell Hoban | *Illustrations by Lillian Hoban*

When our second child joined our family, his older sister was expecting a miniature playmate. Her disappointed response was "It's not that much fun being a big sister." It is common for a child to feel this pain when Mom and Dad are busy with the new baby. In this charming little story, Frances decides the best way out of this dilemma is to run away. She packs her bag and moves in beneath the dining-room table. Within her hearing, the parents discuss the importance of Frances' place in the family and declare how much they will miss her now that she is gone. Enticed by the prospect of a new sweater, chocolate cake (that the baby certainly cannot eat), and a renewed sense of her own value, Frances rejoins the family.

Charlie Needs a Cloak

Tomie dePaola | *Illustrated by Tomie dePaola*

Charlie, a young shepherd, has a basic need. The cloak he wears every day is a tattered mess. He needs a new one, but he must make it himself. In this little book there are few words, but the charming illustrations tell most of this delightful story. Charlie has access to everything he needs to make a new cloak, from the wool of his sheep to the spinning wheel that turns wool into yarn. The problem he faces is a comical little black-faced sheep, who has hastened the ruin of the old cloak by constantly nibbling on it. This book is a delightful celebration of the ordinary.

ENDNOTES

1   Refer to the passage in Jeremiah 29:5–7 (NIV), where God tells his people: "Build houses and settle down; plant gardens and eat what they produce. Marry and have sons and daughters; find wives for your sons and give your daughters in marriage, so that they too may have sons and daughters. Increase in number there; do not decrease. Also, seek the peace and prosperity of the city to which I have carried you into exile. Pray to the Lord for it, because if it prospers, you too will prosper."

2   C.S. Lewis, *The Lion, the Witch and the Wardrobe* (New York: HarperCollins, 1950), p. 82.

WHAT DREAMS MAY COME

SHAKESPEARE

CINDY WARD ROLLINS

I had heard of Shakespeare before junior high, but my first encounter with him came when my eighth-grade class watched the gorgeous Franco Zeffirelli production of *Romeo and Juliet*. Later, as a conscientious seventeen-year-old, I bought *The Complete Shakespeare in One Volume* and proceeded to read the tiny print of *The Taming of the Shrew*. I have no idea why I picked that play, plopped as it was in the middle of the huge volume, but about halfway through the reading I realized that much of it was written in meter. It would be years before I knew to call it iambic pentameter, but from the moment that beat connected to my own heartbeat I was in love with William Shakespeare.

As a young mother I read *For the Children's Sake,* a book about education by Susan Schaeffer Macauley. Susan wrote about sending her little girls to a cottage school in England, run on the principles of a woman named Charlotte Mason, where they came home breathlessly excited each day about reading Shakespeare's plays. Although my first two sons were still quite little, I already knew that I wanted to introduce them to Shakespeare someday. But that seed would lay dormant for many years. Teaching my children Shakespeare when I barely knew anything about him at all seemed too daunting in those years of bearing one child after another.

Eventually, I realized that time was passing quickly, and my children would soon grow up without having ever met Mr. William Shakespeare. In my frustration, I decided to just pick up a play and read it. I picked *A Midsummer*

Night's Dream because it was midsummer, and because it seemed like the perfect choice for reading outside on a summer evening. I was astonished when my boys laughed at the antics of Puck and Bottom. After that success I kept a steady stream of Shakespeare plays going, one scene at a time, until the children were all grown up. Now I read Shakespeare for my own pleasure one scene at a time—a little Shakespeare goes a long way.

Shakespeare's plays are each five acts long, with a varying number of scenes in each act. If you read a scene a day it takes very little time, and you can make your way through the whole canon of thirty-nine plays in a couple of years of light reading. The longest scene is Act 5, Scene II of *Love's Labour's Lost*, coming in at 1,016 lines long. You might want to take a couple days to read that, but most scenes can easily be read in five minutes or less. Technically, all you really need to enjoy Shakespeare with your children is a copy or two of his plays, but sometimes a little help is nice.

I found it helpful to read a synopsis of the play or a story of the play before reading the real thing. My favorite Shakespearean storybook was E. Nesbit's *Beautiful Stories from Shakespeare*, although often we read Charles and Mary Lamb's *Tales from Shakespeare*. Sometimes we even read both. In the last ten years or so, several authors have released storybooks of some of the most popular plays. Marianna Mayer has a lovely edition of *The Tempest*, one of the most accessible of Shakespeare's plays for children, and Bruce Coville has a bevy of well-done retellings in storybook form.

After the children understand the storyline, you can then pick up the play and read it aloud. Depending on the ages of your children, you can either read all the characters yourself—I deadpan the character names—or have everyone take a part or two to read. Or you can use the Arkangel recordings of the play, now free online. (If you use an audiobook form, just make sure that you have the words in front of you so you can see who is speaking.) You can even find the play online and put it on your TV screen while you listen. As with most difficult things, it's better to pick it up and do it in short sections than to have a perfect plan.

After you finish reading the play, you can then find a good production to watch. Some plays have been made into beautiful movies like *Hamlet, Much Ado About Nothing*, and others by Kenneth Branagh or Franco Zeffirelli. All of the plays can be watched as stage plays from various companies and productions. The BBC did them all in the 1980s. These have aged well, and you are sure to recognize an actor or two in their younger years. (Just make sure you read a good review before watching, because some companies take great liberties. I once had to quickly turn off a 1960s stage version of *A Midsummer Night's Dream* because it contained extensive nudity.)

While Shakespeare's plays were meant to be watched, hearing the words plows the ground for understanding, and the most fun way of all to enjoy Shakespeare is through acting out the play with your family and friends, with anything from a full-scale production to a living room read-through. Joyce McPherson has adapted several of the plays for producing with young troupes, and they're quite affordable, so you can buy a copy for each of your actors. Shakespeare is not a one-and-done activity or book; rather, his work makes for a lifetime of reading and enjoying.

I also found it was fun to memorize a section or two of whatever play we were reading. Here are some of my favorite passages to memorize:

1. "The Quality of Mercy" (Portia, *The Merchant of Venice*)
2. "To Be or Not to Be" (*Hamlet*—with its odd words, this is quite delightful)
3. "Friends, Romans, Countrymen" (Marc Antony, *Julius Caesar*)
4. "All the World's a Stage" (Jaques, *As You Like It*)
5. "St. Crispin's Day Speech" (*Henry V*—every boy should know this speech)

But why read Shakespeare at all to children? Childhood is the perfect time to introduce Shakespeare; so many things sound new to children that the plays of Shakespeare will sound no more foreign to them than most other things. Did you know Shakespeare is written in modern English? To read our language in its early modern stage is to be steeped in beauty. Our children deserve to know the full glory of the language we speak. A childhood spent in the King James Bible and Shakespeare will foster a sophisticated use of English with very little training or effort. We also find that knowing key Shakespeare plays opens the door to understanding many modern allusions, sayings, movies, and TV shows. English entertainment and literature is still paying homage to the Bard.

Some worry that Shakespeare is bawdy or has inappropriate or adult themes, and this is true at times, but it's usually far less of a problem than we anticipate. Much that is inappropriate goes right over the heads of children and often moms, too. It's not to hard to leave out things that seem too mature. And as children grow we can use these moments to discuss hard things.

Shakespeare's use of metaphor is another reason to read his plays. Metaphor is a sophisticated tool, but by reading Shakespeare, children can learn organically the concept of comparing unlike things in living ways. And helping us to understand unlike things is one of the main tasks of language. We call that communication. As our language is devolving to an almost barbarian level, reading Shakespeare—even to young children—can go a long way in preserving the culture of our language and promoting true communication and, therefore, communion.

Tales from Shakespeare
Charles and Mary Lamb

Brother-and-sister team Charles and Mary Lamb have narrated twenty plays for us in their classic book. Charles's desire to give his ill sister Mary worthwhile work led them to write these stories; they get the award for being the first on the scene in this genre. The Lambs retain much of the original language of Shakespeare in this collection, making it simultaneously majestic and perhaps too difficult for some beginners. Give it a go, and if you find it rough going pull out my next suggestion instead.

Beautiful Stories from Shakespeare
E. Nesbit

E. Nesbit is a well-known Victorian children's author and mother of many who greatly influenced C.S. Lewis with her numerous fantasy series for children (including our family favorite, the *House of Arden* series). While this book takes the odd angle of making all the characters children for the nursery crowd, it still retains much of the language and beauty of Shakespeare's own words, and the twenty-one stories are quite easy to understand.

William Shakespeare's Macbeth
Adapted by Bruce Coville | *Illustrated by Gary Kelley*

Macbeth is one of Shakespeare's most talked about tragedies. Bruce Coville catches all the eerie wonder of the play in his picture book adaptation. Perhaps this book is not for the small child with its three very wicked-looking hags, but it's a wonderful introduction to the play for most students, capturing the atmosphere and the language of the original. Despite its scary themes, *Macbeth* is easily accessible to young humans who immediately grasp the dilemma Macbeth creates when he hears the witches' prophecies, and Lady Macbeth perfectly illustrates how much of Shakespeare has crept into modern life.

The Tempest
Adapted by Marianna Mayer | *Illustrated by Lynn Bywaters*

The Tempest is Shakespeare's shortest and perhaps most approachable play. Many scholars believe it's his only play based on an original story. With its practical, romantic, and fantastical elements, I've found that it's also an easy one to teach. The ugly Caliban; the sprightly Ariel; the loving daughter, Miranda; her first and only suitor Ferdinand; and the creator of it all, the wizard, father, and former king, Prospero—the characters all move across this story. The scenes change quickly from terror to romance, and even feature quite a bit of high comedy and fantasy. Marianna Mayer's adaptation, accompanied by Lynn Bywater's lush illustrations, makes for a great picture book introduction to *The Tempest*.

Leon Garfield's Shakepeare Stories
Leon Garfield | *Illustrated by Michael Foreman*

Leon Garfield, a British fiction writer, is known for his children's historical novels and for *Shakespeare: The Animated Tales for Television*. His *Shakespeare Stories*, a retelling of twelve of the bard's well-known tales, is perfect for older children. The language, characters, and plot are all deftly captured in each one. This volume—there are two—includes *Twelfth Night, King Lear, Hamlet, Romeo and Juliet*, and *Othello*. Michael Foreman's illustrations, both color and pen-and-ink drawings, add to the drama of each story.

... and an extra recommendation:

Asimov's Guide to Shakespeare
Isaac Asimov

Although this book is out of print, I know of no other commentary on Shakespeare as delightful as Asimov's. His opinionated readings of the plays and his helpful connections open up each play to the average reader where more scholarly works may fail. While I don't recommend you run out and spend hundreds of dollars for this huge volume, I do hope you'll keep your eyes open for it at used bookstores and library sales.

A BEAUTIFUL WORD, BEAUTIFULLY SAID

LATINO LITERATURE

ERÉNDIRA RAMÍREZ-ORTEGA

Worthy books are not companions—they are solitudes:
We lose ourselves in them and all our cares.—P.J. Bailey, *Festus*

Nineteenth-century reformer Charlotte Mason reinforced a full and generous curriculum for children—an educational feast—rich in literature. This feast offers children and parents alike the opportunity to discover and delight in a variety of intellectual food—ideas. Her philosophy informs the read-aloud experience with exquisite literature that both nurtures a love of learning and motivates critical thinking.

In the early years of reading, Mason argued, a child should not consume a diet of what she called twaddle. That is, in a modern sense, literature which is commercial, scrappy, weak. She encouraged parents and educators, rather, to fill their shelves with what she called living books: books that nourish young minds with high-quality, moral, character-building living stories; books that draw us closer together and closer to God.

Living books make a subject come alive for a reader in the following ways: they are written by a single author with a passion for the subject and are usually written in narrative form (as though the author is telling the reader a story); they are written well; they activate the imagination; they eschew stereotypes; and they contain ideas, not dry facts. As born persons, children can appreciate fine art from a young age. It is no surprise then that "children who grow up amongst their elders and are not provided with what are called children's books at all, fare the better on what they are able to glean for themselves from the literature of grown-up people."[1] That is, when a child is given a living book, one that is not diluted with twaddle, he will likely amuse himself with it and gain an appreciation that will lay a foundation for a great love for, say, history. However, when a child is consuming what is commonly thrust on him—twaddle—it may be impossible for him to recall passages from the history book during his childhood, let alone forty years after his reading of the material.

As we equip our children to distinguish between what is twaddle and what is worthy in literature, we are emphasizing this truth: "Whatsoever things are true, whatsoever things *are* honest, whatsoever things *are* just, whatsoever things *are* pure, whatsoever things *are* lovely, whatsoever things *are* of good report; if *there be* any virtue, and if *there be* any praise, think on these things. (Phil. 4:8 KJV)." It is noble for children to read and differentiate the issues of life for themselves as they mature, instead of relying too heavily on others to deposit knowledge into them.

The first step, then, is to supply living books for our children to read themselves, or for us to read aloud to them. But as we choose books, living books that will inform young readers and ignite their interest, we ought to look for books that encourage compassionate awareness of the literature of other cultures—for the purposes of this essay, Latino literature.

In her most profound assessment of school curricula, Mason wrote:

> Perhaps the gravest defect in school curricula is that they fail to give a comprehensive, intelligent and interesting introduction to history. To leave off or even to begin with the history of our own country is fatal. We cannot live sanely unless we know that other peoples are as we are with a difference, that their history is as ours, with a difference, that they too have been represented by their poets and their artists, that they too have their literature and their national life.[2]

We must value the importance of different perspectives within our discussions of history. If we only introduce children to books from within our own tradition, we deny our children encounters with the richness and variety of what exists beyond their atmosphere. The ability to appreciate literature fully develops over time as we continue to expose our children to living literature. "As in a worthy book we leave the author to tell his own tale, so do we trust a picture to tell its tale through the medium the artist gave it."[3]

By introducing our children to the feast of literature by Latino authors, we offer children an opportunity to develop a sensibility about the many distinctions in our culture, and of the times in which a poet or author tells a story. As Mason said, "The more variety you can throw into his reading lessons, the more will the child enjoy them."[4]

The Latino literature we share with young readers should be written with the lucidity, concentration, personal conviction, directness, and admirable simplicity which characterizes a work of literary caliber. We don't need, for instance, to read books that italicize Spanish words in order to distinguish them from English words.

Charlotte Mason considered words as symbols—signs—that the eye can see and associate with an existing idea in the mind. If we take this logic, we see that Spanish words to the English-only reader will be just that—signs. Learning to hold words in esteem is crucial for young readers, especially when approaching the unfamiliar. Have you noticed that when a young child learns a big word, he is delighted and impressed by the new word's sound and tone? It is a novelty, one that takes effort to acquire. Older children should likewise view a new word with excitement, not see it as a confrontation.

Mason writes that words should be a "source of pleasure, . . . worthy of our honor," and that "a beautiful word deserves to be beautifully said, with a certain roundness of tone and precision of utterance."[5] In the case of Spanish words in books written for bilingual readers, English-only readers must render care with words that are unfamiliar by never reducing them to foreign objects to be hurried over. Something incredibly significant occurs when our eyes graze over a set of unfamiliar typographical marks: we compartmentalize and create distance.

But when a reader takes care to enunciate and pronounce the word correctly, the next time she encounters that word, it will no longer be a jarring encounter with the unfamiliar. A child's stock of words takes form, grows, and deepens organically. The power of encountering new words in Spanish warrants a sense of satisfaction that places reading, reasoning, and relating within reach. The child confidently learns to adapt new language into her normative reading. And if the parent enriches the child's learning with moral lessons found in the story, the child may learn empathy as well.

But in a living work of Latino literature, we encounter themes of loyalty, courage, compassion, and the value of trust and honesty. The narrative voice is distinct, personal, and authentic. It doesn't sound borrowed from other traditions; it doesn't mask any truths that need to be expressed. This voice may be lyrical and poignant, or heartbreaking, yet without the melodrama.

As we choose living books that will inform our young readers and ignite their interest, we ought to carefully choose books that encourage compassionate awareness. Take for instance *The House on Mango Street* by Sandra Cisneros. It is acclaimed by critics, beloved by many, and taught in colleges and high schools. It's about a young Latina growing up in Chicago under the pressures of family, friends, and school. It is lyrical, poetic, and minimalist in its vignette storytelling style. It's nostalgic in its tone as well, and memorable most of all.

The theme of family relationships serves as a vehicle for identity in Latino literature. Whether or not the narrator is born in the US, the story is likely rooted in family, and any child can connect with the theme of family because we all share this in common. As we read, we gain insight and depth, and we attain new ideas about the relative value of things—new hope, new vision, newness of sight for us to experience.

An engaging Latino narrative tells a relevant, moving story without sentimentality. It compels the child to appreciate and enjoy the beauty of a culture that has existed in the US for hundreds of years, evolved through the ages, traversed between borderlands, a fixture of American history. Mason said it best when she wrote: "The present writer writes and the reader reads, because we are all moved by the spirit of our time; these things are our secret preoccupation, for we have come out of a long alienation as persons 'wearied with trifles,' and are ready and anxious for a new age."[6]

When a child begins to acquire the habit of reading to herself, she has truly begun her education. When a child reads books with interest and pleasure, true living books, then we can trust that what she is reading has literary power. Selecting books that portray the powerful stories of Latino characters will encourage children to develop a habit of reading for knowledge, delight, and instruction. Children who read with their minds fully engaged, intentional about learning something, will benefit as they narrate in their own words what was impressed upon them. As Mason said, "Just so in their small degree do the children narrate; they see it all so vividly that when you read or hear their versions the theme is illuminated for you too."[7]

Two White Rabbits
Jairo Buitrago | *Illustrated by Rafael Yockteng*

Jairo Buitrago has collaborated with Rafael Yockteng on several award-winning picture books. Although Buitrago lives in Mexico, it is not clear where the little girl in this story is traveling from. We can't be certain it is Mexico. It could be Central America. But as the little girl and her father travel north toward the US border, she counts animals, stars, and clouds along the way, using them as a focal point to help her endure the journey with her father to another land. How she copes in the story with the uncertainty of the long journey is very moving.

While reading, it may be worth noting to children that migrants are not a monolith; a deeper conversation on that matter would be prudent. *Two White Rabbits* has more below the surface, beneath the tale of migration.

That Neighbor Kid
Daniel Miyares | *Illustrated by Daniel Miyares*

A boy, a girl, a surprise, a friendship—this is a tender story of a boy and a girl working together to build, secure, and enjoy the work of their hands. The girl is fascinated with her new neighbor, who is fascinated with building a tree house. The tree is a powerful symbol of a burgeoning encounter that may connect the two neighbors for the course of time. Although this is a wordless picture book, it doesn't fail to be evocative. *That Neighbor Kid* is spare in its presentation, and gorgeously illustrated. It leaves the reader to devise a story based on the theme of collaboration that these two characters embody through the progression of their project. Daniel Miyares is a critically-acclaimed picture book author and illustrator; he has been called a master of visual storytelling. Some of his other books include: *Float, Night Out, That is My Dream*, and *Bring Me A Rock!*

Tomás and the Library Lady
Pat Mora | *Illustrated by Raul Colón*

This biographical tale is about migrant worker Tomás Rivera, who became a writer, professor, national education leader, and chancellor of the University of California, Riverside. It follows the young Rivera on a visit to the library, the impetus to his love for reading and the inspiration for his many imaginative adventures. Colón's exquisitely charming scratchboard illustrations capture the essence of the story. However, this book does italicize the Spanish words and, furthermore, translates them in the narrative voice, which breaks the nuance and voice of the character. These jarring literary and typographical devices are examples of how some books published in the 1990s attempted to draw a non-Spanish speaking readership.

Mango Moon
Diane de Anda | *Illustrated by Sue Cornelison*

This is a beautiful story, illustrated with soft colors, about a young girl whose father is being deported. She learns that she can love him no matter the distance between them. Due to the intensity of her longing for her father and the impact his absence has on her daily life, this story may be a somber read for some children. But it is worth reading, as it is told with the child's narrative voice fully engaged with the issue she is experiencing. I would even give this story a bonus mark for not succumbing to typographical distinctions that would render this story as other, foreign. *Mango Moon* gives us a prime example of the richness of our country and illustrates how in the US we represent a distinct fabric of cultures. We don't need to go far to learn and see that distinction.

On the Other Side of the Garden
By Jairo Buitrago | *Illustrated by Rafael Yockteng*

This book is a bit mysterious, perhaps even a bit broody at the start. When her father must attend to an urgent matter, a girl is left with her grandmother. There appears to be some distance between the two generations, however, which implies that the girl hasn't spent much time, if any, with her grandmother—the story leaves us to wonder why that would be the case. Nevertheless, the story is well carved out, with anthropomorphism thrown in for good storytelling measure. Each of the three creatures—the owl, the frog, and the mouse—are well developed. They are consistent throughout the book (that mouse loves to eat!), and we follow them carefully as they invite the girl to wander through the garden at night. *On the Other Side of the Garden* is a whimsical book that provides an opportunity, with every pause of the page, to admire the exquisite illustrations by Rafael Yockteng—they are a pleasure to explore.

ENDNOTES

1   Charlotte Mason, *Home Education*, 5th ed. (Australia: Living Book Press, 2017, orig. publ. 1886), p. 175.
2   Charlotte Mason, *A Philosophy of Education* (Australia: Living Book Press, 2017, orig. publ. 1923), p. 178.
3   Mason, *A Philosophy of Education*, p. 216.
4   Mason, *Home Education*, p. 204.
5   Mason, *Home Education*, p. 227.
6   Mason, *A Philosophy of Education*, p. 337.
7   Mason, *A Philosophy of Education*, p. 182.

HIDDEN IN PLAIN SIGHT

ALLEGORY

QUANTRILLA ARD

Storytelling has always been my favorite way to learn and share information. Much of what I learned about life, I learned through story. At church, at home, in school—stories were all around me. My love for books, words, and story was established early and firmly fixed. For the majority of the events and happenings that occurred in my life, there is a story attached. The ideologies and belief systems I developed and carried into adulthood were all connected to stories.

Storytelling is a powerful resource in our everyday lives. Language, speech, tone, and inflection are all factors that influence how we understand and assess the world around us. These are integral parts of storytelling. For children especially, listening to stories builds their connection with the literary world. In addition, storytelling helps them gain access to their own history, either by hearing family members discussing "the old days" or by retelling stories about how they grew up and what they enjoyed as children. Storytelling is like a window that transports us from one moment in time to another.

When I was younger, however, I discovered a type of story that impacted me in ways others had not. When I read my very first allegorical book, it instantly grabbed my attention. As I read, I felt the tug of the underlying meaning pulling me along. I was hooked and began to search for other books with a similar structure. At the time, I didn't know what the literary style was called, but I knew that I loved these types of stories, and that both the primary and secondary themes stuck with me long after I closed the back flap.

Allegory is a type of storytelling. It is a literary tool used to convey the deeper meaning of some—often complex—concept by presenting it in a way that is easier for the reader to read and understa-   llegory is an uncomplicated story that may mirror issues in society   at may have characters or elements that represent a person, place.   in the past, present, or future. What makes this type of literature   't all of this is done without the author directly stating these intentic

Many allegories have biblical themes, with hea\   'n the Christian journey, the triumph of good over evil, and light ve.   even have Christ-like figures who sacrifice their lives for others. Som   e God-like qualities or attributes like omnipotence (all-powerful), on   c (always present), and omniscience (all-knowing)—these characters are u.   ately the undisputed savior/hero of the story. These allegories can be overtly spiritual in nature, like John Bunyan's book, *The Pilgrim's Progress*, or decidedly secular with heavy biblical undertones, such as the Warner Brothers movie, *The Matrix*.

Of the two, *The Pilgrim's Progress* is the more obvious allegory, as it uses metaphor and simile to draw a strong connection between the reader and the message. It is the story of Christian, who represents the everyday man, as he travels from the City of Destruction to the Celestial City. Along the way he meets friends and foes who either lead him closer to the Celestial City or who lead him off course and farther away. The story begins when Christian finds a book left behind by a previous traveler to the Celestial City. As Christian reads, he feels a heavy burden. The book informs him that the only way to remove the burden is to travel to a place where he can unload it. He sets off on the journey, determined to get to the Celestial City.

This story is Christian's journey from a life born in sin (the City of Destruction) to salvation in heaven (the Celestial City). The book that makes Christian aware of his sin (heavy burden) is the Bible, and all along the way we can identify both friends (Evangelist, the Interpreter, Faithful, and Hopeful) and foes (Mr. Wordly Wiseman, Mr. Legality). Christian eventually battles Apollyon (Satan), his greatest enemy, in the Valley of Humiliation. After several other grueling snares (the city of Vanity, the Flatterer), Christian has to be rescued by a Shining One (angel). Christian finally crosses the river as a test of faith (death), which then leads him to the Celestial City (heaven).

The plot of the movie *The Matrix* is similarly allegorical, though its parallels are perhaps less obvious. At the start of the movie, all humans are, unbeknownst to them, ensnared in a simulated reality. There are a few who have been freed from this "reality" and who take it upon themselves to return and extricate individuals from "the Matrix." The Matrix is a sophisticated illusion created by extremely intelligent machines who use humanity as a source of energy. The main character, Thomas Anderson, later known as Neo, discovers the sinister plot and is recruited in the resistance against the machines. As Neo is drawn out of the Matrix, he finds that he is "The One"—a savior destined to free humanity from the Matrix. After extensive training and close guidance, he comes into his abilities and is able to manipulate the Matrix, disable the machines, and free humanity.

The main characters, as well as their names, give clues to both their purpose in the story and their similarity to religious themes. Neo, who is constantly referred to as "The One" in the film, is the savior figure. In the movie, he has to "die" before he can be resurrected outside the Matrix in Zion. The freed humans live outside the Matrix, in a place called Zion—the name also used in Scripture to refer to Jerusalem. Here he gains his abilities. He is befriended by a father-figure, Morpheus, who is captain of the ship Nebuchadnezzar. Trinity, Neo's partner and love interest, takes care of him and the others in Zion. A reminder of the Holy Spirit in the Bible, Trinity has the ability to move with agility and precision, without limits. There are other important connections as well: the Oracle is a "prophet" in the Matrix who guides individuals looking for their freedom. And lastly, the intelligent machines endeavor at all costs to maintain the Matrix and are constantly shape-shifting (assuming human form as agents in the Matrix) and re-writing reality in order to keep humans distracted and disoriented so they will not even realize they are in peril.

Both allegorical plots are very similar to the Christian story of salvation. One has a decidedly biblical bent, using strong thematic connections to events and experiences we have in our faith journeys. The other uses indirect correlations between words and names, although its themes are not about Christian salvation. Clearly the creators of The Matrix did not market this movie as a tool to draw others to Christ. As a Christian, however, it is hard to miss the wordplay and overall feel of the progression of the plot. The Pilgrim's Progress was specifically written by John Bunyan to reach and encourage the hearts of believers and is historically considered an allegory. Though The Matrix serves a different purpose, I consider it a modern allegory.

There are also allegories with moral themes such as right versus wrong, telling the truth, doing your best, and making good choices. The intention in these allegories is to share stories that introduce or reinforce character-building. These were some of my favorite types of books to read to my young children when we were learning about a particular topic or concept. My children can distinctly relate certain behaviors or expected behaviors to a story we read in the past. Reading a short, enjoyable story that taught the habits or values I wanted my children to practice was more helpful than repeatedly requesting that they pick up their shoes, clean up their toys, or brush their teeth. These types of allegories are usually simpler and come in the form of poems or short stories. One particular story, *The Two Carolines,* was from a collection of children's books written by Arthur S. Maxwell. It was about a little girl who behaved one way at school and one way at home. The story hinged heavily on the lessons of integrity, honesty, and respect. Allegories of any kind allow children to learn lessons, values, and character traits (biblical and moral) without directly drawing attention to the lesson.

While allegories and stories with moral lessons are not exactly the same thing (they are often used interchangeably, which adds to the confusion), both types of stories accomplish similar purposes. We must remember that, at their core, allegories are stories with deeper or hidden meanings not explicitly laid out in the main text and are not typically aiming at behavioral change. Stories with moral lessons that intentionally teach a value are just that—they are more obvious in their intention to teach a concept or change behavior. For a mama trying to fuss less and teach more, reading this type of story rather feels like sneaking veggies into a favorite meal—a win-win.

The use of allegory is as old as time. The Bible contains many examples of this. Particularly, Jesus' use of parables is an example of teaching with allegory. Jesus often used things and scenarios the people around him could plainly relate to. Many of Jesus' stories involved vineyards—grapes were an important part of His listeners' culture. What better imagery to use than that of vines and branches to illustrate the relationship of abiding in Him?

Jesus admitted to using parables because of their effectiveness in teaching people the mysteries of the kingdom through words and examples they could clearly understand (Matt. 13:34–35). These parables weren't just for those who came to listen to Him by the thousands, but also for those who sought to undermine Him.

Though the use of allegory has been somewhat undervalued or overlooked today, it provides a solid platform for guiding and expanding the minds of our children. Jesus, who knew the hearts of his audience, taught through parables, so we should not discount the use of allegory as we read with our children today. Though *The Pilgrim's Progress* is one of the older examples of allegory, it is one that is being continually retold and updated so audiences of all ages can enjoy its story. This story's persistence shows that its message is worth listening to not just once, but many times—and in many different ways.

Pilgrim's Progress: Updated Edition
John Bunyan

Originally published in 1678, John Bunyan's classic remains a respected and well-loved book, second only in popularity to the Bible. But in its original wording, Bunyan's seventeenth-century text can be difficult to decipher. This edition from Aneko Press features updated language that makes Bunyan's story accessible for modern readers. Though not necessarily written for children, this story can be very valuable in discussions on faith and Christian living.

The Pilgrim's Progress: An Illustrated Christian Classic
John Bunyan, annotated by Carrie Marrs

With beautiful illustrations, nice page layouts, and informative commentary throughout, this hardback version is a lovely way to introduce children to the actual text of *Pilgrim's Progress*. The commentary alone makes this worthwhile to add to your shelves or to give as a gift. I learned Charles Spurgeon read it at least one hundred times; J.I. Packer, over the course of fifty years, read it at least once a year.

Pilgrim's Progress
Retold by Gary D. Schmidt | *Illustrated by Barry Moser*

Newbery Honor-winning author Gary Schmidt has masterfully retold *Pilgrim's Progress* in modern language. Barry Moser's vivid watercolor illustrations invite readers into Christian's story and add an evocative layer to the text. For teenagers (and even adults) who find working through Bunyan's older language difficult, this solid version of *Pilgrim's Progress* will be a welcome addition to the bookshelf.

Little Pilgrim's Big Journey
Adapted by Tyler Van Halteren | *Illustrated by Beatriz Mello*

This retelling of Bunyan's classic tale, intended for children ages 2–10, features engaging text, colorful and captivating illustrations, and thoughtful discussion questions. Of all the editions featured here, Tyler Van Halteren's uses the simplest language to communicate the big truths of Christian's story to young readers. It is also the only one published in two separate volumes: the first volume tells the story of Christian's journey, while the second follows Christiana as she too journeys to the Celestial City.

Little Pilgrim's Progress
Helen L. Taylor | *Illustrated by Joe Sutphin*

This read-aloud edition features the text of Helen Taylor's classic retelling of *Pilgrim's Progress*, accompanied by delightful illustrations from award-winning illustrator Joe Sutphin. While Taylor recast Christian as a young boy rather than a grown man, Sutphin has reimagined the tale further by setting it in a woodland with animal characters. His interpretation of Bunyan's characters makes *Pilgrim's Progress* accessible for even the youngest readers, while the story itself is still full of wisdom for children and parents alike to take to heart.

IN HIS IMAGE

DIVERSE CHARACTERS

DORENA WILLIAMSON, TINA CHO, AND DORINA LAZO GILMORE-YOUNG WITH LESLIE BUSTARD

Three authors—Dorena Williamson, Dorina Lazo Gilmore-Young and Tina Cho—share in their own words what led them to write for children, why they believe it's important to represent diverse people, and what they hope their books will encourage in those who read their words. Their stories reflect the bigness and beauty of God's kingdom and remind us that God is working in our churches and communities to reflect this reality.[1]

DORENA WILLIAMSON

When my daughter Chase was four years old, a sweet book made its debut in our home and found its way into her hands. *I Like Myself,* written by Karen Beaumont, used energetic rhymes to deliver a story that featured a little brown girl with a dynamic personality. David Catrow's whimsical illustrations featured a lead character with spiraling black hair.

I remember Chase walking around and quoting the lines that had been read over and over to her: "I like myself! I'm glad I'm me. There's no one else I'd rather be." She loved this book so much that she felt the need to write a note inside the front cover: *Chase loves this book!*

Sixteen years later, Chase would find her purpose as a skilled painter, passionate about capturing brown-skin-toned beauty on canvas. In an interview upon the release of her first published artistic work, Chase was asked about her inspiration for painting diversity. She mentioned *I Like Myself* and the impact of seeing a character with spirally black hair just like hers.

Educator Rudine Sims Bishop teaches about the need for children to find mirrors of self-affirmation in books. I wanted that for my four Black children as we raised them in a charming southern town. We spent many hours at our local library, pulling books and engaging in storytime. While our diverse church faithfully provided curriculum and images that reflected the beauty of diverse skin tones, I also wanted our home library to give my children affirmation of their God-given beauty and reinforcement of our faith-filled values.

Visits to the local Christian bookstore did not satisfy this need; even the mainstream bookstores only had a few titles that featured characters that looked like my children. When I came across books that satisfied my desire for both ethnic diversity and faith, I grabbed them to stock our home and classrooms.

Five years ago God began giving me story ideas, and I collected them in my journal. I felt called to make a difference by writing books that would impact young hearts. God mined decades of diverse church leadership and shaped a new mid-life adventure for me. And as I began researching and learning about the world of publishing, all the treasured picture books that my kids had outgrown became valuable resources.

I am thankful that there are more examples of representation available for children today. Many forthcoming releases for children feature characters with diverse ethnicities, cultures, abilities, religions, and family backgrounds. It is both an honor and a joy to be one of many who are passionate about providing literary mirrors for children—especially brown and black children who, like my daughter, deserve to feel the delight of seeing characters who look like them.

Parents have shared with me how my book *ColorFull* gave their children a tool to help them describe the shade of skin God made for them. A mother wheeled her toddler son into a hospital book signing for *ThoughtFull* and thanked me for writing a book that included a boy in a wheelchair. Messages have poured in from grateful parents and ministry leaders sharing the need for resources like *GraceFull* that help open up dialogue on difficult and relevant subjects. These words all deeply bless me and remind me that representation impacts both the children who see themselves in the stories and the adults who read alongside them. I treasure the psalmist's reflections in Psalm 104:24 (MSG):

> What a wildly wonderful world, God! You made it all, with Wisdom
> at your side, made earth overflow with your wonderful creations.

Books open up a wonderful world for young minds curious about the diverse people and places around them. There are little girls like my Chase out there. I'm writing for them—for the delight that will fill their eyes and the joy they will feel as they see their beautiful selves on the pages of a story. I hope they know that they are seen, valued, and loved.

TINA M. CHO

Growing up in the Midwest in the 1970s, I don't recall reading any books with characters that looked like me. I think the first time I saw an Asian character was in my daughter's favorite chapter books, *The Cul-de-Sac Kids.* She fell in love with that series because of it. A few years ago, my son enjoyed reading middle grade novels that featured Korean characters. Why? He could relate.

As a teacher, I like sharing picture books with characters that represent my students. Their eyes brighten and they sit up a little taller when they see a character who resembles them. Children gravitate toward characters like them, whether through their looks or through some shared hobby or interest. I want children and their families to respect others and to be globally minded, because God loves everyone no matter their skin color. As a Christian, I want children to realize that God made us all, that we all came from Adam and Eve, and that we all are made in the image of God. One way we can help narrow the racial divide is by sharing diverse books with the children in our lives.

In 2017, my agent suggested I write a story about food, friendship, and hospitality, inspired by Jesus cooking His disciples a fish breakfast in John 21—an idea that was already in my notebook! My picture book *My Breakfast with Jesus,* published by Harvest House in 2020 and illustrated by Guy Wolek, is about children from around the world eating their diverse breakfasts and sharing Jesus' love with others.

Living in South Korea for ten years and teaching at an international school allowed me to see a variety of foods. I had fun writing this nonfiction story, researching breakfasts, and deciding which countries to feature. My hope is that this book would inspire readers to learn about other cultures, taste different foods, and share Jesus' love in creative ways.

My other three picture books feature Korean culture. I wanted children in the US and around the world to hear stories about others who are like them but who are also different. *Rice from Heaven* is about an event I participated in where we sent rice in huge balloons over the border to North Korea. *Korean Celebrations* is a nonfiction picture book featuring holidays and traditions. *The Ocean Calls* is based on the real women divers of Jeju who dive deep into the ocean without breathing equipment.

Stories help to shape who we become. As an author, I want to write stories that not only share my culture and represent who I am but that also honor and glorify God. When a child reads one of my books, I hope they gain a new understanding and appreciation for the people represented in my books. And I hope they come away feeling in awe of our Creator, who made us all unique and in His image.

DORINA LAZO GILMORE-YOUNG

I was a voracious reader when I was young, partly because my mother read books aloud to my brother and me. She invited us to venture through the wardrobe into another world with Lucy, Edmund, Susan, and Peter. A natural teacher, she was able to make the poetry of Robert Frost come alive to us as we imagined those two roads that diverged in a yellow wood.

My favorite picture book when I was a child was *Nine Days to Christmas* by Marie Hall Ets, a Caldecott winner. In the early 80s, this was one of the few books I could find that featured a girl with brown skin like mine and that included rich cultural details.

Although I had never been to Mexico, this book still mesmerized me. It transported me to another place that somehow felt like home. Because my mom had lived in Mexico, she was able to affirm the truthfulness of the storyline, about a girl named Ceci, who eagerly awaits *Las Posadas*—the traditional nine-day series of Christmas celebrations in her village.

I remember carefully examining the illustrations and poring over the pages of that book again and again. I felt like I was going to the market with Ceci and her mother to select the biggest piñata we could find.

As I grew up, I dreamed of one day becoming a children's book author and writing books like this one. However, I ended up pursuing a career in newspaper reporting and teaching.

The summer I discovered a class on writing children's books, I knew it was time to pursue my dream of writing for kids. I enrolled in the MFA in Children's Literature program at Hollins University. As a graduate student, and pregnant with my first baby girl, I spent hours in the library reading children's literature and writing stories. Now, as a mother of three multiracial daughters, my longing to write books that center around characters of color—for the sake of my own children and for others—has come to be.

During that season, I wrote *Cora Cooks Pancit* about a Filipino-American girl learning to cook a traditional noodle dish with her mama. The book was a compilation of my own experiences growing up in the kitchen with my mama, grandmas, and aunties, as well as the stories I had gathered of other Filipino-American families in California's Central Valley. I wanted kids to swirl the pancit noodles in the pot, smell the garlic, and hear the hiss and sizzle of the onions sautéing.

After several years of sending the manuscript of *Cora Cooks Pancit* out to publishing houses and receiving polite rejection letters stating that the book was too niche to publish, editor Renee Ting of Shen's Books (now an imprint of Lee & Low Books) read the manuscript and wanted to publish it. *Cora Cooks Pancit*, with illustrations by Kristi Valiant, hit bookstores in June 2014. Our book was awarded the Picture Book of the Year by the Asian American Librarian's Association. We were invited to Washington, DC to receive the award and give speeches. The most magical part was meeting my illustrator Kristi in person and learning more about her process in creating the beautiful illustrations.

Over the next decade, I read *Cora Cooks Pancit* aloud and spoke at schools up and down the state of California. My greatest joy was seeing the faces of Filipino-American students light up when they recognized the signature dish that represented their culture. On several occasions, I cooked pancit for those classes. Students from all different cultures tasted it for the first time. This was an open door to celebrate diversity and to pivot away from the colorblind rhetoric that so often finds its way into education settings.

Today, my *Cora* book is eleven years old and in her ninth printing. My heart is encouraged as I see a mounting desire among publishers, schools, and readers for books about and for children of color. We have tasted progress like an appetizer but have not been served the full meal. As an author, an educator, and a mother of three brave girls, I want to help serve up new dishes to add to the feast.

Cora Cooks Pancit
Dorina Lazo Gilmore-Young | *Illustrated by Kristi Valiant*

In this story a Filipina girl helps her mother cook *pancit* in the kitchen. Cora's big heart and hardworking hands, her mother's gentle wisdom, and her family's love for each other simply burst out of this charming book. Cora has grown up watching her big brothers and sisters help Mama with the "grown-up" jobs in the kitchen, while she got stuck with the little jobs. But one day Mama lets Cora cook any dish she wants! From soaking the rice noodles to watching her family eat the finished dish, Cora cooks pancit from start to finish, while Mama tells her stories about her grandfather, Lolo, and her family's history. My daughter Carey and I both remember reading a beautifully illustrated about a little girl making pollo en mole years ago, though we could not remember the book's title. *Cora Cooks Pancit* gave me the same delighted feelings as that mystery book from years ago.

The Ocean Calls
Tina Cho | *Illustrated by Jess X. Snow*

A young Korean girl joins her grandmother in the sea off the coast of Jeju Island, learning free-diving techniques, overcoming her fear of the ocean, and strengthening a sweet familial relationship. This story highlights at least three things: honesty about fears, the good help of grandmothers, and the brave work and community of the haenyeo "mermaids." The lush illustrations are factually accurate but give the story a fairy tale feel. They support the story of Dayeon learning to overcome her fears of diving deep into the depths with her grandmother's guidance.

My Breakfast with Jesus
Tina Cho | *Illustrated by Guy Wolek*

This book invites us to enter into the morning routines and meals of eight Christian families around the world. Each double-page spread shows a group of family members or friends in traditional dress, in a home setting, eating breakfast; each includes facts about their food and a way to think about serving and loving others as Jesus did when He gave a breakfast of fish and bread to His tired friends long ago. What a wonderful way to gain a glimpse into the lives of others and to celebrate people around the world—their faith, their foods, and their traditions. *My Breakfast with Jesus* points us to the beauty of God's kingdom here on earth.

ThoughtFull
Dorena Williamson | *Illustrated by Robert Dunn*

In this gentle story, Ahanu, a boy with Down Syndrome, wins an award at school for being thoughtful. But when Joshua, Ahanu's friend, overhears two boys talking about Ahanu on the bus, he is deeply troubled. Readers can celebrate both Ahanu's strength and Joshua's growth and Joshua learns, through his father's wisdom, to better care for his friend.

The Celebration Place
Dorena Williamson | *Illustrated by Erin Bennett Banks*

Ever since God told Abraham . . . and then Moses . . . and then the people of Israel about His intention to bring all nations and tribes on the earth into His kingdom, His chosen people have wrestled with fully obeying and living out God's plan. Dorena Williamson has given us a gift in *The Celebration Place*. Her love for the church is on display through her winsome and joyful words that are simple in their rhyme scheme yet deep in their wisdom. She shows us what worshipping God together can look like and how it points us to eternity. Erin Bennett Banks's illustrations complement and expand Dorena's text.

ENDNOTES

1   Versions of these essays originally appeared on Tina Cho's website, as part of the series |
     "Stories Shape Who We Become."

ORDERING THE SOUL

ART APPRECIATION

ANNIE NARDONE

> In modern times, we have neglected the poetic or musical dimension
> that was presupposed in the Liberal Arts as originally practiced,
> and infused into the Middle Ages by the Benedictines—the need to
> educate the heart and the imagination, not just to feel but to know.
> —Stratford Caldecott, *Beauty for Truth's Sake*

I believe that every education should be grounded in the imaginative arts. Why? Because art aids us in making essential connections between history, the human condition, and our place in both. Artists welcome us to enter their world through the window of their creations. Through their work, we learn of their convictions, their histories, their fears and dreams, as well as their places in the world.

Art doesn't just represent the year of its creation; the images of a work of art can stretch out into our time. How many times have you seen Edward Hopper's *Nighthawks,* with its three customers sitting at the counter of a brightly-lit diner and the guy in a white cap waiting on them, parodied with different characters, be they from *Sesame Street, Star Wars,* or *The Simpsons.* Some parodies are more well-known than the original.

Certain works can prompt a nearly visceral response. When I see the unique styles, colors, techniques, and mediums used by artists like Vermeer or Van Gogh, I am captivated by their beauty. I wonder, "What prompted the artist to paint just like that? I want to know him better."

But sometimes art can intimidate us, especially when we feel like we should know more than we do about famous painters and their work. Unfortunately, not knowing where to start may prevent us from starting altogether!

Without a doubt, childhood is the best time to begin fostering love for the artists who have inspired the world. Yes, children can distinguish Vermeer from Van Gogh and Pollock from Picasso! Young minds can be much more open to imagining and engaging with art, because they have a ready sense of wonder and few preconceptions. Why settle for red and orange when we can show them the lush beauty of alizarin crimson and tangerine? But no matter what our age or experience, well-written picture books can help us navigate the world of art. A simple biography or story, with some of the artist's better-known pieces featured in the text, can provide a fine introduction to the basics.

What qualities make a picture book perfect for sharing in the glory of the visual arts? The best books for children tell a story in such a meaningful way that the message stays in the child's memory. The narrative invites the child into a world that they would love to visit, especially if it is about an artist who paints with whimsy and innocence—children readily relate to, for example, Marc Chagall's brightly colored animals and flying people.

The rhythm of a poetical narrative sounds comforting and enthralling, especially when read aloud. If the author writes in rhyme, the reader picks up on the steady iambic beat or pattern and anticipates continuation with a "what comes next" sense of curiosity. The reader both hears beautiful words and sees beautiful images.

Why is rhyming a wonderful quality? In his book *Beauty for Truth's Sake*, Stratford Caldecott notes:

> Rhythm, harmony, and melody—the subject of formal study at a more ma-
> ture stage of a child's growth—must from the earliest age penetrate deeply
> into mind and soul through imitation and natural enjoyment. Only in this
> way, by ordering the soul in harmony and giving it a sense of the meaning
> of proportion and relationship, can it be induced later to become fully ra-
> tional, and to derive pleasure from the theoretic contemplation of ideas.
> The road to reason leads through the ordering of the soul, which implies
> the necessity of an education in love, in discernment, and in virtue.[1]

A story written in rhyme holds the attention of a child longer than a regular narration, allowing for a lengthier text; however, as Shakespeare tells us, "Brevity is the soul of wit"—which is especially true when choosing a book for a young child.

When I select a book to read to my students or my own family, I look for a few elements that can build a deep-dive learning opportunity. For example, I like to incorporate a composer who lived at the same time as the artist. A study of the French Impressionists pairs well with the music of Claude Debussy. Then we talk about a day in the life of the artist—what would they have ordered at the café down the street when they met with the other artists in the city? We might prepare a light meal using those recipes.

After reading stories of artists—such as *Vincent's Colors*, by Vincent van Gogh— you could visit your local art store and purchase a few items that were used to create the works that you are studying. Did the artist use pastels, oil paints, colored paper, or watercolors? Try unusual media choices like charcoal and colored pastels, which blend easily with a fingertip or tissue; they are very forgiving materials for the beginner. Create like the masters created! Reference the original masterpieces and try to copy one, or create your own masterpiece inspired by what you see. Stretch a canvas; use colored paper and snip out paper shapes, then glue them to drawing paper; mix paint colors to understand color theory.

And remember, creating can be messy, but that is the best way to learn! I have never seen a clean art studio. Drips, and paper scraps are part of the process of learning and understanding. The best, most memorable lessons incorporate many of our senses.

Over time, art will quietly become part of your everyday language. You will notice that so much of what you see and hear has its roots in the creative minds who came before—the pond you walk by may look like a Monet painting, or a dream may remind you of one by Dalí.

Begin with a few books that will color your world and expand your imagination. Start the adventure with the children's books listed here. The qualities I described above are found in these titles—some have a brilliant rhyme scheme, and others have flaps that expand the images and give a clue as to the size of the picture. All of them incorporate paintings or images into the story to help readers make the connection between the artist and their work. The stories and artistic styles mentioned in these books span the centuries from medieval to modern, and each unique style illustrates the imaginative harmony rendered by these artists.

Micawber
John Lithgow | *Illustrated by C.F. Payne*

John Lithgow, an accomplished actor, shares his remarkable gift for writing whimsical picture books. This engaging children's story is written in a lyrical rhyme scheme perfect for reading aloud. Through the art museum adventures of Micawber the squirrel, kids are introduced to the familiar works of several influential artists, spanning the last five hundred years. The story weaves the artwork throughout the delightful illustrations.

Tell Us a Story, Papa Chagall
Laurence Anholt | *Illustrated by Laurence Anholt*

Of all the authors who write about artists on a child's level, Anholt is the best: he always delights and educates the reader with a whimsical tale! In this book, we meet Marc Chagall and his twin grandchildren, who never stop asking Papa to relate stories of his life. Chagall tells them about his childhood in Russia and describes how his first colorful paintings were very unusual for the time. Images of purple cows, pink goats, and green men flew across his canvases. He relates his experience during World War II, when his paintings were ridiculed by the Germans, and about his family's escape to America. The book includes many reproductions of Chagall's fanciful paintings as essential ingredients to the story.

Marguerite Makes a Book
Bruce Robertson | *Illustrated by Kathryn Hewitt*

Books were a precious commodity in medieval Europe, and upon reading this beautiful story, we understand why! Set in the 1400s, the narrative incorporates many topics on the process of creating illuminated manuscripts. The reader follows young Marguerite as she helps her father finish a Book of Hours prayer book for a wealthy benefactor. She collects the materials to make the paints and brushes, quills, and vellum for the pages. Two foldouts include detailed instructions on preparing ink and paints, and several pages are decorated with illuminated borders common to the era.

Matisse's Garden
Samantha Friedman | *Illustrated by Cristina Amodeo*

This colorful and immersive Museum of Modern Art book about Henri Matisse's cut paper art brings attention to this previously unknown art form. What began with a cutout of a bird shape inspired Matisse to explore other basic

shapes and colors—many of them shapes cut from specially painted papers—
and how they interact on a flat surface. The book is filled with beautiful, fold-out
reproductions of Matisse's art. The simple story explains his technique and
encourages the reader to focus on each page. The book inspires us to create our
own cut paper art.

Dalí and the Path of Dreams
Anna Obiols | *Illustrated by Joan Subirana*

This brilliant story invites us into Salvador Dalí's childhood and his unique
way of observing the world. The narrative reads like a dreamy account of little
Dalí, a magic key, fanciful creatures, and an odd miscellany of objects that reflect
his real paintings. Children need to be introduced to more of Dalí's art. Why?
His big, unbound, childlike imagination really speaks to unbridled ideas like
pin-legged elephants, stone men, and butterfly-winged ladies. Each illustration
reflects the text so perfectly that you may start believing that you can lift up the
edge of water or fly through the sky in a boat.

ENDNOTES
1   Stratford Caldecott, *Beauty for Truth's Sake: On the Re-enchantment of Education* (Grand Rapids:
     Brazos Press, 2009), p. 38.

THE FRAGRANCE OF
THE BLESSED REALM

GOODNESS

MATTHEW CLARK

From where I sit writing to you now, I can hear (but cannot see) two, possibly three, windchimes perfuming the air with their music. The wind is filtering through the thick, pale green leaves of an old maple that hunches over my shoulder as I lean back in a chair by the patio table of my friends the Moons. It's easy to imagine how Isaiah could say the trees "clap their hands" (Isa. 55:12); the trees make myriad applause above me as they are blessed by the breeze's breathing. The wind and the leaves are filled like a glass with warm autumn sunlight, and the wavering, water-like overtones of the chimes seem to wing their song through and above everything all at once, as if the beauty of some other world (or some unseen aspect of this one) presides over all of this, singing into it its life, like light beyond the spectrum of human sight making its Presence felt from someplace off-stage.

The chimes I speak of are invisible to me. I hear them; I don't know where they are. But have you ever broken the rind of a nutmeg seed on a grater and breathed in its fragrance? It's like that. The fragrance that escapes *out* of that little spice-stone seems almost rather to have escaped *into* this world from another blessed realm. The simple action of rubbing the nutmeg wakes a kind of communication between a world that looks like a hard, dry seed and a world spilling over with the very fragrance of life and warmth.

Can you think of times you have experienced the beautiful fragrance of the blessed realm "breaking into" this world? Is there a certain place here where the reality of God's goodness becomes palpable, the Kingdom seems truly to be "at hand"? Is there a friend in whose presence you find your shoulders relaxing and your breath deepening, though you hadn't known you were anxious before? Perhaps there is music that, to your surprise, puts a lump in your throat?

> Maybe a there's a story that you've heard
> That opens up an aching in your heart
> Where something like a light behind a door
> Has made it through the cracks to where you are?
> There's a lump in your throat,
> And the tears come to your surprise;
> Like there's someplace that you belong
> With someone who loved you all along.[1]

There are many ways to "break the rind of the nutmeg," so to speak, and one of the most powerful for me has been story. As a child, J.R.R. Tolkien's storytelling both took me into another world and brought me back to this one with renewed vision, capable of detecting "heaven in ordinary," as the poet George Herbert puts it. As a late teen, my youth minister introduced me to G.K. Chesterton. I've read and reread his *Orthodoxy* over the years, particularly stopping to linger over the chapter "The Ethics of Elfland." If ever there was a chapter to shake the dust from an unused imagination and reenchant the heart!

That same youth minister one day handed me his copy of George MacDonald's strange little fiction book *Lilith* to read. I was transported. And bewildered. I really wasn't at all sure what had taken place, in the book or in myself. But some great hand had indeed swept across the dust-crusted glass in the picture frame, and I began to see that new color, form, and images had lain underneath all the while. (Or, as a child of the 80s, I can't help but think of the Goonies finding a fabled treasure map tucked beneath a painting in the attic.)

So, I find myself on edge for those clues strewn about this world; where might I find a loose panel opening into a passageway, or feel fur coats in a wardrobe translating into fir trees in a wood? There is a liturgy that says, "All of us go down to the dust, but even at the grave we make our song." That seems to me to get at the experience we search for—to enter like the child Lucy Pevensie into the wooden casket, to change our garment, and wake walking in another world— but in that case, a world where it is always Christmas.

Occasionally, we get those intimations in this world. Christmas itself arrives through the cracks like "light behind a door," doesn't it? And one of the effects is that the "goodwill toward mankind" that the angels herald to the shepherds of

Bethlehem really does seem to be coaxed to the surface of our own hearts. God has smiled upon us, come to visit as Emmanuel, and it is hard not to offer God's own goodwill in return. Not the small cynical smirk of commercialism, but the great-hearted gladness of grace that marks that season in spite of its secularization. (And Christmas is certainly a time to grate a little nutmeg atop your eggnog.)

Now, Christmas is a high point of the in-breaking of God's presence, but if Tolkien, Chesterton, and MacDonald are correct, it's not meant to be exceptional, but indicative. The realities indicated by the Scriptures fall like snowflakes, each unique, to dissolve into the material of this world and spring up in endless ways through poems, songs, stories, and so on, which draw us toward and into the beauty, goodness, and truth of the Life of the Trinity.

Now, all of that is a big approach to a little book I've been rereading for the third or fourth time called *Sir Gibbie,* by George MacDonald. Since we are looking at books for children, it may help to know that there are a few different versions: the original, due to length and frequent passages written in dialect, isn't the best place to start for a child. Rediscovering that original version as an adult after having grown up with an abridged version would be fun, I think. I'm recommending Michael Phillips's version, *Wee Sir Gibbie of the Highlands,* which has been edited for young readers.

Sir Gibbie is a realistic novel set in the Scottish Highlands, and it follows a mute little boy who, soon after being orphaned, witnesses a murder and runs away from the city. He winds up on the estate and farm of the local Laird (roughly the Scottish equivalent of an English Lord, or landowner). He's run out of there and finds refuge with an older peasant couple, Robert and Janet Grant, in their cottage in the mountains. Without giving away the story, the Grants raise him in dignified poverty, introduce him to life in Jesus, and eventually learn more about his true identity.

Just the action, mystery, and fun of the story would be enough to recommend it, I imagine but, in this story MacDonald has a way of "breaking the rind" of the nutmeg for us. To begin with, Gibbie's character in this story is an experiment in purity and innocence. It's almost as if MacDonald asked, "What if someone could retain the innocence of childlikeness as they grew? What would a story about someone pure look like?" Gibbie is often described in angelic and otherworldly terms with great affection. Put simply, he is good.

One of the great effects this book has on me, personally, is that it makes me desire goodness in myself. It makes goodness immanently attractive, which is a difficult thing to do in storytelling. You may have noticed how easy it is to make badness entertaining in our media? It's easy to take the dried brown stone of nutmeg and throw it at someone, but MacDonald gently scratches its surface to release the delicious fragrance of goodness. We find in Gibbie that the human personality can do so much more than entertain through brashness: it can nourish and delight through goodness and gentleness. With Gibbie, MacDonald allows that warm fragrance of God's goodwill toward mankind to break in on our imaginations—to populate it with new images of how we might live beautifully through goodness.

And Gibbie is not the only character to inspire us in this way: Janet and Robert exhibit faithfulness to one another, joy and contentment in poverty, tenderness, and love toward their children and the orphan Gibbie, and the un-pretentious wisdom that comes from real and regular contact with a living Jesus.

One of the interesting ways that MacDonald affects goodness through Gibbie is by making him mute. Late in the story, Gibbie learns to read, write, and sign, but the majority of the time the only language at his command is action. He of-fers the honest gift of his presence, marked most often by his ready, warm smile and free laughter. Besides that, he serves others. He is joyful and careful with everyone he comes into contact with. MacDonald gives us a character who is literally incapable of "lip-service" to the gospel; Gibbie's faith skips happily over speech directly into loving deeds.

Recently, my friends the Moons and I watched a movie about Fred Rogers of *Mister Rogers' Neighborhood*. Fred Rogers might be a modern-day Sir Gibbie in some ways. I was reminded of a quote from one of Rogers's speeches, where he described a news story of a young boy who kidnapped another child. When the boy was asked why he did it, he said he saw it on television and thought it was something interesting to try. Rogers went on to say,

> Life isn't cheap. It's the greatest mystery of any millennium, and television needs to do all it can to broadcast that—to show and tell what the good in life is all about.
>
> But how do we make goodness attractive? By doing whatever we can to bring courage to those whose lives move near our own—by treating our neighbor at least as well as we treat ourselves and allowing that to inform everything we produce. We all have only one life to live on Earth.
>
> And through television, we have the choice of encouraging others to demean this life or to cherish it in creative, imaginative ways.[2]

The imagination is like a corkboard where we pin images we pick up along the way in life. And it's where we go looking for pictures of how our own lives might possibly look. Those images that populate our imaginations have a lot to do with what we acquire a taste for as well, whether it's goodness or badness. As Fred Rogers indicates, it is very important to collect good images to pin on our corkboard, because they form a taste for the things of God and they bring good choices within reach for us. In other words, if our imagination is atrophied or populated by devastating images, we might say, "I can't imagine myself being loved or loving well." On the other hand, the more good stories, characters, music, and beautiful experiences we internalize, the greater our resource for godly feeling and action becomes (Phil. 4:8).

Reading *Sir Gibbie* helps populate my imagination with goodness. When I go to consult my imaginative corkboard for images of how I might feel and act, I find Gibbie warmly smiling, silently serving, eagerly attending his friend Donal's poetry recitations, gladly freeing an enemy who did him great violence, and embracing the poor.

Often in MacDonald's storytelling, he shows the interpenetration of heaven and earth—how "Earth's crammed with heaven,"[3] as the poet Elizabeth Barrett Browning says. In *Sir Gibbie*, the music of those invisible wind chimes seems always to be present, as is the fragrance of Christ humbly making its way through the world like a ragged, mute orphan boy who carries the goodwill of God in his smile.

The Curdie Books
George MacDonald

While we're on George MacDonald, I can't help but mention his two children's fairy tales, *The Princess and the Goblin* and its sequel, *The Princess and Curdie*. I didn't know about these two as a child, but I was very glad to discover them as an adult. Like Lewis's Narnia stories, these books apply at any age. Curdie is a poor miner's son who must rescue the young princess from plotting goblins living in the mountain. The children's adventures continue in the sequel. In both, MacDonald weaves wisdom, adventure, and transcendent beauty together to shape in our imaginations faith and courage, as well as the knowledge that God is very present and always inviting us into deep participation in His work.

The Magic Carpet and Other Tales
Ellen Douglas | *Illustrated by Walter Inglis Anderson*

I grew up in Mississippi with a grandmother who loved stories and a mother who is an artist, so I've been surrounded by the work of Mississippi Gulf Coast artist Walter Inglis Anderson for as long as I can remember. Anderson's visual art has a strong narrative center, and he illustrated many great myths during his life. Ellen Douglas collected those illustrations and wrote out the stories in this beautiful large format book. For me, Anderson's images, as much or more than the tales themselves, have the effect of making strange and wonderful that which has grown too familiar and opening the imagination to the Greater Story revealed in Scripture.

The Wind in the Willows
Kenneth Grahame

It's a classic, I know, and probably doesn't need recommending. However, it's worth reminding you, if it's been a while since you revisited this one, that *The Wind in the Willows* is such good fun and holds many rich surprises for the heart. The misadventures of Mr. Toad can make you laugh aloud. The friendship of Rat and Mole is so warm. Mole's rediscovery of his old hole-in-the-ground home is a beautiful affirmation of life's simple goodnesses. And the chapter "The Piper at the Gates of Dawn" interpenetrates the wit and fun with a song of transcendent presence and beauty. I also love how the prose is so richly written; it allows us to enter in on our level and be drawn up toward beauty we hadn't imagined.

The Secret Garden
Frances Hodgson Burnett

As an adult who has read about the author's religious beliefs, I see the misguided positivism embedded in this story that doesn't jibe with our need for the saving work of Jesus. As a child, however, that never occurred to me, and I found the story's main effect to be that it made me want to care for the hurting and to bring beauty into the world. Themes of grief, family brokenness, the need for friendship and beauty, and the gift of the natural world all appealed to me. As an artist, the call to cultivate beauty within the givenness of creation as an invitation to participate in God's ongoing redemptive work, whether an intended theme of the author's or not, still strikes me as present and important.

Milly-Molly-Mandy

Joyce Lankester Brisley

Milly-Molly-Mandy lives with her family in a nice white cottage with a thatched roof. In twenty tales, this nearly century-old book shares her everyday adventures, like blackberry picking, going to a fete, visiting the seashore, fixing the roof, and buying a new dress. Without feeling cheesy or saccharine, Milly-Molly-Mandy unapologetically offers the reader good characters and a world of childhood innocence.

ENDNOTES

1   Lyrics from the song "Every Beauty," from Matthew Clark's album *Only the Lover Sings.*
2   Fred Rogers, "How Do We Make Goodness Attractive?," *Federal Communications Law Journal,* Vol. 55 (2003), Iss. 3, Article 23: https://www.repository.law.indiana.edu/fclj/vol55/iss3/23.
3   Elizabeth Barrett Browning, Aurora Leigh, and Other Poems (New York, James Miller: 1872), p. 138.

STORY, VALUE, AND BECOMING MORE REAL

DIFFERENTLY ABLED

COREY LATTA

He had a different look about him. I had seen other babies, of course—
at least three other newborns, if I counted his older siblings and his twin sister—
so I knew what "typical" looked like. But Gus didn't look typical. Something about
the shape of his eyes. His tongue protruded a bit. There was a slow manner to
his movements. And he didn't cry. No screaming. No tears, either. He lay there,
staring up at the unfamiliarity of a world indifferent to what made him different.

I felt desperate to stop one of the nurses who were buzzing around tending
to Gus, then to his sister, then to Gus again. I needed to say something. But what?
I didn't know what to say. That something seemed different about him? That I
was terrified? That I didn't think this story was going to be written quite the way
I'd like? That a reality quite different than my idealized one was setting in?

"Excuse me, can I ask you something? How many babies have you helped
deliver?" I found the courage to ask a nurse.

"Oh, hundreds," she said.

"My son—he doesn't look, uh, typical, does he?"

Her countenance changed. "He looks a little different."

"It's Down Syndrome, isn't it?"

"He looks a little different," she repeated. "Let me go get the doctor."

The rest of the day felt a bit like writing a story that gets out of hand.
I was buried in explanations, confusion, questions, tears, momentary serenity,
an echocardiogram, more questions. Then, the answer: Trisomy 21, a.k.a.

Down Syndrome—a chromosomal anomaly resulting in an extra twenty-first chromosome. Down Syndrome presents as an intellectual disability with developmental delays, distinct physical characteristics, and possible physical defects.

Now, that's a terrible description of how a child with Down Syndrome actually presents. There was nothing in all the scientific literature I was inundated with about how free of malice, full of joy, or prone to the most enviable, unashamed play children with Down Syndrome are.

I'd discover all that about Gus, but I'd have to walk through a lot of fear to get there.

Taking home a child with Down Syndrome felt overwhelming. How or what would I be able to teach him? Would I ever be able to have a conversation with him? Babies with Down Syndrome have floppy muscle tone, so how was I even supposed hold him? Would he be accepted? Would other kids be cruel to him? Would he be happy in the life God's afforded him? How do I steward this life I've been entrusted with?

Some questions have answered themselves. Some will just have to be lived. I still find myself looking for someone to stop and ask how I best parent his differences. But I look for that assurance less and less frequently. I mostly just look at Gus now.

He reminds me of the story Jesus tells about the pearl of great price. The kingdom of God is like a merchant seeking precious pearls. He discovers one of great price, and he sells all he has to buy it. I imagine that pearl being covered in dirt, plain and unremarkable to the eye. Easily judged and dismissed, if seen at all. But once found—the sheer joy of such a rare discovery. The finder's gratitude. The pride that would come from showing others this precious pearl.

I see that discovered beauty in Gus. Not everyone can see it, but I do. I found what others don't know they're looking for. The uncertainty of the delivery room has been transformed by a spell, enchanted into the certainty of discovery. I find myself wanting to tell the story of my pearl. If I tell it enough, will people discover what lies beyond what they see?

Gus's full name is Augustus Stirling James Latta. Augustus after my favorite character in literature and film, Augustus McCrae from *Lonesome Dove*. Stirling for the city in Scotland. James is a centuries-old Latta name. For me, Gus was a continuation of a story I had in mind. He would be strong. A leader. Formidable. Noble. Augustus Stirling James—I mean, that's a president's name! The story I wanted to tell about him wasn't the story he had in him. My narrow story couldn't contain him. I'm learning that he contains a myriad of stories. I'm reminded of all the stories he holds when I come across others just as good, beautiful, and true.

One night, I discovered *The Velveteen Rabbit* in a box of books. Our mundane bedtime routine, liturgized by a story and a quick prayer, unearthed a pearl:

"Real isn't how you are made," said the Skin Horse. "It's a thing that happens to you. When a child loves you for a long, long time, not just to play with, but *really* loves you, then you become Real."

"Does it hurt?" asked the Rabbit.

"Sometimes," said the Skin Horse, for he was always truthful. "When you are Real you don't mind being hurt."

"Does it happen all at once, like being wound up," he asked, "or bit by bit?"

"It doesn't happen all at once," said the Skin Horse. "You become. It takes a long time. That's why it doesn't happen often to people who break easily, or have sharp edges, or who have to be carefully kept. Generally, by the time you are Real, most of your hair has been loved off, and your eyes drop out and you get loose in the joints and very shabby. But these things don't matter at all, because once you are Real you can't be ugly, except to people who don't understand."[1]

I crumbled a bit as I read. Gus looked up at me with the kind of emotional intelligence I've only encountered in children with Down Syndrome.

"Daddy sad?"

"No buddy, Daddy just loves you a lot. You're helping me become real."

"Okay, Daddy."

I'm forty-one now. My hair is thinning, my face more wrinkled, and I'm stiffer, not looser, in the joints. And I don't mind the confusion, the fear, the uncertainty. The reality of the story Gus has brought me into, brought to me, is far greater than all that. The truth is, to love and be loved by a differently abled child is to be brought into a different sort of reality. To know a differently abled child is to be brought from a story of unknowing to an invaluable tale of intimacy, from one of fear to one of joy, from uncertainty to peace, and perhaps most importantly, from the illusion of control to the liberation of surrender. By the time you let the story of a differently abled child become yours, you might have lost some hair or become a little looser in the joints, but you'll have become more real. The pearl of great price might cost you your assumptions and idealized notions of strength, but you'll have traded what you didn't need for something you didn't know you needed so badly.

We'll Paint the Octopus Red
Stephanie Stuve-Bodeen | *Illustrated by Pam Devito*

Six-year-old Emma waits for the birth of her brother Isaac. She imagines all the adventures they'll go on after he's born—all they fun they'll have, all the plans she has for him. But when Isaac is born with Down Syndrome, Emma has to reimagine all of her expectations. She and her parents discover that Isaac is more than they could have ever asked for. The book is a sweet, childlike look at what it means to be in close relationship with a child with Down Syndrome. It captures the uncertainties and the reevaluation that comes from first knowing then loving a differently abled child. Visually, there is a folksy warmth to this book's illustrations that is both peaceful and inviting.

My Friend Isabelle
Eliza Woloson | *Illustrated by Bryan Gough*

Isabelle and Charlie are close friends who love to enjoy activities together, but who have one fundamental difference: Isabelle has Down Syndrome, and Charlie doesn't. Told from the perspective of Charlie, this book is about the nature of friendship. What makes a meaningful relationship a relationship and what should children do in a relationship marked by difference? Woloson's story is paired with inviting and lively illustrations.

Hannah's Down Syndrome Superpowers
Lori Leigh Yarborough | *Illustrated by Roksana Oslizlo*

Written by a mother and pediatric physical therapist, *Hannah's Down Syndrome Superpowers* serves to help people understand Down Syndrome. It's an excellent resource in terms of basic information as well as an invitation for others to learn about Down Syndrome. This resource is impressively informative while also being marked by beauty. The book emphasizes what makes a child with Down Syndrome so special while also emphasizing how similar all children are. The illustrations are bright and engaging and help communicate the book's sweet feel.

Taking Down Syndrome to School
Jenna Glatzer | *Illustrated by Tom Dineen*

This book has an upbeat, positive vibe to it. It's an informative, purpose-driven book about what it means to be proactive in learning what Trisomy 21 is, how it presents, and how to be in relationship with a person with Trisomy 21. Unique to this book is a section devoted to tips for teachers. The emphasis here is practical. The book serves as a humorous visual representation of what children with Down Syndrome are like and what those who love them can expect.

Be Good to Eddie Lee
Virginia Fleming | *Illustrated by Floyd Cooper*

This is a slightly older text about a little girl's annoyance at having to watch after her neighbor Eddie. Christy doesn't want to slow down to take care of Eddie, but over time Eddie's joy and loving nature softens Christy. This text does a great job portraying the child's psychology as they discover what it means to play together. Edifying and heartwarming, this book helps create ideas for how to bridge relationships between typical and differently abled kids. The illustrations feel antiquated, but they're welcoming and give the text more life.

ENDNOTES

1   Margery Williams, *The Velveteen Rabbit or How Toys Become Real*, illus. William Nicholson (New York: Doubleday, 1922), p. 5.

THE WILD SYMPHONY

MUSIC

ELISA CHODAN

One of the earliest things I remember is curling up in the corner of my room with a Little Golden Book and pressing play on my cassette tape player. "This is the story of *The Nutcracker*," said a sparkling voice, and with that the opening measures of Tchaikovsky's famous ballet began. The Little Golden Book Story and Tape series was popular then, and to me, the best cassettes were the ones that read the stories with music, too. The music, illustrations, and stories combined to capture my imagination and make the written book much more entrancing to my young mind. I loved hearing the signal that told me it was time to turn the page; I loved the entirety of the experience of reading, viewing, and listening. It felt like a living and breathing dance. This was one of many aesthetic opportunities I had as a child that subconsciously connected classical music to joy and inexpressible feelings for me.

Twenty-five years later, I am now a full-time music educator. I cannot deny that those early aesthetic experiences laid the foundation for me to value music as essential for life. Books are a bridge to many destinations, and I believe that books that connect readers to music appreciation should be an essential part of each child's literary experience.

But why should children and their parents or teachers care about music? Aesthetic education, or studies of beauty and the arts, connects us to God's nature as a creative, beautiful, and transcendent being. As image-bearers of God, it is essential that we learn to appreciate and articulate thoughts about the arts—those elements of life that exist beyond any utilitarian purpose and that we cannot explain. Music education connects us to these transcendent ideals, specifically through enhancing stories with sounds—or even by telling a story through sound alone. Introducing children to musical stories can bring a nuance to the story that would not exist with just the written word.

By learning to appreciate and participate in music-making, children have the opportunity to partake of God's very nature. They are able to recognize and participate in His creativity, beauty, and transcendence, as well as to understand themselves and those around them in a more complete way.

Music also frees us from thinking in black and white. It is one of the most subjective arts, and thereby reflects meaning in a way that more accurately reflects the experience of everyday life and truth. Music tells a story that is rich and meaningful, yet nuanced and difficult to describe. Though a young child may not immediately recognize music's benefit in this regard, an early introduction of nuanced and subjective music experiences opens the child's mind to the reality that life is not always as it seems.

Children need to associate music with stories early on, not just as something in the background that sets a mood or makes us feel a certain way, but as something transcendent. One practical way of connecting transcendence to a child's experience is through singing stories or by marrying music and story.

John Feierabend, a leading authority on early childhood music education, states in the introduction to *The Book of Children's Songtales:*

> A loving adult who reads to a child with feeling helps that child to understand the expressiveness possible on the printed page. That child will then be more likely to bring the same intuitive understanding to his or her own reading, and will grow up to bring more depth, emotion, and nuance to the words he or she reads . . . Children who hear these songs sung with expression will later be expressive singers themselves and will appreciate the expressiveness in other musical performances.[1]

One can imagine the beautiful fruits of these endeavors in a child's development: not only will the child learn to value and recognize these beautiful and creative elements in stories and song, but she will be more aware of these qualities in those around her as well as in herself.

During my years as a music teacher, I have seen children come to love music because of storytelling and books. As I have sung folk songs and stories to and with children, I have seen them heartily join in the storytelling and laugh as we enjoyed making music together. They began to experience the very normal and human experience of making music as a community.

Once, a father came to me to tell me that his family's Friday night "new music at dinner" tradition had been enlivened by the music of Trombone Shorty—after I had read *Trombone Shorty*, by Troy "Trombone Shorty" Andrews, to his first and fourth grade sons a few weeks before. He had asked his boys if they had any recommendations for music to listen to and was pleasantly surprised when, instead of the usual pop songs, they introduced him to a new jazz artist.

I also love to watch my young students engage with the book *Wild Symphony* by Dan Brown. A sort of modern take on *The Carnival of the Animals*, the book introduces nuanced storytelling about the nature of animals and life through a book and an accompanying app, which includes a professional symphony playing a song for each animal. I always begin by reading the animal's page and sharing the life proverb included with each one; then the students get to identify the animal in the music. The students often smile, shimmy, shout, or sit in silence as the various songs are introduced: the slow, mellow sound of strings as the whale swims by, the beat of a drum to mark the bounce of a kangaroo, or the quick change in tempo as a cheetah pounces and runs. The students, albeit unconsciously, learn to find stories and adventure in the music.

Music books can also help us begin conversations about difficult topics, in age-appropriate ways. As my students learn the story of the development of the song "We Shall Overcome," they get to join in singing the anthem in between brief looks at how race discrimination affected Black Americans in the United States. We get to discuss how singing a song like "We Shall Overcome" could have encouraged those who were being arrested for waiting for a cheeseburger at a restaurant. This opens up opportunities for the students to make connections and discuss these ideas in small ways—like the first grader who mentioned, in one of my classes, that her family listens to Black artists every day as they drive to school during Black History Month.

Books that focus on the lives of the historically recognized composers—like Bach, Haydn, Beethoven, and others—also bring meaning to the music for the children that otherwise would not be there. Learning that Haydn's *Farewell Symphony* was actually a dramatic plea for an orchestra to be reunited with their families after the oppression of a rich ruler brings a fascination and drama to the children's experience of the music. So often orchestral music can feel foreign and far removed from our modern lives, but these books bring a richness of understanding to the listening experience.

Finally, I have found that even books that are not specifically music books but perhaps have a repeated refrain or rhyme can also be made into meaningful music experiences for the students. One book called *Peanut Butter and Cupcake*, by Terry Border, shares a heartwarming story about the challenge of making new friends. I have been able to use this with young students by singing the repeated refrain in the book to a short tune and having the students play along to the beat on classroom instruments. I hope in some small way, this simple aesthetic experience helps them remember the message of friendship in the book, as well as the experience of joy in making music within a community.

Books make wonderful bridges. Time and time again I have seen books become the means to student engagement with music. They begin to understand the nature of stories in both a subjective and objective manner. They hear and see the stories in a multi-dimensional way; their view of the world and of others begins to become multi-dimensional as well. Instead of music simply being an "extra" that enhances an experience, children begin to see it as essential to storytelling. Then, the transcendent parts of our human experiences are no longer expendable but essential to both our learning to love others and to our own personal flourishing. In this small way, our children can begin to love others well as they recognize this nuance in themselves and in others. Ultimately they mirror God in His creative nature.

The Book of Children's Songtales
Compiled by John Feierabend | *Illustrated by Tim Caton*

This 96-page compilation of children's story songs is an absolute gem of a resource for both teachers and parents. The songs are loosely divided up by theme: "Love and Marriage," "Who's Who," "A Riddle and Three Swaps," and "Going Going." I love using this resource to learn and re-learn American folk songs and share them with children. The songs can be excellent tools to awaken children's imaginations to the expressivity of music and music making. This book includes simple notations for each song's melody and does require the adult to have a basic ability to read music in order to learn and share the songs.

The Music in George's Head
Suzanne Slade | *Illustrated by Stacy Innerst*

This book is such a beautiful marriage of images and text, and it easily leads into a listening of George Gershwin's masterpiece, *Rhapsody in Blue*. The fonts used in the book appear almost as a tension between the music that already existed in George's time and the music in his head—which pioneered into newer and freer musical territory. The illustrations especially provide that link to the transcendent element inherent in the music, and the cool, curved, blue-hued pictures will capture the imagination of the reader.

Beethoven's Heroic Symphony
Anna Harwell Celenza | *Illustrated by JoAnn E. Kitchel*

This book follows Ludwig van Beethoven's journey to write his third symphony, *The Heroic Symphony*. Throughout much of the book, Beethoven is driven by a desire to honor Napoleon Bonaparte's accomplishments with a symphony, but there is an unexpected and meaningful twist to the story near the end. The book and its message may sit best with middle and upper elementary-aged children. The author includes additional fascinating biographical facts at the end of the book. Imaginative yet easy-to-understand descriptions of the symphony movements are included in the book and provide helpful background that enhances the experience of listening to the symphony. The original publication includes a CD of the symphony.

We Shall Overcome
Debbie Levy | *Illustrated by Vanessa Brantley-Newton*

"We Shall Overcome" continues to be an anthem of hope for so many in the United States and across the world. Debbie Levy beautifully captures the roots of this music and skillfully relates the changing aspects of race relations in the United States over the last two centuries. Various portions of the song lyrics are included on every page—inviting the storyteller to sing the anthem to the listeners in small and meaningful phrases. This provides an immediate connection to the song as you read, and by bringing in the element of music, it enhances the written word from the very first page. Levy gives several recording suggestions for listening as well as a timeline of the development of the song in relation to events within the United States' Black community and beyond.

Because

Mo Willems | *Illustrated by Amber Ren*

Because traces the path of one musician's journey toward becoming a world-famous composer. The path begins with a man named Ludwig, and a beautifully illustrated musical staff glides the story through many other people, both musicians and non-musicians, toward a young girl. I love how the story highlights the diversity of influences that all converge into making us who we are. The story ends with a young woman choosing to become a full-time composer, but the people and situations that got her there include composers, music librarians, graphic designers, transportation officers, janitors, and more. The various types of music that are mentioned in the story provide plenty of ideas for music to listen to with children as you read.

ENDNOTES

1   John Feierabend, *The Book of Children's Songtales* (Chicago; GIA Publications, 2003), p. 3.

SYMBOLS ON THE DOORFRAME

RACE

SHANIKA CHURCHVILLE

In Deuteronomy 6:4–9 and 11:18–21, as well as throughout the Pentateuch, God encourages the use of concrete images and tangible symbols.[1] Symbols on hands, between eyes, and on doorposts would mark these ragtag nomads as the people of God and create a basis for lessons and conversations between parents and children, ones full of stories of God's goodness and faithfulness.[2]

I suggest that Deuteronomy provides modern-day readers not only with examples of how to talk with our children about God's protection and provision but also with a model for conversations about race. The Black Church has historically claimed as its own the story of the 400-year enslavement of God's people and His liberation of them in Exodus.[3] Following in its steps, we can use Deuteronomy to frame conversations with children about race.

While I write this, America is grappling with issues of race. Many are awakening to the experiences and realities faced by people of color related to racial injustice and centuries-old oppression. Some white friends and acquaintances have confided to my husband and me that they have never talked or thought about race and feel ignorant of the perspectives, experiences, and history of Black people. I'd like to suggest that God has given Christians of all races, but particularly white Christians, a pivotal opportunity to think and talk about race. If we want our children to grow into adults who can lovingly and respectfully engage across racial or cultural lines, we must begin by having conversations about race with them at home.

With Deuteronomy as our guide, I'd like to offer myself to you as a fellow learner on this journey. I am Sri Lankan American and have had the privilege of living in both Sri Lanka and the United States. While I've had to navigate life as a person of color in largely white spaces in the United States, I've also lived as a member of a privileged family of a majority culture in Sri Lanka.

Two decades ago, I married my husband, who is Black. Over our years together, I have learned much about the history of this country and the beauty and suffering of Black people. I have had to learn the painful realities of historic and systemic racism. I have had to grapple with my own prejudice and ignorance and acknowledge the unearned benefits accorded me by my privileged background. God has blessed us with two sons. In raising them, I have had to become more intentional about learning and teaching them their history and the realities of living in a society that might misunderstand them at best and seek to destroy them at worst. It has been both exhilarating and incredibly painful, and it has been one of the most profound experiences of my life.

I recognize that I have kept my focus very narrow here. I've chosen to share how I celebrate Black history and experience with my sons. I haven't shared about how I communicate Sri Lankan culture to my sons or how a parent could teach their children about the varied ethnic and cultural experiences of white, Asian, Latino, Native, or multi-racial peoples. However, I believe the following principles hold true when making any intentional choice to enrich children's reading experiences and expand their cultural competence and sensitivity.

BE CONCRETE

You shall bind them as a sign on your hand, and they shall be as frontlets between your eyes. (Deuteronomy 6:8)

God reinforces the power of the concrete in his exhortation to parents. The beauty of children's books is their power to deliver the loftiest truths and the deepest sorrows with simple stories and vivid imagery. I love sharing Faith Ringgold's books with my boys. Her gorgeous, vibrant artwork provides a stunning and fanciful backdrop to her depiction of the Underground Railroad in *Aunt Harriet's Underground Railroad in the Sky*. Picture books provide a solid, touchable, engage in conversations about race with your children about race with your children. Research shows that children as young as six months begin to

nonverbally categorize race and that toddlers begin to make inferences connected to racial categories.[4] It is never too early to begin talking about race in open,
affirming, and age-appropriate ways. Books, particularly picture books, provide a
marvelous way to do that.[5]

BE HUMBLE

> Know, therefore, that the Lord your God is not giving you this good land
> to possess because of your righteousness, for you are a stubborn people.
> Remember and do not forget how you provoked the Lord your God to
> wrath in the wilderness. From the day you came out of the land of Egypt
> until you came to this place, you have been rebellious against the Lord.
> (Deuteronomy 9:6–8)

God reminds His people that their possession of good land had nothing to do
with their faithfulness or goodness. He calls them to humility and to recognize
Himself as the source of their blessings. As Americans, we have also been given
"this good land" and the accompanying freedoms many of our global neighbors
do not enjoy. While we may enjoy certain rights and privileges, God calls us to
remember that *He* is the source of those blessings, not our own goodness.

In Deuteronomy 9, God also calls His people to remember their sins of
stubbornness and rebellion. Our country's history, while full of evidence of God's
goodness, has also been marked by a stubborn refusal to face and change deeply
held beliefs about race. To engage with children about this stubbornness in our
racial divide is to exercise humility. It is humbling to face the guilt of oppression
and injustice built over centuries. Books provide an age-appropriate way to exercise this humility, along with our children. Read books such as Jeannette Winter's
Follow the Drinking Gourd and Deborah Hopkinson's *Sweet Clara and the Freedom
Quilt* and open your children's eyes to the specifics of slavery and the Underground Railroad. Read Jacqueline Woodson's *The Other Side* and Margaret Mason's *These Hands* and facilitate discussions about the indignities of segregation.

God does not protect His people from memories of disobedience and waywardness but recounts a story of both blessings and rebellion. Neither should
we, in an effort to protect our children, whitewash memories of our disobedience
to God's commandments—disobedience that has included the subjugation and
oppression of Black people.[6]

For your eyes have seen all the great work of the LORD that he did. (Deuteronomy 11:7)

Any hearer of Moses' words would be amazed, contemplating God's "mighty deed and his outstretched arm" (Deut. 11: 2). Towards the end of Deuteronomy, we hear Moses praising God for his faithfulness (Deut. 32:1–4). Indeed, the book of Deuteronomy is a hymn to the amazing deeds of the Lord.

When I look at my sons, I see in them the sheer determination and triumph of their ancestors who overcame historic hardships. I think of the following from Maya Angelou's "Still I Rise":

Bringing the gifts that my ancestors gave,
I am the dream and the hope of the slave.
I rise
I rise
I rise.[7]

Don't settle for the abridged and anesthetized version of Black history served up in elementary schools every February. Open your family to the glory and beauty of Black history. In our house we celebrate Martin and Malcolm, Rosa Parks and Harriet Tubman, Jackie Robinson and Muhammad Ali, as well as our Black students, colleagues, family members, and friends. Fight against the prevailing narratives, both the paternalistic ones that caricature *all* Black people as helpless and hopeless and the destructive ones that depict *all* Black people as dangerous and criminal. Share books with your children like Derrick Barnes's *I Am Every Good Thing* and be amazed!

"More More More" Said the Baby
Vera B. Williams | *Illustrated by Vera B. Williams*

I have fond memories of sharing this book with both of our sons when they were babies. It's a rambunctious celebration of the love between energetic toddlers and their grown-ups. There's swinging in the air, chasing and chanting, and kissing of belly buttons. This wonderful book naturally introduces children and adults of different skin colors and backgrounds into the young reader's visual landscape. As you read, draw your child's attention to Little Pumpkin's light brown skin, his grandmother's blond hair, Little Bird's shiny black hair. Help them notice the differences but also the similarities—the energy, the deep love, and the exuberance—of Williams's characters.

Tar Beach
Faith Ringgold | *Illustrated by Faith Ringgold*
   This dreamy book, which incorporates images from Ringgold's quilts, showcases her rich and layered artwork. Cassie Louise Lightfoot flies above Harlem and looks down upon the tar roof of her family's apartment building. She soars above the George Washington bridge and the Union Building that her father helped to build. She talks of the union that denied her father membership because of the color of his skin. She celebrates the friends and family that gather on "Tar Beach." There's plenty to observe and talk about in this gorgeous book, whose story of a dream of freedom can be paired with Ringgold's *Aunt Harriet's Underground Railroad in the Sky.*

God Made Me and You
Shai Linne | *Illustrated by Trish Mahoney*
   Linne opens his book with the picture in Revelation 7 of a great and diverse multitude praising God, thus reminding us that racial and ethnic diversity is not just a good idea but God's grand vision for His people. In the context of a teacher addressing a classroom incident, Linne presents the narrative of creation, with all its diversity; the fall, with its resulting hatred and racism; and God's redemption through Jesus. He uses rhyme to translate profound truths into language that is accessible to young readers and listeners. However, he does not minimize the complicated challenges of acknowledging and addressing racism. My favorite parts of the book are Linne's gracious but sober closing letter to parents and caregivers and the concrete tools to help children "appreciate God's design for ethnic diversity."

The Beatitudes from Slavery to Civil Rights
Carole Boston Weatherford | *Illustrated by Tim Ladwig*
   This beautiful book honors the unique faith built over centuries of Black history, from the moment that Africans were stolen from the Motherland to the inauguration of Barack Obama. It speaks with the voice of a compassionate

God who has always championed justice for His people. Alongside the stories of figures important to the history of slavery and Civil Rights, Boston Weatherford includes lines from the Beatitudes, pairing anecdotes of resistance and bravery with the words of Jesus. She gives us a wonderful lens through which to read the Sermon on the Mount. The book closes with biographies of key figures mentioned in the book, providing parents with plenty of material for deeper learning with their children.

Can I Touch Your Hair?
Irene Latham and Charles Waters | *Illustrated by Sean Qualls and Selina Alko*

This book of poems frames conversations between two students: Irene, who is white, and Charles, who is Black. It captures their questions and experiences with what may seem mundane—hair and church and parents and recess. However, in the context of the everyday, without drama or apology, this book honestly depicts Irene's and Charles's struggles, including those deep hurts and misunderstandings related to race. The poems portray what children and adolescents may be thinking and feeling about race outside of the interfering narrative of well-meaning adults. They also show what is possible between children of different races when honesty and communication, questioning and listening, are affirmed and encouraged.

ENDNOTES

1   See Numbers 10:1–10 for use of silver trumpets; Numbers 15:38–40 for tassels on garments; Numbers 16:16–19, 36–40 for censers.

2   It is not unreasonable to assume that hearers of these words would have taken them literally based on the practices of contemporary Ancient Near Eastern peoples. See Ajith Fernando, *Deuteronomy, Loving Obedience to a Loving God* (Wheaton, IL: Crossway, 2012), pp. 268–271.

3   Esau McCaulley, *Reading While Black* (Downers Grove, IL: InterVarsity Press, 2020), p. 17.

4   Erin N. Winkler, "Children Are Not Colorblind: How Young Children Learn Race," accessed September 16, 2021, https://inclusions.org/wp-content/uploads/2017/11/Children-are-Not-Colorblind.pdf.

5   For an overview of children's attitudes towards race along stages of development, parents' assumptions about those attitudes, and the mistakes that spring from those assumptions, see Po Bronson and Ashley Merryman, "Why White Parents Don't Talk About Race," in *Nurture Shock: New Thinking About Children* (New York: Twelve, 2009), pp. 47–69.

6   One example of this history is the American church's complicity in racism. See Jemar Tisby, *The Color of Compromise* (Grand Rapids, MI: Zondervan, 2019).

7   Maya Angelou, "Still I Rise," *Poetry Foundation,* accessed November 18, 2021, https://www.poetry-foundation.org/poems/46446/still-i-rise.

WHY SHOULD CHILDREN BE GIVEN OLD BOOKS?

ANTIQUARIAN BOOKS

ANNE KENNEDY

Why should children be given old books? As a fun little exercise, I typed that line into Google before really getting down to work, thinking I would come up with hundreds of good answers, all better than this one. Unfortunately, Google chiefly delivered up to me several articles of warning. Old books will be anachronistic, they cautioned, they may not reflect the values of today that you desire to impress upon the minds and souls of your children. Be careful! You might come across some upsetting turns of phrase or expression. You may have some explaining to do.

I should not have been surprised. Current expectations about what children should think and feel have narrowed considerably over the last decade. Anxiety that the youth of today will be exposed to ideas or modes of expression that we are culturally not accustomed to, or that we disagree with, is why books like *The Adventures of Huckleberry Finn* have been controversially edited, and why the Laura Ingalls Wilder Award was renamed the Children's Literature Legacy Award.

These cautions are not entirely wrong. As I have read my favorite books to my children over the last two decades, I have often had to stop and explain words or phrases that are no longer in common use. I have even, when I am tired and not up to a big explanation, changed words as I read aloud, or fudged over bits of text that I knew might shock their little ears. There are all kinds of words and ideas that even I find myself shocked by, and I grew up on old books. In fact, all my favorites are basically out of print, which means spending hours online trying to get copies of them to give away to people I love.

Nevertheless, there are at least three good reasons to read books that are old or out of fashion. The first reason has to do with the caution itself. Yes, you will come across the values and beliefs of people from long ago. All the more reason to crack open books born of a lost way of seeing the world and to discover what those ideas and values were. Most of us take our children into unfamiliar environments when we are able, exposing them to people and experiences that will expand their horizons, enlarging their hearts and their ways of organizing their perceptions of the world. I don't know of anyone who thinks that traveling to other places is wrong. On the contrary, most modern parenting guides preach the importance of teaching children to be tolerant of others, of getting to know people different from themselves. If you are looking for some kind of cross-cultural experience for your child but have very little money, read books aloud to them that hold ideas and customs that have long since disappeared. If you are able to translate to your children the feelings and behaviors of people whom they do not yet know, it will not be too hard to do the same with a book, to stop and explain that not everyone is the same.

The second reason to read old books has to do with affection and speaks again to the caution named above. Reading books is dangerous because children easily fall in love. They will become enthralled with the characters and people they encounter if you aren't careful. For me, this is a feature, not a bug. I don't want my children to have all the same loves as their peers. I want them to live in some kind of other world—an angular Christian world, where they feel slightly out of sorts with the prevailing culture that presses in on them from every side. Short of only reading the Bible on a loop—or *The Chronicles of Narnia*—reading old books from which the categories of today have been borrowed but not fully understood has given my children their own kind of anachronism. They are not really at home in the world. They would prefer to live—though they cannot—in ancient times. All their convictions are formed in other eras. They are always wistfully looking out of the window for the chance to live elsewhere. They are vaguely discontented, but not in an easily remediated way—by buying more things or making more money. The only thing that makes them feel better is writing new ancient worlds in their heads.

Which is part of the third reason—that children need to rebel against something. A good and safe focus of rebellion is all the books that everyone else is reading. Not wanting my children to rebel against *me*, I have always tried to direct their disdain towards anything overtly "mainstream." This isn't an absolute rule, of course. If a book is good, it is good no matter when it is written. But while the whole world was reading *Harry Potter*, I managed to get my children hooked on Anthony Trollope's *Chronicles of Barsetshire*. While other people read *The Hunger Games*, I read them *My Family and Other Animals*. When my girls were little and people kept trying to give me *Junie B. Jones* and *Fancy Nancy*, I fed them shovelfuls of *Bread and Jam for Frances* and *The Princess and the Goblin*. I wanted children who would be rebellious about books that always insisted that they "get" the moral; I wanted them to revile humorless, flat writing; I wanted them to be completely fed up with boring rhymes and garish, fatuous color-schemes.

Perhaps there is a good fourth reason to read old books. Besides the mental and emotional furniture of another age, I have found the pacing and cadence of older books to be vastly preferable to those of newer ones (though there are, of course, notable and beloved exceptions). Most of my children have learned to speak with an elegance of language that wouldn't have been available to them if they hadn't been read piles of Wodehouse and Austen. They wouldn't be as good at spinning off epic metaphors if they weren't listening to *The Lord of the Rings* on a loop. And they wouldn't laugh as loudly as they do if they didn't know and love Gerald Durrell.

The Church Mouse

Graham Oakley | *Illustrated by Graham Oakley*

In *The Church Mouse*, Graham Oakley introduces Sampson, the church cat, who "had listened to so many sermons about the meek being blessed and everybody really being brothers that he had grown quite frighteningly meek and treated Arthur [the church mouse] just like a brother." The *Church Mice* books— the first was published in 1972 and the last in 2000—are not very old, but they do belong to a bygone era. Oakley's artwork is minutely detailed, its beauty matched by his humor. These books bear being read over and over for the simple reason that most of the jokes fly right over the head of the child and send the adult into regularly punctuated groans and occasional peels of laughter. This is the book I always give away. It's not the book you long for when your baby is born, but it is the one you reach for on the thousandth night of having to face bedtime yet again, when everything else sounds like sawdust and ennui.

The Fantastic Flying Journey
Gerald Durrell | *Illustrated by Graham Percy*

Gerald Durrell is my favorite, though many people today would be put off by not only his wordiness, but also by the colonialist world in which he found his voice. But his descriptions of the natural world are unparalleled, and his desire for all people to love and care about animals in their various ecosystems, not to mention his flashes of literary brilliance and humor, make him a staple in our household. *The Fantastic Flying Journey* is charming not for its writing, but for its sheer fun. Uncle Lancelot wrests his niece and nephews out of their boring English life and takes them around the world in a hot air balloon called The Belladonna, powered by friendly electrical eels, in search of his brother Percival. In the narrow way between proper care for the earth and ideologically dubious cries for green energy and environmental activism, Durrell (an admitted atheist) unwittingly articulates lyrical praise about the natural world. Here is no anger, no guilt, just sheer joy.

The Donkey Rustlers
Gerald Durrell

Durrell, during his life, was an excessively prolific writer. His humor and his descriptions are unparalleled. My favorites of his are his books for children. While *The Fantastic Flying Journey* is highly, as they say, "educational," full of facts about animals (a sort of pre-Wild Kratts, if you will), books like *The Donkey Rustlers* are for the story and the humor. When the evil village mayor wants to take away Yani's fields, Yani, David, and Amanda stop him—by stealing all the village donkeys. Donkeys, it turns out, can swim, and this unusual fact, along with a little arithmetic and many meetings in the cypress groves under the stars, turn the three children into heroes. When you've read it, rush out and buy *The Battle for Castle Cockatrice* for an extra thrill.

The Giant Golden Book Treasury of Elves and Fairies, with Assorted Pixies, Mermaids, Brownies, Witches, and Leprechaun
Edited by Jane Werner | *Illustrated by Garth Williams*

"The Fairy Book," as it is known in our house—mercifully available for purchase, though first published in 1951—is full of wide-mouthed children and cunning fairies. Though chock full of poems and stories, of particular importance to me is "The Cannery Bear," about a starving bear whose shoes don't fit and who can't eat regular fish because he just can't. He likes his fish canned. Fortunately for him, the fairy bear, who is pink, gives him wings and radar, so that he is able to fly over the sea and give correct nautical information to the foreman of the salmon canning plant so that, when the ship replete with salmon sails into the harbor, he has everything ready to process all that fish, stuffing it into the cans that make it so particularly delicious. This book is rightly called a "treasure" because if you don't have it, I don't see how you can possibly be happy in your life.

Kim
Rudyard Kipling

One of the values that I most hope to instill in my children is an affectionate curiosity for the world—the natural world, the world of people and cultures. This, for me, is that old-fashioned liberal virtue of "tolerance," but it is also something beyond that: it is looking out at the wide world and, like Kim, stepping out to taste all its delights, being caught up in the Great Game—not of the British and Russians spying on each other, but of the adventure of life itself. Growing up as I did in another culture, feeling that my own "ethnic" home was not really my own, I found that Kipling's Kim pushed away the dark loneliness of alienation and ushered in the bright majesty of a complex and vibrant world.

I do not believe that the cluttered accusations of colonialism and imperialism undermine this beautiful book. Certainly, as we age, it is worth wondering about the conquering and domineering enterprise of one nation unjustly occupying another. Those conversations are necessary and critical. But the backdrop should be one of affection, of having a cultural fluency to discover that life, in all its complexity, cannot be cut evenly into neat and tidy boxes. Rather, Kim is the story of the heart of a disciple for his master, of a little boy who grows into a man, of falling into the river of life and being saved.

A DRAGON IN THE HAND IS WORTH TWO IN THE BUSH

FANTASY

JUNIUS JOHNSON

Fantasy literature is that set of stories that have to do with myth, magic, and other worlds. Fantasy may affect all aspects of a story: the characters (which may include mythological creatures such as fauns and magical creatures such as unicorns and dragons), the setting (which may be a hidden world within our own, or an alternate version of our own, or another world entirely), and the plot (which often incorporates magical or mythological features as central to its unfolding).

Fantasy thrives on and specializes in the unaccustomed. This must not be mistaken for novelty: fantasy does not have to create something *new*. (A dragon, though the oldest fantastical beast in human literature, is no less exciting in fantasy now than it was in myth millennia ago.) Its job is not to innovate *per se*, but rather to shift our gaze from the ordinary to the extraordinary.

Thus, fantasy is an especially concentrated use of the imagination; its bread and butter is possibility. Fantasy is in many ways the native language of children, both in their own creative play and in the stories they are drawn to. When we invite children into fantasy worlds, therefore, we feed them with a food to which their souls are well suited and for which their hearts long.

Yet before we strap on our swords and set off to fight dragons, there are objections to the use of fantasy which deserve to be taken seriously. The first concern is the claim that fantasy is a negative moral influence. The concern is this: magic and witches are condemned in the Scriptures,[1] and it is likely that any such power that does exist in the world has its origin in demons. So, in reading stories that glorify such things, are we not perhaps opening ourselves to their influence? The problem with trafficking in mediums and spirits in our world is that in doing so we attempt to bypass the Holy Spirit, our true teacher. These worldly spirits stand against God, so to side with them is to oppose God. But is this true in a novel? In the *Harry Potter* novels, for instance, magic is not the seizing of demonic power; it is simply a force, like gravity, that has specific rules and that can be deployed for good or evil. If "any sufficiently advanced technology is indistinguishable from magic,"[2] then magic in fantasy is an expression and manipulation of the laws of that world, just as science is in our world. The fantastic notions of Harry disapparating or James T. Kirk "beaming up" using the transporter are equally imaginative and equally benign.

The second objection to fantasy is that it is escapism. Certainly some people do use fantasy literature in an escapist way, but this is not a problem unique to fantasy. Many a child has hidden from the "real world" in the novels of Laura Ingalls Wilder or Lucy Maud Montgomery, or in the pages of *The Hardy Boys*, or even in military histories of the Civil War. The imagination, like every human faculty, is always open to abuse. And this is where fantasy literature can be helpful: it flows from and back into reality. The dragon is drawn from the colossal impossibilities of living the diminished life we adults call "real"; the struggle to overcome it inspires and equips us to face that "real" world. As Chesterton has it, "Fairy tales do not give the child his first idea of bogey. What fairy tales give the child is his first clear idea of the possible defeat of bogey. The baby has known the dragon intimately ever since he had an imagination. What the fairy tale provides for him is a Saint George to kill the dragon."[3]

In short, to understand fantasy rightly and to use it well, one must take it neither too seriously nor too lightly. If taken too lightly, it appears frivolous, a distraction, and we fear that our children are wasting their time and not getting about the serious business of growing up. But if it is taken too seriously, then we fear that it is a bog in which our children will get mired, magnifying their darkest tendencies and training them to brood upon the morose or the occult.

Childhood is filled with molehills that have been made into mountains, what Chesterton calls "tremendous trifles": that is the particular gift of childhood, and it is as natural to it as trust and dependence. It is not just because the child is small that all things look big: it is also because the child looks at each thing in wonder, and wonder is a spell that enlarges whatever its gaze stays upon. It won't do to forget that in seeing each thing thus magnified, children are seeing things *better* than adults, for each thing, seen in its proper relation to God, is magnificent and expansive. Childhood takes the world very seriously, and childhood is to be taken seriously.

But children also flit nearly effortlessly across the surface of this world. We often envy them, thinking they go so far so fast so *constantly* because they have more energy in their bodies. But this is only part of their secret; the other is that they are *lighter* than we are. Not yet weighed down by experience, tragedy, grief, guilt, and, worst of all, self-importance, they are freed to take themselves and their world lightly. Even when they deify something with their gravest attention, they hold it lightly. This leaf is the most important thing ever, but in five minutes it will be forgotten, and released back into the world. In this way childhood takes itself and the world very lightly, and is itself to be taken somewhat lightly. But we falsely interpret this to mean that the problems of childhood are not real, or do not matter much. Childhood is not to be taken *only* lightly.

Fantasy is a metaphor for childhood because in it everything is magnified, anything is possible, and the stakes always feel ultimate; and yet, one person can make a difference, and the world is not only dangerous and dark, but also mischievous, bright, and *delightful.*

Now, of course childhood may grow very dark indeed; it may become a serious, dour affair. We have, perhaps, all met with serious, joyless children, and perhaps every child at some point experiments in being such. Likewise there are serious, dour fantasies that have not realized that levity and gravity are not incompatible. This is as much a disease of fantasy as it is a disease of childhood: the dour child is precocious in the worst way, for running ahead to seize what it means to be an adult, he has lost what it is to be a child at the only time when the adults around him will indulge him in that condition. Dark fantasy, not content with offering us an alternate world, tries to be *all the world*, and by throwing out levity in the name of realism, it also lessens its relevance to real people.

C.S. Lewis's *Chronicles of Narnia* has always been for me ground zero of the imagination. Since the first moment the first book was read to me in kindergarten, I have returned to it at regular intervals. Every adult should reread the *Chronicles* every couple of years to be reminded of the child they were and still must, in some significant sense, be. These books will teach bravery, integrity, and loyalty. But they also teach the cost of betrayal, the terrible price that can fall on others because of one's actions, and the indescribable clash of joy and horror at seeing one much worthier than you pay the debt you owe. They teach that beauty and goodness are terrifying and unsafe, but nevertheless desirable. They teach that it is not courage but silliness to stand when you should kneel in awe, and that there is no distance you can fall from which you cannot be lifted if you will let yourself be undone first. There are perhaps no books in all of literature I would recommend more highly than these.

As I said before, Fantasy is in many ways the native language of children. This is because it so nearly imitates the dynamics of childhood. "Could there be another world just around the corner? Obviously! Nothing is more likely." When you tell a child that someone has stepped into a puddle and fallen into the ocean, they don't ask "How can that be?" They ask, "What happened next?" This is not just adorable—it is indispensable to viewing the world rightly. Fantasy literature isn't simply an acceptable genre to enjoy, it is a necessary genre to experience, for it allows a child to speak their native language with grammatical correctness and grace.

The Chronicles of Narnia
C.S. Lewis | *Illustrated by Pauline Baynes*

When it comes to fantasy for children, this series defines the list.[4] The stories have all the elements of high fantasy: unicorns, dragons, talking animals, another world that touches upon ours, magic, and quests to break curses and rescue princes. But you can't just live your life in Narnia: you have to go home. Indeed, you were only brought to Narnia in order to learn how better to live in England. These books do all of this while embodying in their narratives powerful witnesses to a Christian worldview. This is part of their charm; even as a non-Christian child, I was deeply attracted to the elusive *meaning* that obviously underlay so much of the imagery and action.

Harry Potter Series
J.K. Rowling | *Illustrated by Jim Kay*

The world of Harry Potter is one of the most immersive and compelling I have come across since Narnia. This is the story of a boy who, through a mother's act of love and sacrifice, is destined to be the downfall of a great dark wizard. Our hero has had to grow up away from magic, so he knows as little as we do about it, and we experience with him the wonder of learning everything for the first time. This is like entering a second childhood, for everything is marvelous and new to us but so familiar to the other characters that they take it for granted. And like real children, we know that we are right: Ron has seen moving photos before, but Harry is right to be astounded.

The Young Wizards Series
Diane Duane

This series follows two children on their journey to being wizards of great power. The series combines elements of science fiction with its fantasy and, importantly, certain religious themes. Parents will want to consider carefully how to think about these, and when the right time is to introduce them to the child, but the series is as a whole quite positive towards traditional Christian notions of sacrifice and redemption, and even the delayed outworking of an accomplished victory.

There is a natural arc to the first three books in this series, which can stand alone. The third book is simply breathtaking, and is a wonderful example of the coexistence of levity and delight with ultimate gravity and danger.

The Seventh Tower Series and *Keys to the Kingdom Series*
Garth Nix

Garth Nix has emerged as one of the more consistent and prolific fantasy writers living today. I have chosen these two series to highlight because they are suitable for children and display outstanding immersive world-building.

The Seventh Tower tells of a world divided between the Chosen, who dwell in a castle and wield light magic, and the Icecarls, a nomadic people who travel the perpetual oceans of ice on ice-sailing ships. It falls to a child from each race to uncover the threat that looms over the entire world and stop it. The characters are depicted lovingly and sympathetically, and they pull me effortlessly into their rich and unusual world.

The Keys to the Kingdom focuses on a young boy who is mistakenly named the heir to the Architect of all reality, inheriting the right to rule the seven realms of existence. The Architect's faithless trustees, who were charged with facilitating the transfer of power, have instead hoarded the power for themselves, and have brought reality to the verge of collapse. Our hero must embark on a quest through each of the realms in order to gain the power that is rightfully his and set things to rights.

The story values honesty, loyalty, and goodness, while also deeply valuing the importance of being *human*, even in the midst of beings with superhuman power.

The Dark is Rising Sequence
Susan Cooper

This series is nestled deep in the folklore of Britain. The story, which details the final stages of an age-old battle between Light and Dark, uses our world as its main setting, while creating fantastical pockets and intrusions within it. This blending of our world with both its own past and with fantastic elements of popular lore invites us to look at the world anew.

Beautiful and cosmic, Cooper's tale also never loses sight of the particular and the domestic: it is often those accounted little who play great roles in the events that unfold.

ENDNOTES

1   The witch of Endor in 1 Samuel 28, for example.

2   Arthur C. Clarke, *Profiles of the Future: An Inquiry into the Limits of the Possible* (New York: Harper and Row, 1973), p. 21, n. 1.

3   G.K. Chesterton, "The Red Angel," in *Tremendous Trifles*, (Bulgaria: Demetra Publishing, 1909), pp. 62-63.

4   *Editors' note:* Speaking of lists, although the series is currently organized chronologically, the best way for a child to first read them (or hear them first read aloud) is in the initial sequence in which they were published: *The Lion, the Witch and the Wardrobe* (1950), *Prince Caspian: The Return to Narnia* (1951), *The Voyage of the* Dawn Treader (1952), *The Silver Chair* (1953), *The Horse and His Boy* (1954), *The Magician's Nephew* (1955), *The Last Battle* (1956). Devin Brown, author of *Inside Narnia,* has observed that "one need not be a Lewis scholar or an English professor to see that *The Lion, the Witch and the Wardrobe* must be read first if we want to walk with and not ahead of the four Pevensie children as they hide inside the Professor's strange wardrobe and enter an enchanted land called Narnia. Reading this story first is the only way we can share their wonder." Alister McGrath, author of *C.S. Lewis—A Life,* has written that "To read [*The Magician's Nephew*] first completely destroys the literary integrity of *The Lion, the Witch and the Wardrobe,* which emphasises the mysteriousness of Aslan. It introduces him slowly and carefully, building up a sense of expectation that is clearly based on the assumption that the readers know nothing of the name, identity, or significance of this magnificent creature."

SI SE PUEDE

MIRROR BOOKS

ARACELI CRUZ

I am an only child. I am all alone. These were the thoughts I had throughout grade school. I am not an only child, but the youngest of five. *She was an accident,* I heard them say. My siblings were much older than me. While they got to go to the mall, I had to stay at home. I was spoiled. I was *little Cheli.* Always little. Always too young to do anything. And so I would sulk. I created my own world filled with fantasy, music, writing, and books. My imagination became my escape and my diary—my confidante.

I would daydream about life in a big city, and me on the way to somewhere very important, perhaps in a cab or on the subway. It's not like I grew up on a farm, out in the middle of nowhere, but Montebello, a city just ten miles from downtown Los Angeles, still felt like a world away from anything relevant. Either way, it's not like I could roam around freely. I was stuck and there wasn't anything I could do about it. Then my world got a little bit bigger.

My mother, an assertive, Spanish-speaking Latina, enrolled me at Greenwood Elementary. The school staff assumed that, because my mother spoke very broken English, I should be placed in an ESL class. I wasn't paying attention to anything they spoke about, and it's not like they were asking me any questions. I soon realized the error when I got to class and the teacher handed me a book in Spanish.

"Araceli, you can start."

I looked at the first line and could not interpret the words in front of me. So, I did what anyone in my position would do—I started to cry.

"She doesn't belong here," the teacher whispered to another adult.

I was quickly pulled from the class and placed in another.

"I can read this!" I told my new teacher after she handed me a worksheet.

You could say my life began at Greenwood Elementary, because it was the first place I felt that I was being heard. It was also the only place I could actually do fun things like shop—at the book fair!

That is where I met two rambunctious little girls who seemed bigger than life itself and who were—the best part—just like me. I can't recall how I first encountered Ramona and Pippi. Maybe from the book jacket, or maybe they were recommended to me by a teacher. All I know is when I read the first lines of each book, I was hooked.

"I am not a pest" were the first words I ever read by Beverly Cleary. I looked around as I read, thinking someone was on to me. *Did someone read my diary? Ramona the Pest* was obviously about me, and my Beezus was my sister Mari, whose real name was Maria Alicia. Ramona also went to Glenwood Elementary. I mean, could the fiction be more perfect? Ramona and I were similar in a lot of ways. She was insecure, curious, and silly. But unlike Ramona, I wasn't adventurous or opinionated.

My family, like many Latino families, taught children to speak only when spoken to. Ramona's parents made time for her. They showed her love and kindness. While I wasn't neglected, I also wasn't encouraged. My parents were hardworking people, all they did was work—so how could I complain? I couldn't, but I also didn't say much at all.

Around the same time, at another book fair, I bought *Pippi Longstocking,* by Astrid Lindgren. Now Pippi and I could not have been more different. Yes, we both had pigtails, but Pippi was a girl on another level. "Pippi was a very remarkable child," Lindgren wrote. *Am I remarkable?* I wondered. *Am I special like Pippi?* I wasn't entirely sure. My eldest sister said many times that I was a miracle child. I had survived getting run over by a drunk driver when I was four. I was left crippled and bedridden for six months. But I got through it, thanks to Van Halen and Michael Jackson—and lots of physical therapy. Could Pippi have survived what I had? Certainly. She probably would have stopped the car with one hand.

Pippi became my idol. She was fierce, independent, fearless, strong, and willful. While I dreamed of being as assertive as Pippi, I was actually more like Annika, Pippi's demure neighbor. Annika was always well-dressed, neatly groomed, and respectful of her parents. Every picture of me as a young child shows me looking like a Mexican doll. My mom would dress me in poofy dresses, tight curls, and shiny Mary Jane shoes. In church, if I even attempted to utter a single word, my mom would tell me to sit still. Pippi would not last a minute in a church. That I knew for sure. Annika and I were followers, and believe me, I wasn't proud of it, but I didn't know how to get out of the hole.

How could a little girl like Pippi possess so much power? For starters, her dad was her biggest cheerleader. My dad was (and continues to be) my central advocate. I, however, didn't realize I had his support until I pushed myself to take more risks.

Through Cleary's series of Ramona books and Lindgren's Pippi volumes, I was able to find my inner strength. I was still little, and still a nuisance to my siblings, but I wasn't as quiet or scared as before. I was ready to take on the world—or, in this case, fifth grade.

I tried out for everything under the sun: softball, cheerleading, band, choir, dance. And I didn't succeed at *anything*. But the most incredible aspect of it all was that it didn't bother me that I didn't make it. I was trying. I was putting myself out there—largely because of Ramona and Pippi. When I began to take risks, my parents embraced it. Every time I showed enthusiasm for something new, they showed support.

As my senior year in high school approached, I knew, very firmly, that I was destined for bigger things. At seventeen, I left for college at San Francisco State and began my journey away from anything or anyone I had ever known. But I kept my inspiration close. When I moved into my first apartment sophomore year, I named it "Villa Villekulla"—an homage to Pippi, my fearless leader who would get me through life on my own.

Years later, when I finally began my life as a journalist in New York City, I often caught myself, while walking swiftly on Fifth Avenue, thinking of myself as an insecure and lonely kid. I'd smile and think to myself, *All Araceli needed was some encouragement, some support, and a bit of bravery to get going.*

Last Stop on Market Street
Matt de la Peña | *Illustrated by Christian Robinson*

When CJ and his grandma ride the bus across town one day after church, what should have been an ordinary bus ride becomes a critical moment of self-reflection as CJ becomes aware of the world outside his own. CJ reminds me a lot of myself as a child, wondering why I didn't have cool things and why my life wasn't like those around me. The difference between CJ and myself is that he has a grandmother to help guide him through his deep questions about life. *Last Stop on Market Street* shows why it is important for children to have a trusted adult that they can turn to with significant questions.

The Storyteller's Candle/La velita de los cuentos
Lucia Gonzalez | *Illustrated by Lulu Delacre*

This story beautifully shares what it is like to be uprooted from a home and transplanted to a new place that has an unfamiliar language and another culture. But there is one place where the characters feel at home: the public library. This book reminds me of what it felt like to feel safe in a place filled with books, stories, and characters that welcomed me as one of their own.

Lola Levine Is Not Mean!
Monica Brown | *Illustrated by Angela Dominguez*

Lola is introspective and, like me, loves to write in her journal. But like Pippi and Ramona, Lola is an assertive young girl who is often misunderstood as mean and aggressive. This book is perfect for young kids who are often encouraged to be strong but who question themselves after others peg them as too assertive and strong-willed.

Separate Is Never Equal
Duncan Tonatiuh | *Illustrated by Duncan Tonatiuh*

I wish I would have learned about Sylvia Mendez, an extraordinary Mexican Puerto Rican young girl who made history in a city not far from where I grew up. Almost ten years before Brown vs. the Board of Education, Sylvia Mendez and her family ended segregated schools in California. Knowing her story at an earlier age could have changed the perception of my own strength. This book helps children understand the importance of the contribution of Latino people in the US.

Esperanza Rising
Pam Muñoz Ryan

Esperanza may have come from a life of wealth and privilege, but after her father's murder, she moves from Mexico to California, where she is instantly grouped with hardworking Latinos who are treated like second-class citizens. I wasn't born into a life of privilege, but I did understand early on that I had more than others. And as a child, it was hard to be appreciative of what we had. But while Esperanza doesn't like her new life, she faces her difficult reality and learns to appreciate the things that truly matter in life.

SILVER AND GOLD

NEWBERY BOOKS

GYPSY MARTIN

Being dragged along to run errands with my mom when I was a kid was the worst—unless we got to make a stop at the library. Then it was the best. Our public library was a small white stucco building with a red-tiled roof, and it smelled of mildew, probably due to the effect of our damp coastal air on the old building and on the books it contained. I was allowed to check out as many books as I could carry back to the car.

We didn't have a TV at home to compete for our attention, and our book collection was small, so my armful of borrowed library books never lasted long. Once I'd read all the books from authors I knew I liked, along with every Nancy Drew mystery in the library—I even tried a few Hardy Boys in desperation— I was stumped as to what to read next.

I knew there must be books in those musty stacks that were worth reading, but the librarian didn't know enough about children's books to be of any help. I trolled the shelves without guidance and with little hope, squinting at the rows of titles in the glare of the florescent lights. But every once in a while I would pull out a book with a gold or silver seal on the cover, and I would feel a little frisson of possibility. An award-winner! I wasn't sure exactly *which* award (I always got the Newbery and Caldecott confused), and I had no idea who gave them, or how often, or how many. To me, that seal meant just one of two things: either the book was going to be very good or, more likely, it was going to be very good *for* me.

I loved the Newbery winners *Island of the Blue Dolphins* and *From the Mixed-*

Up Files of Mrs. Basil E. Frankweiler. A Wrinkle in Time was one of the books of my heart, as I imagine it was for many girls of my generation. But titles like *Roller Skates* and *Strawberry Girl* sounded suspiciously sappy. *The Matchlock Gun, Daniel Boone,* and *The Codfish Musket*? No way was I reading any of those unless a teacher made me. *Bridge to Terabithia*? It tells you right on the back cover that a terrible tragedy occurs! No thank you. I was looking for an escape from my own bad feelings, not an escape into someone else's.

I wasn't the first person to find the Newbery winners a mixed bag, and I am confident I won't be the last; ample room for disagreement is baked right into the broad criteria for the award. In 1921, editor and later publisher Frederic G. Melcher proposed to the American Library Association meeting of the Children's Librarians' Section that they give a yearly award to the author of "the most distinguished contribution to American literature for children." Melcher hoped that the recognition provided by the award would raise the standing and quality of children's literature in America. The Newbery Medal, named by Melcher after the eighteenth-century English bookseller and publisher John Newbery, was adopted and established in 1922.

"Most distinguished" is a very broad criterion, and this definition from the American Library Services to Children (the current name of the body that governs the award) doesn't do much to narrow it down:

- Marked by eminence and distinction; noted for significant achievement.
- Marked by excellence in quality.
- Marked by conspicuous excellence or eminence.
- Individually distinct.[1]

Even with this clarification, determining the one book that best exemplifies these qualities remains a subjective endeavor. The pool of eligible books is enormous—it includes any book for children up to the age of fourteen published in America and written by an American resident—making it unsurprising that there is often lively disagreement about which book deserves the Newbery Medal.

Fortunately, the rules allow the committee to recognize additional books from among the nominees. These books receive a silver seal rather than gold, and were known as "runners-up" until 1971, when the term was changed to "honor books."

The first Newbery Medal was awarded to Hendrik Willem van Loon, PhD, for *The Story of Mankind*, which is worth taking a look at if only to appreciate how much children's literature has changed since 1922. A peek should be enough.

Here's what the professor had to say about the Hebrew people: "They had wandered far and wide, and after many years of dreary peregrinations they had been given shelter in Egypt."[2] And regarding the ancient Greeks:

> Every year they held solemn processions in honor of Dionysos, the god of the wine. As everybody in Greece drank wine (the Greeks thought water only useful for the purpose of swimming and sailing) this particular divinity was as popular as a god of the soda-fountain would be in our own land.[3]

While the list of Newbery winners is a great resource for discovering good books (and one I could have used in my never-ending quest to find something to read), I hope the above excerpt suffices to dissuade anyone but the most ardent completist from the idea of reading the entire list of winners straight through. Anyone doing so would be forgiven for quitting before she got very far. In approaching the list, there are a few things it is helpful to know in order to get the most out of it.

First, don't exclude the honor books. It's a given that one book will be awarded the Newbery Medal every year, but an honor book must be championed by the committee in order to be named. The honor book choices are also less likely to be influenced by cultural trends and singled out as the "kind of book" that should win in any given year. This may have been the case in 1953, when *Charlotte's Web* was one of five Newbery Honor Books and *Secret of the Andes*, which is now primarily known for beating out *Charlotte's Web*, won the Newbery Medal. Just as one might prefer a different nominee to the movie that ultimately wins the Oscar for Best Picture, an individual reader may find more merit in the honor book than in the medal book.

Next, bear in mind that the distribution of award books is lopsided across age groups and genres, which makes the list great for finding books in some categories, and not at all helpful in others. While picture books, chapter books, nonfiction, and poetry collections are all eligible, the majority of awards have gone to middle grade novels "by white people about white people,"[4] a concern I'll come back to. If you're looking for something other than that, your choices will be scanty.

So what is the list particularly good for? As a treasure trove of well-written middle grade fiction, it is the perfect place to find books for kids whose reading skills outstrip their readiness for mature themes and subject matter. Not that Newbery books don't deal with difficult subjects or contain controversial language. But with such a big pool to draw from, one is bound to find something suitable. When my own voracious reader was in fourth grade, I struggled to find books for him that weren't too easy on the one hand or too adult on the other. It was a frustration I heard echoed by many other parents. I got caught up in trying to find new releases for him, never once thinking to consult the list of Newbery winners. If I'd done so, I would have discovered that the kinds of books I was looking for were not unicorns, but Newbery books.

There's another "unicorn" category that the Newbery list can help with, and that is books that engage teens but that don't push boundaries as insistently as contemporary young adult literature tends to. There aren't many true YA books on the list, but two I can recommend are *The Thief*, by Megan Whalen Turner, and Robin McKinley's *The Hero and the Crown*. And, because the middle grade winners tend to skew toward the older end of the age range, the list contains plenty to interest teen and even older readers. I've read more Newbery books as an adult than I did as child, and I enjoyed *When You Reach Me*, *The Giver*, *The Graveyard Book*, and *Holes* (a book that's as close to perfect as a book can be) just as much as I would have as a younger reader.

Finally, it's important to know that in the past five years the Newbery committee has increasingly recognized books that are diverse in both genre and ethnicity. So if you are looking for stories from diverse viewpoints told in a variety of genres, the Newbery list is becoming a place where you can find them. *Merci Suárez Changes Gears* is a middle grade novel about a girl and her Cuban-American family. *Other Words for Home* is a novel in free verse about a family of Syrian refugees. The picture book *Last Stop on Market Street* by Matt de la Peña was the first book by a Hispanic author to win the Newbery Medal. *New Kid*, a story about a Black student navigating his home and school cultures, is the first graphic novel to win the top prize. These books provide much-needed windows for some readers, and buoying mirrors for others. They give readers an opportunity to appreciate a diversity of storytelling styles and lived experiences, and they connect us by showing how much we have in common.

Today's readers are fortunate to have almost a century of Newbery books to choose from and the benefit of online reviews to help weed out books that aren't of interest. Because the committee does not consider a book's popularity when selecting winners, some children's librarians have raised the concern that the awards are going to books that children don't want to read. Consulting a combination of reader reviews like those at Goodreads and industry reviews from places like *Kirkus* can help you determine which books you *should* read, which books you *want* to read, and which books you might skip altogether.

It's not unlike referring to the inner menu card in a box of chocolates: is this book a strawberry cream (yikes), a chocolate caramel (yum), or a butterscotch square (huzzah)? Or perhaps you want to choose blindly—that can be its own kind of fun. The good news is that no matter which Newbery book you land on, you can most likely borrow it from your public library.

So enjoy exploring the Newbery list; catch up on the good books that you missed while you were busy being an adult, and if you have young people in your life floundering to find something good to read, point them to the list and encourage them to read widely. What a joy to be introduced to the wry humor of E.L. Konigsburg, the Welsh-flavored fantasy of Lloyd Alexander, and the luminous stories of Kate DiCamillo. There are new favorite books just waiting to be discovered on the ever-growing list of Newbery Medal and Newbery Honor books.

Bud, Not Buddy
Christopher Paul Curtis

This Coretta Scott King Award-winner is exactly the sort of book I, as a young reader, would have assumed belonged in the "good for me" category and avoided—which would have been a shame. *Bud, Not Buddy* is the story of a Black ten-year-old boy named Bud Caldwell in depression-era Michigan. Bud runs away from an abusive foster family and sets out from Flint to find the musician he's decided is his father.

Bud's uncommon mix of experience and naiveté make him a winsome narrator. His voice and humor leaven the heaviness of the injury, hunger, and grief he endures, and Curtis refrains from digging deeply into their effect on Bud's psyche. At its heart this is a book about love and belonging, and readers will enjoy cheering Bud on as he journeys to find family and home.

Gone-Away Lake
Elizabeth Enright

In *Gone-Away Lake*, ten-and-a-half-year-old Portia and her little brother go to the country to stay with family for the summer. Portia and her cousin Julian are exploring the woods when they come upon a swamp—and on the far edge of the swamp, a ghost town! Soon Portia and Julian encounter the two remaining residents of this ramshackle row of formerly grand houses.

This gentle, old-fashioned book evokes in the reader a longing for the kind of summer it recounts. *Gone-Away Lake* is for everyone who's ever wanted to explore a ruin, or have a secret clubhouse, or sit in the sun on a big rock that "smelled of baked moss." And if you haven't ever wanted to do those things, reading this book will fix that. While the plot is light on conflict (and on consequences for bad decisions), *Gone-Away Lake* is saved from saccharinity by being beautifully written and by being *funny*. It's not a fantasy book, but this engaging tale of summer at Gone-Away Lake is so far removed from our own day and age that it has a magic all its own.

The Ear, the Eye, and the Arm
Nancy Farmer

This might be the oddest book ever honored by the Newbery Committee. This soft science fiction tale takes place in Zimbabwe in the year 2194. When thirteen-year-old Tendai and his younger siblings sneak out of their family compound to traverse the dangerous city of Harare, their mother solicits help from the Ear, the Eye, and the Arm—a team of private detectives who each possess a unique ability. This book is a bit of a mess at times—its faults include a weak opening, uneven tone, and some pacing issues—but it's a *fun* mess that succeeds in the end. Its eccentric hodge-podge of memorable settings, characters, and themes will continue to engage the reader's imagination long after more conventional award-winners have been forgotten.

The spiritual elements integral to this story (demons, witchcraft, and ancestral spirit possession among them) are based on Shona religious beliefs, and Farmer's chilling portrayal of demonic evil warrants the book's YA classification. While the tribal religious setting isn't for everyone, I appreciate that the conflict within it is a contest between a clear good and a clear evil. And by putting the spirit world front and center, it reminds western Christian readers that materialism is an inadequate view of reality and encourages us to examine our own beliefs.

Breaking Stalin's Nose
Eugene Velchin

Ten-year-old Sasha Zaichik reveres Joseph Stalin. But on the night before Sasha scheduled to join the Young Pioneers, the secret police arrest his Communist official father and take him from their communal apartment. Over the course of two days Sasha's world is upended, and he confronts choices that may have life-or-death stakes.

Short and grim, *Breaking Stalin's Nose* concisely and powerfully communicates the nature of totalitarianism and the horrors that ensue when citizens are

turned against one another. Yelchin illustrates the book extensively with drawings that convey the menace of Stalin's rule in the Soviet Union. Parents should
preview the book (which can easily be read in one sitting) and be prepared to
talk about it afterwards. Or, better yet, read it with your child. The book doesn't
explore much emotional territory, but I don't think it intends to. It is, instead, an
extremely effective introduction for young readers to the travails and abuses of
life in Russia under Stalin.

Splendors and Glooms
Laura Amy Schlitz

When young Clara Wintermute goes missing from her stately family
home, suspicion falls on the performers who entertained at her birthday party:
puppet-master Grisini and his charges Lizzie Rose and Parsefall. Then the ma-
levolent Grisini vanishes, and the children are left to make their own way as they
puzzle out what's happened. This intricately plotted gothic novel set in Victorian
London is dark, moody, witty, and exquisitely written, like a junior version of
Susanna Clarke's *Jonathan Strange and Mr. Norrell*.

Only the disreputable characters in the book use magic, which stands in contrast
to Lizzie Rose's Christian faith. This faith explicitly informs her character in a way
that one rarely encounters in children's literature, and the conflict between good
and evil sparks with truth. Schlitz's deft writing sweeps the reader into this strange
and thrilling story of hardship, friendship, and avarice, and she resolves the book's
complex plot by piling happiness upon happiness in a deeply satisfying way.

ENDNOTES

1   See "John Newbery Medal," *Association for Library Service to Children*, accessed October 18, 2021,
    https://www.ala.org/alsc/awardsgrants/bookmedia/newbery.
2   Hendrik van Loon, *The Story of Mankind* (New York: Liveright, 1921, updated 2014), p. 39.
3   Van Loon, *Story of Mankind*, p. 73.
4   Roger Sutton, "Editorial: 'Last Stop, First Steps'," *The Horn Book*, June 24, 2016, https://www.
    hbook.com/story/editorial-last-stop-first-steps.

WELCOME HOME

MARRIED AUTHORS & ILLUSTRATORS

CINDY WARD ROLLINS

"Mawwage is what bwings us together..."

Perhaps we all remember *The Princess Bride*'s take on the Anglican wedding ceremony. That comical movie scene is often coupled in my mind with the much more sobering and brilliant scene from the BBC 1995 *Pride and Prejudice* finale where the vicar preaches through the Anglican service while we see both the smiles of the happily married and the wistful looks of those not so happily joined. We hear the vicar proclaim the words that marriage "is an honorable estate, instituted of God in the time of man's innocency, signifying unto us the mystical union that is betwixt Christ and his Church."

From the very first book sale my oldest son, Timothy, and I stumbled upon at the library to my continuing book purchases over the years, I noticed that some of my favorite children's books were written and illustrated by married couples. Over and over again these couples brought something of the mystical union to their work together. And while the Anglican service tells us that marriage was ordained first for the procreation of children, it is profound to see it birthing other creations such as books and illustrations as well. Most of the married couples referred to here have won the prestigious Randolph Caldecott Award for best picture book in a given year, not to mention countless other nominations, and these couples are not the only married couples listed for that award. Marriage is a union of creation.

One of the very first children's books I owned was *A Book of Seasons* by Alice and Martin Provensen. I didn't even have children yet when I stumbled across this paperback in a bookstore. You could almost say the joy of that little book made me long to have a child to share it with. That longing was fulfilled when my own children were born. Eventually, I had to replace my old tattered copy with a new one ready for my grandchildren. I also began to look for other books by the Provensens and found they had quite a catalog of collaborations. The Provensens won the Caldecott for their lovely book *The Glorious Flight*, but *The Year at Maple Hill Farm* became our favorite, along with *Our Animal Friends at Maple Hill Farm*. Wrapped up in the Provensens' world of Maple Hill Farm was a whole ethos for living. A child without a farm to grow up in could find a home in these books—a home with dogs, cats, goats, and pigs, each as unique as any other family member.

Home is exactly what I found over the years in books written and illustrated by married couples. Berta and Elmer Hader invite us into just such another world in their Willow Hill tales such as *The Big Snow* and *Little White Foot*. Elmer and Berta wrote more than seventy books together from their artistic haven in Rockland County, New York. Through their books, we can walk right out of their kitchen into the great big snowy world outside or right up their stairs to the dark attic where a little mouse lives rather harmlessly with his family—except for when he ventures into the kitchen below. In the Haders' books, nature confronts us both indoors and out, and if our lives happen to be barren of such things then all the better that we can meet an older ethos amongst our books. While our own homes may be collapsing around us, we can step into the homes brought to us by couples who lived and worked together.

These married couples seem to bring a real world of home and family to their stories and illustrations, even when their work is fantastical or historical. Ingri and Edgar Parin d'Aulaire use bold color to pull us into the worlds of historical figures such as Leif Erikson. Lucky indeed is the child who enters the Norse world of *Leif the Lucky*. The d'Aulaires were considered part of the Golden Age of Picture Books, and just thumbing through one of their oversized picture books explains why. This naturalized American couple brought us *Pocahontas, Abraham Lincoln* (a Caldecott winner), *Buffalo Bill*, and other books about American historical characters that help us grasp that these were real people. But the d'Aulaires hit their stride when they brought us the fantastical world of Greek myths with this same lavish use of color. Their words and illustrations captured the strangeness of Greek and Norse gods and goddesses and at the same time brought real historical figures into technicolor reality.

The brilliant books of Leo and Diane Dillon take us to diverse places and cultures in their extraordinary imitation of art from around the world. Culture is transmitted to our own children through art. The Dillons are the winners of two Caldecott Medals in consecutive years for their illustrations in the books *Why Mosquitos Buzz in People's Ears* and *Ashanti to Zulu*. The Dillons lived and created together for more than fifty years, producing hundreds of illustrations and books. The Dillons' art is truly seamless. One never knows where Leo's hand began or Diane's finished. The two have become one in their books.

In the works of Russell and Lillian Hoban we find something else unique to married people—children. We meet Frances, a young badger, and her delightful family. Over and over again in the Frances books, Mother and Father Badger deal with Frances's childhood problems with wisdom and love. I learned to be a better parent from these badgers. And while Frances never does get a spanking, the fact that her parents consider it is one of the few places in children's literature where we see a child not punished but disciplined with wisdom. One of the most delightful surprises in the Frances books is the little songs Frances, like so many human children, sings. Frances often sings her frustrations. For example, when it is her little sister Gloria's birthday—and not hers—she sings:

Everybody makes a fuss
For Birthday girls who are not us.
Girls who take your pail away
Eat cake and q-p-m all day.

"Qpm," as Mother Badger discerns, is ice cream. I once heard a man reading aloud a Frances book and was quite astonished and appalled that he used a different tune than I did when singing Frances's little songs. I had so lost myself in the books I forgot the tunes were made up in my own head.

But that is how stories work; we get lost in other worlds, and when we return to reality we find we have brought new ideas, tools, or even tunes with us. As we grab the hands of our children and enter these other worlds, we often find the very things our families lack or need.

The mystical union of marriage can bring creative works into the lives of our families that can help us cover a multitude of sins. We all fall short. We all err in many ways. Introducing our children to other times, places, and homes can help them repair the ruins of their own parents—us. It is not so astonishing that artists who marry one another find themselves creating works together and that those works often transcend what each of them could do on their own. Marriage does indeed bring us together to create as we were meant to create: as children made in the image of our Father.

Our Animal Friends at Maple Hill Farm
Alice and Martin Provensen | *Illustrated by Alice and Martin Provensen*

This is a world to be savored, more than a story to be checked off the reading list. From Eggnog the ancient Siamese to the tracks of the unseen porcupine, the lives of all who come and go at Maple Hill Farm walk across the pages of this endearing book, making us feel they are our animals and it is our farm.

The Big Snow
Berta and Elmer Hader | *Illustrated by Berta and Elmer Hader*

Of all their wonderful books together, *The Big Snow* earned the Haders a well-deserved Caldecott Award. From the moment the geese begin to fly south until Groundhog Day, we see the lives of animals preparing and surviving a big winter. I believe we even get a glimpse of Elmer and Berta themselves as they help the animals through the winter with seeds, nuts, and breadcrumbs. Interspersing color and black-and-white illustrations, this book is a treasure of nature study.

Bread and Jam for Frances
Russell Hoban | *Illustrated by Lillian Hoban*

There is something about a family meal table that communicates deep moral values. I have noticed this on TV shows too. When families sit down to a meal together it is a spiritual discipline. *Bread and Jam for Frances* captures all the nuances of this phenomenon. It begins at family breakfast and ends with a school lunch complete with a doily, flowers, thermos, and a friend. We can call this communion on some level. A fine array of Frances's songs complement this book, and she is very fond of jam!

Leif the Lucky
Ingri and Edgar Parin d'Aulaire

Like the Haders, Provensens, and Dillons, the d'Aulaires also won a Caldecott Medal—for their 1940 illustrated biography *Abraham Lincoln*—but the book that sticks with me most is their biography of Leif Erikson, *Leif the Lucky*. The Norse world of the Vikings comes to life in the pages of this book as blonde, blue-eyed Leif, son of Eric the Red, discovers the coast of North America and the natives living there—natives who would get a chance to live in peace for a few hundred more years after the Vikings left. The antics of Leif and his discoveries remind us that history is often a clash of cultures.

To Everything There is a Season
Leo and Diane Dillon | *Illustrated by Leo and Diane Dillon*

Using the biblical book of Ecclesiastes in *To Everything There is a Season*, the Dillons take us on a journey to different times and places, from Ancient Egypt (wall murals) to Europe (woodcuts), from Ireland (illuminated manuscripts) to Ethiopia (book illustration), from Thailand (shadow art) to Mexico (screen folds), and many more, at the same time sharing with us the unique lifestyles and artifacts of diverse peoples of the world all created in the image of God. As we lose ourselves in each page we find these people are very different from us and yet not quite so different after all. Here we find sowing and planting, living and dying, working and playing, and marriage and family life—familiar things in unfamiliar paintings that remind us we are one blood.

HEALING GARDENS
AND TWILIT VALLEYS

NATURE

AMY BAIK LEE

One night while running errands, not very long ago, I turned my car onto the long road heading home and gasped.

The moon was low in the sky, four times its usual size, a three-quarter disc of hammered light. Black shadow sliced across its upper right quadrant so that it hung like an immense and luminous chipped pearl above the darkening skyline.

Perhaps because my mind was fresh from journeying through C.S. Lewis's *Out of the Silent Planet,* I paused to marvel at length when I stopped at a red light—and with a start, I realized I was looking upon an object older than the history of men. This was the same coracle that once sailed between the stars as Abraham counted; it was the same face that Adam might have gazed upon that first long night outside Eden. I tried not to stare too long as I drove.

I have since surprised myself by committing similar little acts of madness. I've pulled the car over to the side of the street a mere forty yards from home to point out striations of sunset color to my daughters; I've knelt in the dirt to photograph the first iris of spring with an enthusiasm that would put celebrity paparazzi to shame. These are glad moments that bring a certain childlikeness to the fore—moments when I can hardly help celebrating life and being alive. And when they occur around my children, I'm aware that I am planting seeds for the habitual close observation and exploration of nature. A realm of marvels and mysteries and hidden Fibonacci sequences awaits them, and my mother-heart hopes they will never shy from seeking adventure there.

At the same time, I am learning that nature is a force that often needs to be narrated. We mortals live in a world regularly marred by hurricanes and avalanches, tsunamis and earthquakes, and our reactions to nature's violence range from fear to recklessness. What should I say, I sometimes wonder, when two uncertain faces turn to me from a darkly overcast window? Which words will secure and settle their hearts as high winds clamor at the panes?

The apostle Paul reminds me that God's "invisible attributes, namely, his eternal power and divine nature, have been clearly perceived, ever since the creation of the world, in the things that have been made" (Rom. 1:20). Coming to know His character through the lens of His word has made all the difference in my own life, affecting even my perspective on the vastness of creation. The power of sea tempests and the infinitude of space, whose sheer existence might otherwise be too terrible to consider, are not senseless and overwhelming—for I know their Maker, and He is not capricious.

This, therefore, is what I find myself searching for in the books I read with my children: not didactic bullet points, but stories and art that show us our place under the sovereign hand of our King and in His creation. Literary scenes can display the might of the One who laid the foundations of the earth, as when Laura Ingalls Wilder describes the pounding and howling of prairie blizzards in an interminable winter. E.B. White places us in a barn at Zuckerman's farm to watch the clear passage of seasons with Wilbur: one rich tableau after another from a surprisingly slim window on the world. A silent nighttime walk through a snow-covered wood in the pages of *Owl Moon* leaves us hushed and better prepared for our next encounter with small wild creatures.

But the prose and poetry we read also do more: they show us the freedom and responsibility that mankind is meant to take up in the natural world. In Frances Hodgson Burnett's *The Secret Garden*, Mary Lennox confronts her cousin about his fear of becoming a hunchback and demands to examine his back herself. "There's not a single lump there!" she declares, and threatens to laugh him to scorn if he ever mentions such a suspicion again. The consequences are both immediate and jarring:

> No one but Colin himself knew what effect those crossly spoken childish words had on him. If he had ever had any one to talk to about his secret terrors—if he had ever dared to let himself ask questions—if he had had childish companions and had not lain on his back in the huge closed house, breathing an atmosphere heavy with the fears of people who were

most of them ignorant and tired of him, he would have found out that
most of his fright and illness was created by himself. But he had lain and
thought of himself and his aches and weariness for hours and days and
months and years. And now that an angry unsympathetic little girl insisted
obstinately that he was not as ill as he thought he was he actually felt as if
she might be speaking the truth.[1]

In this moment, Colin begins to believe that the doubts and fears that have
taken hold of his isolated mind are not his true reality. Little by little the sunlight
and the soft approach of Spring are let into his room, bringing him rumors of life
and animals and "green and growing things," until one day Mary and Dickon
wheel him at last into the storied secret garden. There he falls backward in astonished rapture and dares to believe, at last, that he might *live* after all.

I strongly believe that Colin's recuperation mirrors the benefit that books
on nature and place offer to the developing mind. Their influence is vital in
numerous ways—for while such books are excellent for nurturing wonder and
childlikeness, their true subject matter is not childish in the least.

Take, for example, the exquisite simplicity of Patricia MacLachlan's *All the
Places to Love*. With MacLachlan's trademark lyricism, a small boy details his
entrance into the world and the home his family has made. Each family member
loves a different aspect of the farm and the surrounding countryside, and Eli
ponders which experience or site he might pass on as his own favorite to his
baby sister. The book is a tender catalog of objects and locations beautified
by familiarity and by their connections to Eli's memories: the river where his
grandmother sails bark boats downriver to him, the barn rafter on which his
grandfather has carved each family member's name, the blueberry barren where
his mother watches both sunrise and sunset.

Implicit in the story is the understanding that our lives can be deeply marked
by physical places, and that physical places often give us the rootedness we need
to feel that we belong. This sense of belonging is a step that cannot be skipped
in a healthy life; it gives people of all ages a base from which to offer hospitality,
and, quite simply, to love.

A second example, Lucy Maud Montgomery's *Rainbow Valley*, depicts the
great potential of nature to be a shelter for our bodies and a refuge for our
imaginations. A little valley beloved by Gilbert and Anne Blythe's children hosts
countless tangible experiences, including a tantalizing fish fry seasoned with
"fresh air and appetite of youth, which [gives] to everything a divine flavour":

To sit in Rainbow Valley, steeped in a twilight half gold, half amethyst, rife with the odours of balsam-fir and woodsy growing things in their spring-time prime, with pale stars of wild strawberry blossoms all around you, and with the sough of the wind and tinkle of bells in the shaking treetops, and eat fried trout and dry bread, was something which the mighty of the earth might have envied them.[2]

But it is also a place where an old string of sleigh bells, strung from two trees, rings with fairy melodies—a place where children and adults alike retreat to compose their thoughts, dreams, and hopes in solitude.

In our increasingly digitized age, we stand in great need of sharpening both our physical senses and our imaginations. A child feeling rejected on social media—if she can be persuaded to leave the screen—may yet go out to a field to see buttercups nodding at her and a robin skittering unafraid nearby. She might approach a dragonfly sunning on a warm wooden post, only to be astonished as it sails a full circle around the garden and alights again a scant two inches away. A book with such scenes is no substitute for real experiences, but it can teach the reader how to watch for them; it can train her vision and remind her that she is more than a mere conglomerate of likes and comments and shares and avatars. Fried trout and fairy bells, even glimpsed through the pages of a story, help us to recover the knowledge that we have faces, souls, ears, minds, hearts, fingertips, stomachs, and eyelashes. We are red-blooded creatures, not merely online specters. And it's only when we recover our faculties that we begin to understand our role as imaginative caretakers of creation.

To return briefly to *The Secret Garden*: when Colin's father enters the once-neglected garden for the first time in ten years, he is awestruck by the late roses, the golden-hued trees, and the lovely "wilderness of autumn gold and purple and violet blue and flaming scarlet."

"I thought it would be dead," he says, and Colin replies, "Mary thought so at first, but it came alive."[3] Indeed it has. Mary's first tentative act of clearing grass away from the roots of early spring flowers has traveled like a spark along a fuse, making way for growth and flourishing. Planting, pruning, coaxing, and weeding are the actions that have increased the children's appetites and their delight in being alive, and they are acts befitting the charge given to all humans at the dawn of the world.

Burnett's tale calls us to remember that we are meant to be caretakers who reawaken dead spaces and cultivate beauty in tandem with the ultimate Creator.

Like children discovering green shoots in a withered garden, we are spurred on to imagine things not as they are, but as they shall be in the day when death is no more. As we read books that encourage us to encounter nature for ourselves, we gain a sense of wonder that calls us to engage in the work of redemption and restoration.

As I write this, a child's laugh floats in from the garden, the blithe sound piercing the gray chill of this autumn day. I watch as one daughter collects a bouquet of emerald clover leaves. The other tends to a play kitchen made of bricks and pebbles and clamshells, inspired by Alice McLerran's *Roxaboxen*. I'll hear further details about these at the dinner table, I'm sure.

But though I've opened the windows to keep an eye on my daughters, hoping for some free time to espalier words along the rough-hewn trellis of my thoughts, I'm aware that the tables have turned. *Will the salvia live through the winter? Come look at the size of these clovers! What is that tiny unmoving light in the sky at dusk?* (I don't know.) *Could it be a planet?* (Let's look it up!) *Guess what I've decided to plant in my raised bed next year!* Their words beckon me to look, to delight, to remember where I am. And as I do, I pause for a grateful laugh.

They are narrating our surroundings back to me, opening a casement of wonder through which I am invited to become like a child—and enter the unceasing joy of a deathless kingdom.

Little Men
Louisa May Alcott

A lesser-known sequel to *Little Women,* this story of the rambunctious and lovable children of Jo Bhaer's Plumfield school involves a rich range of outdoor settings. But these are more than mere backgrounds; the beloved old willow tree, a huckleberry field, and the individual garden plots for each child all prove to be integral to the shaping of the children's hearts and minds. I've found this book to be as cheering in parenthood as in childhood, and I still find inspiration in its pages to create, revel, and wander.

The Gardener
Sarah Stewart | *Illustrated by David Small*

Told through a series of poignant letters, *The Gardener* traces the journey of a young girl who goes to live in the city during the Great Depression. In her suitcase are seed packets from her grandmother; in her heart, a "dream of gardens." Her efforts and triumphs remind me that the cultivation of nature isn't limited to the countryside, and that the city might even be a more fertile place for enjoying the fruits of gardening in community with others.

The Wishes of the Fish King
Douglas McKelvey | Illustrated by Jamin Still

"Come to the window, Mansi," begins this whimsical bedtime tale. The first time I read this book, I was surprised to find it had no plot—at least, not one in the usual sense of children's literature. But it offers a splendid path winding through forest and pond and fantasy that my children and I have now followed countless times, emerging from it better fit to spot the mysteries and magnificence in the landscapes around our own home.

James Herriot's Treasury for Children
James Herriot | Illustrated by Ruth Brown and Peter Barrett

Nature includes fauna as well as flora, and few authors describe the quirks and personalities of animals as winsomely as veterinarian James Herriot does. (One of the stories in this treasury is even told from the perspective of a lost lamb.) Herriot's humor and kind attentiveness have set us an excellent standard regarding the treatment of animals.

The Lost Words
Robert Macfarlane | Illustrated by Jackie Morris

Bluebell. Fern. Heather. Kingfisher. "The only words that ever satisfied me as describing Nature are the terms used in the fairy books, 'charm,' 'spell,' 'enchantment,'" wrote G.K. Chesterton. These acrostic poems illuminate the enchantment in each of the featured words, unfolding them one by one between breathtaking illustrations. Reading this book, for our family, is an experience akin to taking a walk through a quiet wood in the late afternoon—we meander, linger, and watch with bated breath. The Lost Words imparts a love of nature through immersion.

ENDNOTES

1 Frances Hodgson Burnett, The Secret Garden (London: Penguin Books, 1911), p. 203.
2 L.M. Montgomery, Rainbow Valley (New York: Bantam Books, 1919), p. 19.
3 Burnett, Secret Garden, p. 338.

IMAGINATION. MYSTERY. WONDER.

AFTERWORD

JUNIUS JOHNSON

When I was a child, the world seemed infinite. The horizon seemed literal: perhaps the world really *did* go on forever. Omniscience was easy to envision: perhaps my dad really *did* know everything. When I learned from the old professor in *The Lion, The Witch and the Wardrobe* that nothing was more likely than that "there could be other worlds—all over the place, just round the corner,"[1] this was not much of a surprise. My response, though not in these words, was something like: "I knew it!" The excitement immediately turned into action—of course I began looking for them. Many a closet failed to yield to my questing hands as I sought passage into the world of magic and talking animals. Of course, the professor had warned that we shouldn't go looking for them, that if we were patient and lived our lives, they would come to us;[2] but how could I be sure they would find me if I *didn't* look? I never succeeded, of course, but it always felt like I might. Like Lucy in *Prince Caspian*, I felt that I had come just a little too late or had not asked in quite the right way.[3] The reality I sought had always just disappeared around the corner as I came into the room: you could still smell its scent. And so the search continued.

But as I grew older, the world began to shrink. The horizon was just a trick of optics, weather, and topography; my dad was a mere mortal, and a flawed one at that; a closet was just a closet. Gradually but relentlessly every gateway to another world was closed in my face, proven never to have really existed. The tantalizing sense of *more* that had kept the search going was just my own wishful thinking. It was time to accept that there was no world but this one, and to get down to the grim and dull reality of dealing with a world insufficiently populated with wondrous things, marvelous people, and, most heartbreakingly, *meaning*.

This story, I'm given to understand, is a common one. Growing up seems to mean letting go of the way we want the world to be and accepting the way it is. The only problem is that this whole view of the world that we grow into is dead wrong.

The children have it right, and this is their birthright: to see what adults have, through disillusionment, neglect, and a misdirected sense of duty, trained themselves not to see. That is why children flock to Jesus in the Gospels, even as the religious experts scratch their heads in consternation. That is why Isaiah says "a little child shall lead them" (Isa. 11:6). Theology teaches us that the world is, at every level, *more* than we adults consider it to be. The natural world is a ceaseless trove of wonders (water falls from the sky! Birds bright as candies fill the air, and our days and nights are lit by massive explosions in space); we are surrounded by hosts of strange and magnificent people (the saints and angels); there are monsters and dragons to be slain (demons); and above it all is another world, unimaginable in its richness and joy. This world is creeping into our own—around every corner, behind every leaf or blade of grass, is a possible glimpse of it and entry to it. I had the world right all along, though I was off on some of the details. The task of growing up is not to learn to let go of this way of seeing the world, but to learn to recognize what all this *means*.

As adults, we have to help children along this path. That is what the essays in this book do: they point the way along various roads that will lead children to grow up to have childlike eyes with mature hearts. The paths laid out here are numerous, because what calls to one soul will not call to another. Also, these paths are not exhaustive: we cannot show all the ways, but by showing some it will be easier to recognize others. There are commonalities in the things presented here, derived from the nature of human thought and desire. Some of the most important ideas that animate these paths are imagination, wonder, and mystery.

When I speak of imagination in conjunction with literature, the mind may first turn to fairies and goblins, dragons and knights, wizards and enchantments. And yet, we should think of the imagination no less when speaking of historical fiction, or a book about nature, or a biography. The imagination is fundamentally about the possible, and what is real and every day is no less possible than what is fanciful and out of the ordinary.

For example: where Tolkien builds his world from the ground up, or Rowling crafts a world parallel to and intertwined with our own, historical fiction builds upon the things that were possible, the technology that was available, and the structures that made up society at a particular time in our past. This by no means limits the imagination, for its work is not just in building the stage, but also in figuring the characters and contouring the plot. Even when Napoleon or Julius Caesar come into the tale, they come not in their historical form, but are recast by the imagination of the author. There is always this sense of seeing between the pages of history, catching action and conversation that never made it into the official record. This is of course what makes it fiction; the imagination is freed rather than hampered by the historical starting point.

In the case of biography, it might seem that the imagination is squeezed out by the necessity to faithfully present the actual person in question. Here the goal is not to slip between the pages of history but to fill out those pages. While it may be a virtue in historical fiction to reimagine Napoleon, this is a vice in biography. And yet a biography is no bare listing of deeds done. Rather, every biography is a story—but not the same story experienced by the subject of the biography. As with historical fiction, the writer's imagination takes what is given but can only create a whole by creative interaction with it.

The imagination is as active in appreciating our world as it is in making new ones. It produces not only dragons and wizards, but also new ways of telling a story, as well as perspectives on history. Indeed, all crafting, all creation, is a work of the imagination. Every story, whether it tells of things true or make believe, is a fruit of the imagination.

We see countless miracles every day. As Chesterton puts it: "Fairy tales say that apples were golden only to refresh the forgotten moment when we found that they were green. They make rivers run with wine only to make us remember, for one wild moment, that they run with water."[4] And yet, we take the vast majority of these marvels for granted. Of *course* rivers run with water: that's nothing special. But it *is*. Imagine how differently we would feel if we came across a river of liquid gold—yet water is much more precious and no less marvelous.

Sometimes we are arrested by a marvel, and we linger over it. The attitude that lingers over the marvel is wonder. Wonder is the way we honor the strange, the otherworldly, or the *magnificent*. We love this experience so much that "wonderful" far exceeds "good."

Wonder raptures us out of the commonplace, out of the false confidence with which we approach the world as a known thing. This is because wonder arises as a result of perplexity: this can be, as Aristotle thought, because we are ignorant of the cause of something,[5] or because we are perplexed and astounded by the greatness of something. When I see a massive mountain, I am not so much perplexed by how such a thing can be as I am awed by the sheer immensity of it. When an angel appears, it must say "do not be afraid" because its very being so greatly exceeds our own that we are overcome by a wonder that quickly slides into dread. It is this type of wonder that stories evoke in us: the grandness or even strangeness they present cracks open our understanding of what is possible.

When awakened by the products of the imagination (human imagination in the case of stories and art; divine imagination in the case of beings and places), wonder itself awakens the imagination. Wonder forces us to realize that the boundaries of the possible are not where we thought they were. When faced with an enlarged sense of possibility, we must call upon the imagination as a guide through these new vistas.

And so we are brought to mystery. Though we come to it last, mystery is really first, because it is mystery that gets the whole process going. Let me explain with a personal example.

When I was in college, my life revolved around our library and classroom building. It was a majestic building: a row of tall columns that supported a golden roof dozens of feet above and through which one had to pass to enter the building. Inside the colonnade, the ground was paved with tiles, and at the center was a fountain. Water flowed from the top level down to the bottom through twelve channels (symbolizing the twelve apostles). In the midst of the water in the upper level was a torch that was always lit. I passed in and out of this gateway several times a day, and it became a sort of temple of knowledge, the emblem of my daytime world.

But one night I wandered around to the back of the building and discovered that the building was symmetrical—there was an identical "temple" in the rear. But the rear looked out over a field that ran down to the stream that marked the edge of campus: no one ever needed to go that way, so the university chose not to spend money on the needed upkeep. The fountain was dry, the torch unlit, and the tiles were broken in places, the tesserae lying about as if discarded by a disinterested child. It was a ruin, and I *loved* it. I went there often, almost exclusively at night, where I could have the illusion that I had stepped through a mirror from my daylight world into its dark reflection in another world.

I was drawn to this place because it was a tangible instance of what I had so long looked for—a door into another world. Every time I stepped onto those broken tiles, I felt transported to a world where I was the only living thing. It reminded me of the dead world in *The Magician's Nephew*, where Digory and

Polly unwittingly awaken the White Witch.[6] There was nothing mysterious about it *really*, of course: the university had been in financial difficulty for many years, and so had no money to waste on unseen parts of the campus. But it was possible to ignore all that and pretend that there was a great history here, a great civilization that had fallen.

The strangeness of the place awakened my sense of mystery, which moved me to wonder, which engaged my imagination. The process was so seamless that it seemed to take no time at all: it was as if I were plunged headlong into the sea of mystery, wonder, and imagination the moment my eyes laid hold of that marvelous desolation.

We adults often fail to be on the lookout for wonder and imagination. We approach the world as though we fundamentally understand it, and so we do not wonder at it; we solve problems by reason, and so we do not feel the need to bring imagination to bear. But mystery interrupts this: when we encounter mystery, we are immediately moved to wonder. And when we try to unravel a mystery, we are forced to use our imaginations, precisely because the mysterious nature of the thing in question defies our normal intellectual categories.

If our job as adults with children in our lives is to guide them down paths of maturity that will leave imagination and wonder intact, then our great weapon in selecting books for them is mystery. Mystery has a gravity to it, and if we can bring our children within its influence, it will draw them inevitably deeper. This is why the approach must be varied: we must learn what will grab each child and offer that, so that we provide channels for their wonder and imagination. Each book opens another channel, and we want to open as many as we can, for the Spirit of God is abundant enough to flow through infinitely many. These things hold open the spaces in our soul where the Spirit inspires and encourages us. They make us magnanimous, and on this spiritual immensity we can build the character that will help our children grow into the fullness of virtue. Good stories keep the soul awake, forewarning it of danger and populating it with heroes and heroines whose examples of courage and character give us strength to see ourselves standing against similar foes and refusing to yield to evil. Story has always been and remains our greatest tool in crafting wise and great people.

Story reminds us, too, that there *is* more—a world beyond the one we see. Through these channels of imagination, mystery, and wonder, the Spirit keeps our desire for that other world alive and reminds us that it is worth pursuing, however perilous the path ahead.

ENDNOTES

1   C.S. Lewis, *The Lion, the Witch and the Wardrobe* (New York: Macmillan
     Publishing, 1970), p. 46.
2   Lewis, *The Lion, the Witch and the Wardrobe*, p. 186.
3   C.S. Lewis, *Prince Caspian*, (New York: Macmillan Publishing, 1951),
     pp. 112–113.
4   G.K. Chesterton, *Orthodoxy: Centennial Edition* (Nashville, TN: Sam Torode Book Arts, 2008, orig.
     publ. 1908), p. 49.
5   Aristotle, *Metaphysics*, Book I, 982b.
6   C.S. Lewis, *The Magician's Nephew*, (New York: Macmillan Publishing, 1955), pp. 41–53.

EDITORS' EXTRAS

APPENDIX I

THÉA ROSENBURG

The closer we got to the end of this project, the harder it got to stop. Leslie mentioned Kate DiCamillo's name wistfully—surely we'd included one of her books? Carey showed up for a meeting with a pile of holiday books—we couldn't forget those! And I stopped short each time I passed one of our bookshelves, arrested by the sight of yet another title I hadn't seen mentioned in any of the essays.

Because the truth is that there is no end to book lists, and anyone who sets out to write one must be a Particular Sort of Person. If you ask us what we're reading, we're liable to start filling your arms with books. So, as a way of getting ourselves out the door gracefully before we overstayed our welcome, we allowed ourselves ten "extras"—titles that hadn't been recommended anywhere else in the anthology but that we think you need to know about. May you find among them books you can't resist sharing with your loved ones.

LESLIE BUSTARD

A Hole is to Dig
Ruth Kraus | *Illustrated Maurice Sendak*

The Lord's Prayer
Illustrated by Tim Ladwig

Island Boy
Barabara Cooney | *Illustrated by Barabara Cooney* (tied with
Ox-Cart Man, the book that she illustrated by Donald Hall)

Charlie and Lola: I Will Never, Not Ever Eat a Tomato
Lauren Child | *Illustrated by Lauren Child*

The O in Hope
Luci Shaw | *Illustrated by Ned Bustard*

Cobble Street Cousins: In Aunt Lucy's Kitchen
Cythnia Rylant | *Illustrated by Wendy Anderson Halperin*

Beowulf the Warrior
Ian Serrailier | *Illustrated by Mark Severin* (tied with ***The Dream Keeper
and Other Poems,*** by Langston Hughes | Illustrated by Brian Pinkney)

Because of Winn-Dixie
Kate DiCamillo (tied with ***The Angel Knew Papa and
the Dog*** by Douglas McKelvey)

Alex Rider: Stormbreaker
Anthony Horowitz (tied with ***Jane Austen's Northanger Abbey***
by Nancy Butler and illustrated by Janet Lee)

The Exact Place (Book One of the Place trilogy)
Margie Haack

CAREY BUSTARD

The Shape Books: *Triangle, Square,* and *Circle*
Mac Barnett | *Illustrated by Jon Klassen*

Strega Nona
Tomie dePaola | *Illustrated by Tomie dePaola*

Inch by Inch
Leo Lionni | *Illustrated by Leo Lionni*

A Big Mooncake for Little Star
Grace Lin | *Illustrated by Grace Lin*

Windows
Julia Denos | *Illustrated by E.B. Goodale*

Imaginary Fred
Eoin Colfer | *Illustrated by Oliver Jeffers* (*The Heart and the Bottle* and
This Moose Belongs to Me by Oliver Jeffers are good, too.)

A Sick Day for Amos McGee
Philip C. Stead | *Illustrated by Erin E. Stead*

Tom's Midnight Garden
Philippa Pearce

Ella Enchanted
Gail Carson Levine

The Joys of Love
Madeleine L'Engle (but also *Meet the Austins* and *The Small Rain*)

THÉA ROSENBURG

The Mistmantle Chronicles
M.I. McAllister (see also: **Redwall,** by Brian Jacques)

The Railway Children
E. Nesbit

Miracle Man
John Hendrix | *Illustrated by John Hendrix* (see also: *everything else by John Hendrix*)

All the Small Poems and Fourteen More
Valerie Worth | *Illustrated by Natalie Babbitt*

Building Our House
Jonathan Bean | *Illustrated by Jonathan Bean*

Treasures of the Snow
Patricia St. John

The Wilderking Trilogy
Jonathan Rogers

Hinds' Feet on High Places
Hannah Hurnard | *Illustrated by Jill De Haan & Rachel McNaughton*

A Year in the Big Old Garden
James D. Witmer | *Illustrated by Joe Sutphin*

The Little White Horse
Elizabeth Goudge (and, of course, L.M. Montgomery's **Emily of New Moon**)

HOLIDAY BOOKS

CAREY BUSTARD

Growing up, my family was known as the family that celebrated *everything*. Saint Patrick's Day? Of course, we're Irish! Book Release Days? We celebrated every *Harry Potter* release at midnight, not to mention the books my parents published. Birthdays—not just our own, but also C.S. Lewis's and Bilbo Baggins's. Thanksgiving and Christmas were stacked with traditions, as were Valentine's Day, Easter, and Reformation Day. Everything must be celebrated and celebrated hard. As a teacher, it has been my great joy to bring this propensity towards celebration into my classroom. Much of that includes reading a book that goes with the holiday. I wanted to share some of those nuggets with you. This is by no means a full, comprehensive list of every fantastic holiday book, but it is a carefully curated collection of favorites. I hope it helps inspire celebration and tradition in your home, as much as it has in mine.

VALENTINE'S DAY

Cranberry Valentine
   Wende Devlin | *Harry Devlin*
Rome Antics
   David McCauley | *David McCauley*
Saint Valentine
   Robert Sabuda | *Robert Sabuda*
XO, OX: A Love Story
   Adam Rex | *Scott Campbell*

ST. PATRICK'S DAY

Fin M'Coul: The Giant of Knockmany Hill
   Tomie dePaola | *Tomie dePaola*
Jamie O'Rourke and the Big Potato
   Tomie dePaola | *Tomie dePaola*
Patrick: Patron Saint of Ireland
   Tomie dePaola | *Tomie dePaola*
A Pot of Gold
   Kathleen Krull | *David McPhail*

EASTER

At Jerusalem's Gate
Nikki Grimes | *David Frampton*

The Country Bunny and the Little Gold Shoes
DuBose Heyword | *Marjorie Flack*

The Donkey Who Carried a King
R.C. Sproul | *Chuck Groeninck*

The Easter Egg
Jan Brett | *Jan Brett*

Max's Chocolate Chicken
Rosemary Wells | *Rosemary Wells*

Petook
Caryll Houselander | *Tomie dePaola*

THANKSGIVING

Cranberry Thanksgiving
Wende Devlin | *Harry Devlin*

Milly and the Macy's Parade
Shana Corey | *Brett Helquist*

This First Thanksgiving Day
Laura Krauss Melmed | *Mark Buehner*

Thankful
Eileen Spinelli | *Archie Preston*

Thanksgiving in the Woods
Phyllis Alsdurf | *Jenny Lovlie*

Thank You, Sarah
Laurie Halse Anderson | *Matt Faulkner*

HALLOWEEN

Cranberry Halloween
Wende Devlin | *Harry Devlin*

**The Little Old Lady Who Was
Not Afraid of Anything**
Linda Williams | *Megan Lloyd*

Stumpkin
Lucy Ruth Cummins | *Lucy Ruth Cummins*

Too Many Pumpkins
Linda White | *Megan Lloyd*

The Vanishing Pumpkin
Tony Johnson | *Tomie dePaola*

CHRISTMAS

The Best Christmas Pageant Ever
Barbara Robinson

The Birds of Bethlehem
Tomie dePaola | *Tomie dePaola*

Christmas in the Country
Cynthia Rylant | *Diane Goode*

The Christmas Miracle of Jonathan Toomey
Susan Wojciechowski | *P.J. Lynch*

Christmas Tapestry
Patricia Polacco | *Patricia Polacco*

Cranberry Christmas
Wende Devlin | *Harry Devlin*

The Little Drummer Boy
Ezra Jack Keats

Lucy and Tom at Christmas
Shirley Hughes | *Shirley Hughes*

Nativity
Cynthia Rylant | *Cynthia Rylant*

Peter Spier's Christmas
Peter Spier

Pick a Pine Tree
Patricia Toht | *Jarvis*

Saint Nicholas the Giftgiver
Ned Bustard | *Ned Bustard*

Santa Calls
William Joyce | *William Joyce*

Shooting at the Stars
John Hendrix | *John Hendrix*

Silent Night
Lara Hawthorne

Song of the Stars
Sally Lloyd-Jones | *Alison Jay*

The Story of the Three Wise Kings
Tomie dePaola | *Tomie dePaola*

Toot & Puddle: I'll Be Home for Christmas
Holly Hobbie | *Holly Hobbie*

Tree of Cranes
Allen Say | *Allen Say*

The Twelve Days of Christmas
Jack Kent

Who is Coming to Our House?
Joseph Slate | *Ashley Wolff*

Mr. Willowby's Christmas Tree
Robert Barry | *Robert Barry*

The Year of the Perfect Christmas Tree
Gloria Houston | *Barbara Cooney*

SEQUENCE

APPENDIX III

LESLIE BUSTARD

We've included a list of our recommendations, organized by reading level, just for you. Of course, every child is a special creation with his or her own needs and gifts, so this appendix can only be a starting point. Special thanks to Laura Peterson, this project's in-house librarian, for her work helping us sort out the many piles of books lying around on the floor ...

TODDLER (T)

Barnyard Dance (T)
Sandra Boynton | *Sandra Boynton*

Bear Snores On (T)
Karma Wilson | *Jane Chapman*

Found (T)
Sally Lloyd-Jones | *Jago*

God's Very Colorful Creation (T)
Tim Thornborough | *Jennifer Davison*

Let the Whole Earth Sing Praise (T)
Tomie dePaola | *Tomie dePaola*

The Little Black Truck (T)
Libba Moore Gray | *Elizabeth Sayles*

Little Seed: A Life (T)
Callie Grant | *Suzanne Etienne*

"More More More" Said the Baby (T)
Vera B. Williams | *Vera B. Williams*

My Very First Mother Goose (T)
Iona Opie | *Rosemary Wells*

Prayer for a Child (T)
Rachel Field | *Elizabeth Orton Jones*

The Runaway Bunny (T)
Margaret Wise Brown | *Clement Hurd*

EARLY (PK-2)

The Adventures of Mali & Keela (PK-2)
Jonathan Collins | *Jenny Cooper*

After the Fall (PK-2)
Dan Santat | *Dan Santat*

The Alfie Books (PK-2)
Shirley Hughes | *Shirley Hughes*

Autumn Story (PK-2)
Jill Barklem | *Jill Barklem*

A Baby Sister for Frances (PK-2)
Russell Hoban | *Lillian Hoban*

Baby Wren and the Great Gift (PK-2)
Sally Lloyd-Jones | *Jen Corace*

Be Good To Eddie Lee (PK-2)
Virginia Fleming | *Floyd Cooper*

A Big Mooncake for Little Star (PK-1)

CONTRIBUTORS

MISSY ANDREWS is a veteran homeschool parent of six and co-author of *Teaching the Classics* literature curriculum. She and her husband Adam run *CenterForLit.com*, a family business offering curriculum materials, book-lists, an online Lit Academy, a membership community for homeschool parents and classical educators, a sister website (*CenterForLitSchools.com*), and *BiblioFiles*, a literary podcast for the entire family. Missy has authored two books: *Wild Bells: A Literary Advent* and *My Divine Comedy: A Mother's Homeschool Journey*. She nests in eastern Washington overlooking the Columbia River, where she reads and scribbles and thinks.

QUANTRILLA ARD lives in the Atlanta area with her husband and three littles. A passionate creative at heart, she has answered the call to encourage women in all stages of life and of various backgrounds through empathy, transparency, and love. She is a faith-based personal and spiritual development writer and speaker who believes in the power of collective strength, community, and fellowship. She recently graduated from Walden University with a PhD in Health Psychology and is an advocate for social justice, with a focus on Black maternal and infant health and mortality. You can find her at *ThePHDMamma.com*.

ANDI ASHWORTH is the author of *Real Love for Real Life: The Art and Work of Caring*, an essayist and diarist, and co-creator of the blog, *The Writer & The Husband*. She is co-founder of the Art House in Nashville where she served for over two decades through hospitality and mentoring. Andi was editor-in-chief of the Art House America literary blog from 2010–2018. She holds an MA in Theological Studies from Covenant Theological Seminary. Andi and her musical husband, Charlie Peacock, have two grown, married children and four grandchildren.

REBECCA BECKER graduated with a BSEd and MSEd from Bloomsburg University. She and her husband Tom raised five children. Becky home-schooled her children and then, for six years, directed a Charlotte Mason school. She now works as a postpartum doula in Lancaster County, PA.

Becky has also worked the last few years helping to direct a women's Bible study. She loves on her grandchildren in Denver and Philadelphia.

LESLIE ANNE BUSTARD spent much of her adult years homeschooling her three girls, and teaching literature, poetry, art appreciation, and writing to other children in various homeschooling co-ops. She also taught middle school literature and writing at a local classical school, as well as produced high school and children's theater. She currently writes for The Cultivating Project and The Black Barn Collective. Leslie loves museum-ing and watching movies with her family. You can find her musings on beauty, truth, and goodness at *PoeticUnderpinnings.com.*

CAREY BUSTARD is passionate about diversity in classical education and celebrating the image of God in every child. She is currently living that vision out as she teaches Junior Kindergarten at The Geneva School of Manhattan. Carey was homeschooled classically and earned a degree in Media, Culture, and the Arts with a theology minor from The King's College, NYC. Her deep loves include children's literature, Spotify playlists, and traveling with friends. She is originally from Lancaster, PA, but has called New York City home for the last decade.

TINA CHO is the author of four picture books and an upcoming middle grade graphic novel. After living in South Korea for ten years, Tina, her husband, and two teenagers reside in Iowa where she also teaches kindergarten. Learn more at her website, *TinaMCho.com.*

ELISA CHODAN holds a bachelor of science in Music Education and a master of music in Voice Performance. She teaches hundreds of students weekly in general music and choir classes; she also maintains a private vocal studio. Elisa is an active member of the American Choral Directors Association, National Association for Music Education, and the Pennsylvania Music Educators Association. She has completed multiple internships with the British vocal ensemble VOCES8, including the 2019–2020 VOCES8 Choral Scholar. She lives in Lititz, PA, with her cat, Tigger.

SHANIKA CHURCHVILLE has a BA in English from Swarthmore College and an MSEd in Instructional Leadership from Neumann University.

She has taught middle elementary grades in private, public, and charter schools. She currently teaches writing and coordinates writing services at Lancaster Bible College. She enjoys running, yoga, reading, and cooking and sharing Sri Lankan cuisine. Shanika, her husband, and their two sons make their home in Lancaster, PA.

MATTHEW CLARK is a singer/songwriter and storyteller. He has recorded several full-length albums, including a Bible walk-through called *Bright Came the Word from His Mouth* and *Beautiful Secret Life*, a collection of songs highlighting "heaven in ordinary." Matthew hosts *One Thousand Words—Stories on the Way*, a weekly podcast featuring essay reflections on faith-keeping, and writes regularly for The Cultivating Project. A touring musician and speaker, he is currently recording a 33-song trilogy of concept albums to begin releasing in 2022.

ARACELI CRUZ is a writer and journalist. A native of Montebello, CA, she holds a BA in Journalism from San Francisco State University and has written for *Village Voice*, *The Guardian*, *New York*, *Teen Vogue*, *Rolling Stone*, and elsewhere. She's currently working on an MFA in Writing at the Savannah College of Art and Design and has a new piece of short fiction included in *Palabritas* from Harvard University. She lives with her husband, the poet Aaron Belz, and their dog, Wikus, in St. Louis, MO.

MATTHEW DICKERSON has authored numerous books including a recent work on spiritual theology (*Disciple-Making in a Culture of Power, Comfort, and Fear*), a medieval historical novel (*The Rood and the Torc*), a three-volume fantasy novel (*The Gift*, *The Betrayed*, and *Illengond*), several books about trout, rivers, and ecology, and books about fantasy literature. He lives in Vermont with his wife and is a professor at Middlebury College.

SARAH ETTER is currently a student at Cedarville University pursuing a degree in International Studies. She hopes to work with refugees and human trafficking survivors. She grew up with her parents and four brothers in Lancaster, PA, and graduated from Wilson Hill Academy, where she learned to love literature, history, and philosophy. This is the second Square Halo title in which she has appeared, the first being *Bigger on the Inside: Christianity and Doctor Who.*

CAROLYN CLARE GIVENS lives in Charlotte, NC, with her cats, Lord Peter Wimsey and Harriet Vane. Carrie holds a BS in Bible from Cairn University and a MA in English from Arcadia University. She is the author of *The King's Messenger* and *Rosefire*. Carrie is the CEO of Bandersnatch Books, a small publisher of treasures found off the beaten path and is a contributor to Story Warren. She works in communications at New City Church in Charlotte. You can learn more about her work at *CarolynCGivens.com*.

KIMBERLY GILLESPIE graduated from Loyola University-Chicago with a degree in economics an MA in Christian Education from Dallas Theological Seminary. After being an educator for almost ten years, she served as a conference event planner with a college ministry. Kim's love for writing and equipping led her to contribute to various publications and websites including Urban Ministries, Inc.; Precepts for Living; *A Moment to Breathe* daily devotional; *(in)courage Devotional Bible;* and Beloved Women. She is currently the director of operations at Cornerstone Church and resides in Atlanta, GA, with her husband, son, and twin girls.

DORINA LAZO GILMORE-YOUNG is an award-winning author, speaker, Bible teacher, and podcaster. She helps people chase God's glory down unexpected trails and flourish in their God-given callings. She and her husband, Shawn, are raising three brave daughters in central California, who love to travel and learn about different cultures. Connect with her at *DorinaGilmore.com*.

MARGIE HAACK lives in Savage, MN, with husband Denis, where she tries to attract bumblebees and hummingbirds with marginal success. Nature and place connect her to the spiritual geography that has shaped her life. Margie's writing includes the *Place* trilogy, published by Square Halo Books. Her work has appeared in Art House America, *Comment Magazine,* and other publications. Recently, she shattered a favorite platter, sucked her socks into the vacuum cleaner, and backed into a parked car—proving that safety lies in writing more and leaving the desk less. You can find her blogging occasionally at *Critique-Letters.com*.

ELIZABETH HARWELL is the author of *The Good Shepherd's Pasture* and *The Good King's Feast*. She and her husband, Andrew, are currently planting a church in the northern suburbs of Atlanta, where they live with their three kids and an exceptionally curious dog named Louie. She loves the writing of Wendell Berry, the pluckiness of bluegrass music, the sight of lightening bugs over a soybean field, and she doesn't think you'll need to see her Kentucky birth certificate after that. You can find more of Elizabeth's writing at *Elizabeth-Harwell.com.*

KATY BOWSER HUTSON is a songwriter and writer. She is the co-author, along with Flo Paris Oakes and Tish Harrison Warren, of *Little Prayers for Ordinary Days.* She is one of the founding creators of Rain for Roots, a musical group that tells God's big story for little ones and their grownups. Katy also wrote a collection of poetry from her time with cancer, *Now I Lay Me Down To Fight.* She lives in Nashville, TN, with her husband and two children.

K.C. IRETON is an essayist, storywriter, and poet. She is the author of two nonfiction books, has written for numerous print publications and online venues, and currently serves as a contributing editor for The Cultivating Project. She holds an MA in Apologetics from Houston Baptist University and is a founding member of Seattle Classical Co-op, where she teaches high school history, literature, and writing. An avid reader, she enjoys sharing good books with anyone who will listen, which usually ends up being her husband and four children. Besides books, she also likes gardens, long walks, Oxford commas, and tea.

JUNIUS JOHNSON is a scholar, musician, and writer with expertise in historical and systematic theology. He performs professionally on the French horn and electric bass. He holds a BA from Oral Roberts University (English Lit), an MAR from Yale Divinity School (Historical Theology), and an MA, two MPhils, and a PhD (Philosophical Theology) from Yale University. He is the author of four books, including *The Father of Lights: A Theology of Beauty.* He is a frequent guest contributor to blogs and podcasts on faith and culture and is a regular contributor to The Cultivating Project.

ANNE KENNEDY has an MDiv and is the author of *Nailed It: 365 Readings for Angry or Worn-Out People,* from Square Halo Books. She blogs about current events and theological trends at *Preventing Grace* on *Patheos.com.*

AMY KNORR is an educator, speaker, spiritual director, and writer who loves to create and nurture face-to-face and virtual contemplative spaces. She received her BA in English and Linguistics along with Secondary English and ESL teaching certificates, taught at the high school and community college level for a decade, transitioned to designing and writing curriculum, and is currently pursuing a masters degree. She is a mom to two girls growing tall and a son she will hold again someday. She enjoys a good laugh, a quiet moment, a furry doggy face, a challenging trail, and a cup of hot tea.

COREY LATTA earned an undergraduate degree in Biblical Studies, am MA in New Testament studies, am MA in Counseling, as well as am MA and PhD in English. He has taught in higher education in the areas of theology, philosophy, literature, and counseling for over fifteen years. Corey is the author of four books, including *C.S. Lewis and the Art of Writing*. Corey lives, writes, and parents his four children in Memphis, TN.

AMY BAIK LEE holds an MA in English Literature from the University of Virginia. She is a writer and managing editor for Cultivating Magazine, and a contributing writer at The Rabbit Room. She lives with her husband and two daughters in Colorado. Ever seeking to "press on to [her] true country and to help others to do the same" (C.S. Lewis), Amy posts essays and stories about Homeward longing at *AmyBaikLee.com*.

CAROLYN LEILOGLOU is the author of *Library's Most Wanted* and the *Noah Green: Junior Zookeeper Series*. She was a finalist for the 2021 WILLA Award and the 2018 Katherine Paterson Prize, and her poems and stories have appeared in award-winning children's magazines around the world. When she's not writing, Carolyn can be found homeschooling her four children in their house full of bookworms, which also happens to be the name of her blog. You can find her at HouseFullOfBookworms.com and CarolynLeiloglou.com and on social media as House Full of Bookworms.

CHRISTIAN LEITHART lives with his wife, Tara, in Birmingham, AL. They both teach full-time but somehow find the hours to raise their daughter and newborn son, read piles of books, and go outside occasionally.

Christian contributed to a previous Square Halo volume, *Bigger on the Inside: Christianity and Doctor Who*. He writes for the Theopolis Institute and blogs intermittently.

GYPSY MARTIN lives with her husband and two teenage sons in the beautiful Pacific Northwest. You will likely find her walking the trails in the woods or trolling the aisles of a local thrift store, depending on the weather. Gypsy's short fiction and creative nonfiction have been published in various literary journals, including *The Timberline Review*, and in the anthology *Flash in the Attic 2* from Fiction Attic Press.

PAHTYANA MOORE is a wife, mama to two ninja princesses, author, artist, and international speaker. She has written for Velvet Ashes, an international online community for women overseas and for Transpositions, the online journal for the Institute for Theology, Imagination and the Arts at St. Andrews University. She sits on the Advisory Board for The Cultivating Project. She and her family called Kenya home for over five years and currently reside in Thailand where she and her husband coach and mentor overseas workers and ministry leaders.

ANNIE NARDONE is a two-year C.S. Lewis Institute Fellow with an MA in Cultural Apologetics from Houston Baptist University. She homeschooled her three kids for twenty-five years and teaches art, creative writing, and humanities at her co-op. Annie contributes to and edits *AnUnexpectedJournal.com* and is a managing editor for The Cultivating Project. Annie lives with her Middle-earth/Narnia/Hogwarts-loving family, piles of books, and an assemblage of cats who read with her daily but don't give a tick about her ramblings. You can find her at *LiteraryLife.org*.

ASHLEY ARTAVIA NOVALIS has spent a decade working in early childhood settings through non-profits and public school programs. Most recently, she has worked in child and adolescent behavioral health through a local counseling agency. Ashley is passionate about mental health advocacy, social justice, and good empanadas. She lives with her husband, Joshua, in the East Side of Lancaster City, PA, where they love reading books, watching Netflix, and attempting to garden.

MITALI PERKINS has written many books for young readers including *You Bring the Distant Near* (nominated for a National Book Award) and *Rickshaw Girl* (adapted into a film by Sleeperware Productions). Mitali's fiction explores poverty, immigration, child soldiers, microcredit, and human suffering, thanks to living overseas for many years and studying Political Science at Stanford and Public Policy at UC Berkley. Her goal is to make readers laugh or cry, preferable both, as long as their hearts are widening. She lives and writes in the East Bay. Learn more at *MitaliPerkins.com*

LAURA PETERSON holds a master's degree in library and information science. She currently works as a children's librarian at a public library in northern Virginia, where she loves sharing her favorite picture books at story-time and chatting about new middle grade novels. A former editor, Laura combines her love of writing and of children's books as a frequent contributor to Story Warren.

ERÉNDIRA RAMÍREZ-ORTEGA has an MFA from Mills College and a BA from UCLA. Her fiction, essays, and poetry appear widely in various publications. She is the co-founder of Burning Bush Press. Eréndira and her husband live in California. They have been homeschooling their children since 2013. You can subscribe to her semi-monthly newsletter, *Lovely Things*, at *EROrtega.com*, or visit her page at *EROcreative.com* to learn more about her other work.

CINDY ROLLINS homeschooled her nine children for over thirty years using Charlotte Mason's timeless ideas. She is the author of *Mere Motherhood: Morning Time, Nursery Rhymes, and My Journey Toward Sanctification*, and *Hallelujah, Cultivating Advent Traditions with Handel's Messiah*. She co-hosts *The Literary Life* podcast with Angelina Stanford and Thomas Banks. She is also the owner of the Mere Motherhood Facebook group and runs an active mom's discipleship group on Patreon. She lives in her sometimes empty nest in Chattanooga, TN, with her husband, Tim, and dog, Max. You can also find her at *CindyRollins.net* .

THÉA ROSENBURG, since graduating with a degree in creative writing, has worked as a dental assistant, an indie musician, a peddler of hand-knit gifts, an art teacher, an informal librarian, and an editor. She is a regular contributor to Story Warren and has served as content editor for *Deeply Rooted Magazine*. Her writing has also appeared on The Rabbit Room and Risen Motherhood. Théa lives with her husband and four daughters in Bellingham, WA, where, when the wind blows from the right direction, she can smell the ocean from her front yard. She reviews children's books for her blog, *LittleBookBigStory.com.*

LYNETTE STONE has her MEd and is a Literacy Coach, training teachers in language arts instruction. She has taught in grades 4–8 and has a special love for middle schoolers. An active member of her church for the last twenty-six years, she has been particularly involved with youth and music ministries as well as writing for their online devotionals. Lynette and her husband, Chris, are currently raising their high school daughter in central west New Jersey. They have raised two sons, both now married, and are enjoying the antics of their first grandson.

JOY STRAWBRIDGE reads and writes in Nashville, TN, where she spends most days caring for her littlest neighbors as a nanny. She has had the privilege of teaching elementary, middle, and high school students at classical Christian schools in Pennsylvania and Oregon. She has worked as an editor for Square Halo Books and The Row House, and is proud to call Carey Bustard a lifelong kindred spirit.

DORENA WILLIAMSON loves the power of a good story and writes children's books that adults need too. She is the author of *ColorFull, ThoughtFull, GraceFull,* and *The Celebration Place*—children's books that feature diverse ethnicity and shape perspective on relevant topics with biblical truth. She is the co-planter of multiracial Strong Tower Bible Church in Nashville, and her writing has been featured in Christianity Today, Facts and Trends, and Crosswalk. She and her family live in Franklin, TN. Visit her at *DorenaWilliamson.com.*

WHAT? YOU WANT **MORE** BOOK RECOMMENDATIONS? WELL, OKAY . . .

A BOOK FOR HEARTS & MINDS: WHAT YOU SHOULD READ AND WHY

"Curators of the imagination, stewards of the tradition, priests of print, [Beth and Byron Borger] have always done more than sold books: they have furnished faithful minds and hearts. This book is a lovely testimony to that good work."

—James K.A. Smith, Calvin College, author of *You Are What You Love*

NAILED IT: 365 READINGS FOR ANGRY OR WORN-OUT PEOPLE

". . . if you, like me, long for a devotional that is sharpening, witty, and downright real, well then, you simply must read this book."

—Karen Swallow Prior, author of *On Reading Well*

SPEAKING CODE: UNRAVELING PAST BONDS TO REDEEM BROKEN CONVERSATIONS

"If you've ever longed for an effective tool to help replace hurtful speech or deadly silence with words that give life and heal hearts, *Speaking Code* is a must-read."

—Kimberly Miller, author of *Boundaries for Your Soul*

THE EXACT PLACE: A SEARCH FOR FATHER

"As I read the story of Margie's life, I reflected on my own, and wondered at the goodness in the ordinary—land well-tended, food well-prepared, children sheltered and fed with sweat and tears—and at the unfolding of hope in the midst of hardship and heartbreak."

—Gideon Strauss, academic dean of the Institute for Christian Studies

GODLY CHARACTER(S): INSIGHTS FOR SPIRITUAL PASSION FROM THE LIVES OF 8 WOMEN IN THE BIBLE

". . . these 'great eight' propel you towards habits of godliness—putting you in a place to receive grace and fall more deeply in love with your savior—and that in His love you might be re-shaped and re-formed."

—Robert William Alexander, author of *The Gospel-Centered Life at Work*

SQUAREHALOBOOKS.COM